TIMING
THE
DE-ESCALATION
OF
INTERNATIONAL
CONFLICTS

Syracuse Studies on Peace and Conflict Resolution
HARRIET HYMAN ALONSO, CHARLES CHATFIELD, and LOUIS KRIESBERG
Series Editors

TIMING
THE
DE-ESCALATION
OF
INTERNATIONAL
CONFLICTS

Edited by
LOUIS KRIESBERG
STUART J. THORSON

SYRACUSE UNIVERSITY PRESS

Copyright © 1991 by Syracuse University Press
Syracuse, New York 13244-5160
All Rights Reserved

First Edition 1991
91 92 93 94 95 96 97 98 99   6 5 4 3 2 1

The paper used in this publication meets the minimum requirements of
American National Standard for Information Sciences—
Permanence of Paper for Printed Materials, ANSI Z39.48-1984. ∞™

Library of Congress Cataloging-in-Publication Data
Timing the de-escalation of international conflicts / edited by
Louis Kriesberg and Stuart J. Thorson. — 1st ed.
    p.   cm. — (Syracuse studies on peace and conflict resolution)
Includes bibliographical references and index.
ISBN 0-8156-2521-9 (cloth : alk. paper). — ISBN 0-8156-2523-5
(paper : alk. paper)
    1. Pacific settlement of international disputes. 2. Diplomatic
negotiations in international disputes. 3. Conflict management.
I. Kriesberg, Louis. II. Thorson, Stuart J. III. Series.
JX4473.T56 1991
341.5'2—dc20   91-9810
                                       CIP

Manufactured in the United States of America

CONTENTS

FOREWORD

Louis Kriesberg's and Stuart J. Thorson's edited volume on *Timing the De-escalation of International Conflicts* is an important and frequently original contribution to the theory and practice of international politics.

The cause for this is not simply the professional distinction of the individual contributors—although many readers will turn with justified high expectation from the authors listed in the contents to the essays themselves. But what earns this symposium a special place among those projects that the U.S. Institute of Peace is proud to have supported is its particular theme: timing.

In politics as in baseball, timing can make the difference. Without superb timing, Joe DiMaggio's perfect swing could have produced a record crop of strikeouts and foul balls instead of a never-to-be-repeated fifty-seven-game hitting streak in that historic summer fifty years ago. Likewise, in politics, President Carter's Camp David diplomacy was well timed to take advantage of a new state of "ripeness" in the long-running conflict between Egypt and Israel. Kriesberg notes that prospects for de-escalation improve when a conflict has become stalemated at a high level of antagonism—when it has in fact become a "hurting"stalemate. (In a more recent case, Chancellor Kohl acted wisely to seize the available moment to reunite West and East Germany. Had he delayed, second thoughts in either Moscow or Bonn might have produced a different outcome.) Conversely, a policy initiative may on its face appear to address a critical international issue (e.g., France's Security Council proposals of 1982 and 1984 regarding Lebanon) but have little effect, because of its "asynchrony" with the policies of other powers.

Thus a principal lesson of the book for both statesmen and scholars (and they will find many useful lessons and insights in the book) is that policies are never "correct" in an abstract, timeless manner. There are no "school solutions" in life, and this book does not offer any.

vii

Instead, it makes clear that a correct policy of de-escalation should be neither premature (as some U.S. confidence-building measures with the USSR might have been prior to the Cuban missile crisis) nor miss the tide (as peacemakers in the Middle East perhaps did in the summer of 1967). A correct policy of de-escalation should, in other words, above all be rightly timed.

My own years of toil in diplomatic vineyards have taught me that, of all the variables with which a diplomat contends, time is the source of the greatest frustration and the greatest opportunity. With the help of Louis Kriesberg and Stuart J. Thorson, and their able collaborators, however, both analysts and practitioners of the de-escalation of international conflict will be able to aim "Time's Arrow" more precisely at its mark.

Washington, D.C.   SAMUEL W. LEWIS
June 1991   President
                              United States Institute of Peace

ACKNOWLEDGMENTS

THE WORK upon which this book is based was supported by a grant from the United States Institute of Peace. The opinions, findings, and conclusions or recommendations expressed in this book are those of the authors and do not necessarily reflect the views of the United States Institute of Peace.

We also wish to acknowledge with thanks the many persons who cooperated in the work resulting in this book. In addition to the contributors to this volume, many Syracuse University faculty and graduate students participated in the meeting at which drafts of the contributions were discussed and during other stages of the project. The graduate students who served as rapporteurs were: Bhavna Dave, James Downes, Susan French, John Lawyer, and Denise Williams. The faculty members who collaborated in the project included John Nagle, Terrell A. Northrup, and Howard Tamashiro.

In addition, we wish to thank Anica Sturdivant for her thoughtful management of the considerable secretarial and organizational tasks of the project. We also wish to thank Nancy Morrell for her skilled help in the final editing of the book.

CONTRIBUTORS

JAMES P. BENNETT, who received his Ph.D. from MIT in 1978, is Associate Professor of Political Science at the Maxwell School of Citizenship and Public Affairs at Syracuse University. He has served as a consultant to numerous businesses, governments, and research institutes. His publications have focused on areas of discourse theory in examining national security debates, resource allocation, and terrorism.

GOODWIN COOKE is Vice-President for International Affairs at Syracuse University and an adjunct professor at the Maxwell School of Citizenship and Public Affairs. Before coming to Syracuse, Ambassador Cooke served for twenty-five years as a Foreign Service officer with the Department of State, including positions as Deputy Chief of Mission, Ivory Coast, and as ambassador to the Central African Republic. His articles appear in numerous newspapers throughout the country.

JUERGEN DEDRING earned his Diplom-Politologe at the Free University in Berlin and his Ph.D. in Government at Harvard in 1974. His most recent post is that of Senior Political Affairs Officer in the United Nations Office for Research and the Collection of Information. He has authored a book entitled *Recent Advances in Peace and Conflict Research: A Critical Survey* (1976), and articles and papers about peace research, Morgenthau's political realism, the European parliament, and the functions of United Nations organs.

AMBASSADOR RALPH EARLE II, a graduate of Harvard College and Harvard Law School, is currently the National Policy Director of the Lawyers Alliance for Nuclear Arms Control, a nonpartisan arms control research and public information organization. From 1980 to 1981, Ambassador Earle was Director of the U.S. Arms Control and Disarmament Agency (ACDA), where he was the principal advisor to the president, National Security Council, and secretary of state on matters involving arms control and disarmament.

SUSAN FRENCH is pursuing a Ph.D. in Social Science with an emphasis in Conflict Resolution at the Maxwell School of Citizenship and Public Affairs at Syracuse University. In addition to her studies, she works as an applied social scientist in energy deficiency, education, and conflict resolution.

RICHARD N. HAASS is a member of the United States National Security Council and a former lecturer in Public Policy at Harvard University's John F. Kennedy School of Government and Senior Research Associate at Harvard University's Center for Science and International Affairs. Dr. Haass has held several high positions on international policy within the U.S. government. Dr. Haass is the author of *Congressional Power: Implications for American Security Policy* (1979) and *Beyond the INF Treaty: Arms, Arms Control and the Atlantic Alliance* (1988), as well as coeditor of *Superpower Arms Control: Setting the Record Straight* (1987).

P. TERRENCE HOPMANN (Ph.D., Stanford University, 1969) is Professor of Political Science at Brown University and Director of Brown's International Relations Program. He also serves as research associate with the Center for Foreign Policy Development. Professor Hopmann has published *Rethinking the Nuclear Weapons Dilemma in Europe*, coedited with Frank Barnaby (1987), *Cumulation in International Relations Research* (1981), and *Unity and Disintegration in International Alliances: Comparative Studies* (1973). He serves as coeditor of the *International Studies Quarterly* and has published extensively on such topics as conventional and strategic arms control, third-state nuclear systems, and the history of U.S.-Soviet arms negotiations.

ROGER HURWITZ has taught political science and history at the Hebrew University, Massachusetts Institute of Technology, and Northeastern University. He was a research fellow at MIT's Center for International Studies and is currently an associate of MIT's research program on Communications Policy. He also works on Relatus, a project at MIT's Artificial Intelligence Laboratory, which is building an environment for the computerized analysis of social science–oriented natural language texts. Hurwitz's research has focused on theories and methods of international relations, Middle East politics, and patterns of mass communication.

Jo L. HUSBANDS is currently a Senior Research Associate at the National Academy of Sciences, in Washington, D.C. She received her doctorate in 1977 at the University of Minnesota and has held positions as Deputy Director of the Committee for National Security (1982–86), Senior Research Associate with CACI, Inc. (1978–82), and Senior Analyst at the Center for Defense Information in Washington (1978–82). Dr. Husbands has published extensively on topics such as U.S. and Soviet arms trading, the impact of nuclear proliferation on areas of national interest and international influence, and increasing security while reducing military spending.

LOUIS KRIESBERG (Ph.D., University of Chicago, 1953) is currently Director of the Program on the Analysis and Resolution of Conflicts, and Professor of Sociology at Syracuse University. Professor Kriesberg's books include *Social Conflicts* (1973, rev. 1982) and *Social Inequality* (1979); he edited *Social Processes in International Relations* (1968), *Intractable Conflicts and Their Transformation* (Syracuse University Press, 1989), and since 1978, has edited an annual series in *Social Movements, Conflicts, and Change*.

AMBASSADOR JOHN W. MCDONALD is a lawyer, diplomat, former international civil servant, and development expert concerned about the economic and social problems of the Third World. Ambassador McDonald is currently President of the Iowa Peace Institute and has served as an adjunct professor at George Washington University Law School, the Senior Adviser to George Mason University's Center for Conflict Analysis and Resolution, and is lecturer at the Foreign Service Institute and the Center for the Study of Foreign Affairs.

MAJ. GEN. INDAR JIT RIKHYE graduated from the Indian Military Academy in 1939 and served in World War II in the Middle East and Italy and in the northwest frontier of India from 1945–47. His ten years of service with the United Nations included posts as Chief of Staff of the U.N. Emergency Force in Gaza (1958–60), and Military Adviser to Dag Hammarskjold and U Thant. General Rikhye left the United Nations in 1969 and became founding President of the International Peace Academy. He is the author of *The Sinai Blunder: Withdrawal of the United Nations Emergency Force* (1980), *The Theory and Practice of Peacekeeping* (1984), and has coauthored other publications. He was awarded the UNESCO Prize for Peace Education in 1985.

JEFFREY Z. RUBIN is Professor of Psychology at Tufts University and Executive Director of the Program on Negotiation at the Harvard Law School. The author, coauthor, or editor of ten books and numerous articles, Rubin is also editor of *Negotiation Journal: On the Process of Dispute Settlement*, a quarterly journal focusing on the theory and practice of negotiation.

STUART J. THORSON is Chair of Political Science and Director of the International Relations Program at the Maxwell School of Citizenship and Public Affairs at Syracuse University. Professor Thorson has published several articles in his fields of current research: computational models of politics, foreign policy decision-making, and formal models of politics; in addition to work in such areas as congressional turnover and the election of women, the Cuban Missile Crisis, public opinion, election prediction, and weapons procurement.

I. WILLIAM ZARTMAN teaches at the School of Advanced International Studies, African Studies Program, at Johns Hopkins University (1980–). Professor Zartman has authored ten books, among them *The Practical Negotiator* (1981) and *Ripe for Resolution: Conflict and Intervention in Africa* (1985), and he has coauthored, edited, or appeared in more than sixty additional volumes.

TIMING
THE
DE-ESCALATION
OF
INTERNATIONAL
CONFLICTS

INTRODUCTION
Timing Conditions, Strategies, and Errors

Louis Kriesberg

THAT TIMING IS IMPORTANT in international de-escalating efforts is widely asserted. For example, Elmore Jackson, reflecting on his mediating efforts, observes, "There are times and seasons for everything, and often if opportunity is not seized, malleable political and personal contexts that could have been shaped to a larger and more significant purpose can quickly disappear" (Jackson 1983, 85).

The importance of timing is also indicated by the frequent reference to it by officials, who are either urging someone else to act or justifying their own inaction. Thus political leaders may say to an adversary, "Now is an opportunity that will soon be lost; seize it by making the concession we have been urging." On the other hand, political leaders often explain their own inaction by pointing out that the time is not ripe, observing that the adversary is not yet ready to make the necessary concessions.

The polemical use of the concept of timing, or ripeness, is based on preferences and also on conventional beliefs about when de-escalation efforts are likely to be effective. Relatively little research has been done, however, upon which those beliefs could confidently rest. This book offers assessments of when the time is actually right for a de-escalatory effort. No amount of research will ever make it clear to everyone that a given historical circumstance is or is not ripe for de-escalation. This is true for two reasons.

First, analyses only can be done about past events and about conditions prevailing in the past. Furthermore, even if generalizations can be drawn that go beyond a historical moment, they only pertain to

1

a few factors. Making good decisions about a single case requires clinical wisdom that combines detailed knowledge of the case and of scientific generalizations. Second, whether the time is right for de-escalation efforts does not depend only on the factual analyses. It depends, too, on the values and preferences of those who make the assessments.

Assertions that the time is or is not right for de-escalating a conflict are always conditioned by preferences about the nature of the settlement being sought. This observation is evident in the urgings by some adversaries for certain kinds of interventions or in admonitions by others that the time is not right for intervention. For example, consider the reactions to the efforts in early 1988 by Secretary of State George Shultz to renew the peace process in the Middle East. The spokesperson for Prime Minister Yitzhak Shamir said that the timing of the Shultz initiative was inopportune. He noted that in the wake of the disturbances in the occupied territories "Israel is perceived as divided and weakened and this is not a good atmosphere in which to start talks." (*Jerusalem Post* 1988).

At the same time, the spokesperson for Foreign Minister Peres exuded a sense of urgency, arguing that the current U.S. administration is "very friendly to Israel and . . . it is doubtful that a similar degree of intimacy can be achieved with any administration in the foreseeable future. We are the ones who should be interested in this administration getting involved in the peace process." (*Jerusalem Post* 1988)

Such rhetorical uses of the concept of timing should alert one to the possibility that whether one regards a particular set of conditions as propitious for de-escalation depends not only on the conflict conditions but also on the interests and values one is trying to preserve. In this book conditions are specified conducive to effective de-escalation efforts for *particular objectives*. Such specification will also enhance one's understanding of conflict de-escalation.

This approach implies that it is not always correct to de-escalate, even when the time appears ripe for de-escalation. De-escalation is not always desirable. For many people, fighting for a better settlement in the future is the correct policy, and that assessment should not be disregarded. On the other hand, trying to de-escalate even when the time is not right may be correct; it may be useful in the long run or may build constituency support.

In this introduction, I first discuss the concepts of de-escalation and timing. Then I map out the three sets of questions addressed in this book and examine the major considerations relevant to answering them. The questions pertain to the conditions that constitute good timing, de-escalation, strategies and policy choices.

THE CONCEPTS OF TIMING AND DE-ESCALATION

The terms *de-escalation* and *timing* require explication. De-escalation should be recognized as a multidimensional phenomenon. In this book, it refers to a reduction in one or more dimensions of the intensity of the conflict behavior between adversaries. Not necessarily co-varying with intensity, de-escalation also refers to a contraction in the extent of the conflict, including the number of parties engaged in the struggle. In addition, it refers to efforts to move toward a settlement of the dispute. Such efforts include tacit bargaining and implicit understandings of mutual benefits. They also include explicit peace initiatives, negotiations about a possible de-escalation agreement, and the reaching of an agreement that settles a particular desire.

Most attention in this book is on de-escalation efforts that lead to formal negotiations and to explicit agreements. This phase of de-escalation is similar to the increasingly recognized stage of prenegotiation. There are ambiguities in assessing the de-escalation character of conduct by adversaries or by intermediaries. For example, many de-escalation initiatives or proposals are meant to deflect or assuage domestic or coalition pressure in order to allow the proposer to continue a fundamental escalation. Even negotiations may not constitute de-escalation when they go on for years without any concluding agreement. Such negotiations, unmarked by significant progress toward agreement, are not regarded in this book as de-escalation. On the other hand, the process of getting negotiations started when the parties previously would not meet to negotiate clearly is de-escalation. Negotiations that conclude with agreements are also regarded as de-escalating, even if previous negotiations had persisted for a long time without reaching an explicit agreement.

De-escalation may follow from episodes of increasingly intense hostility, including war-threatening crises or escalating wars. It may also occur after the conflict is stalemated at a high, mutually hurting level of antagonism (Touval and Zartman 1985). De-escalation may also follow from frozen adversarial relations, as in cases of a cold war or a cold peace.

De-escalation can be directed toward increased cooperation or away from intense animosity. Explicit de-escalation may be efforts to get adversaries to the negotiating table, or it may be negotiations to settle a particular dispute. De-escalation may also be a step toward reconciliation and the resolution of the basic conflict in which the major adversaries are engaged, or it may be the settlement of a peripheral issue. De-escalation may be viewed as a stage in the course of a conflict, which, itself, incorporates several stages. The stages include signaling or probing by one party, exploratory discussions about possible agendas for negotiations, conducting negotiations, and concluding and sustaining agreements.

The concepts of *timing* and *ripeness* also have several meanings relevant to the concerns discussed in this book. Ripeness usually refers to circumstances when the conflict is ready for an effort to bring about a particular change. Timing has a broader meaning, encompassing circumstances that are and are not appropriate for particular efforts. Ripeness, then, is a metaphorical way to refer to the *right* time to undertake an effort to make a desired change.

One meaning of timing is that events and changes occur in sequence and, therefore, a particular de-escalation effort must be made at the appropriate time in the sequence of developments. In another meaning, timing refers to an irreversible series of events that suggests that, to be effective, a de-escalation effort must be made when the conditions are appropriate because the conditions will change and not recur.

These characteristics may appear to have a reality independent of the adversaries. However, in a fundamental sense, they do not. What is the natural sequence and what is or is not reversible depend on subjective beliefs of adversaries and intermediaries. These beliefs change over time, reflecting changes in experience and in external circumstances.

Some conditions certainly seem to have a readily observable time characteristic independent of subjective judgments. For example, many government officials hold office for fixed terms. All the actors are aware of such terms; hence, these office terms may set time limits for many kinds of relations. Even in these cases, however, people may disagree about how different a successor to the office is likely to be. Depending on perceptions of how different the new government will be, the foreseen change in government head may or may not be regarded as a changed condition.

The contributions in this book are relevant to three sets of questions. The first pertains to the conditions affecting what constitutes readiness for de-escalation efforts. What conditions are conducive to de-escalation efforts? Are they inherent in the conflict or are they created by the partisans and the intermediaries? Are such conditions recognizable independently from observing successful de-escalation efforts?

The second set of questions refers to the strategies used to bring about de-escalation under varying conditions. What de-escalation strategies are effective in varying circumstances? Which strategies are different parties able to use effectively? The parties include nongovernmental as well as governmental actors, interveners as well as adversaries, and weak as well as powerful actors.

The third set of questions addresses policy matters. What are the likely consequences for various parties of missing the opportunity to make a de-escalation effort when the time is right? What are the risks of trying to de-escalate a conflict when the time is not right? What are the consequences for different parties of effectively de-escalating a conflict at a given time?

These questions cannot be answered by any simple generalization. The answers vary with who is undertaking the de-escalation effort, for what objective, and with which adversary. I shall note such variation while discussing the conditions of a conflict that make it ready for de-escalation, the strategies appropriate for different conditions, and the consequences of trying to de-escalate both when the conditions are and are not appropriate.

CONDITIONS

When outlining the conditions that are and are not conducive to de-escalating a conflict, I treat the conditions as if they were not manipulable by the parties whose perspective is taken. When I turn later to discuss strategies, some of these same conditions will be regarded as modifiable. In an extended time perspective, of course, many of these conditions are alterable by some actors. In a short time perspective, most actors must accept them as part of an unalterable reality.

Three major sets of conditions warrant discussion: relations between the adversaries, domestic circumstances, and the international context.

Adversary Relations

A conflict between adversaries varies in intensity over time. Particular disputes may lie dormant for years, then emerge into awareness, escalate in intensity, begin to de-escalate, and be settled or resolved, perhaps to emerge in a different form years later (Kriesberg 1982). These disputes are embedded in more general conflicts that have their own course of development, as is evident in the U.S.-Soviet conflict.

The nature of the adversarial relationship in a conflict certainly affects the possibility of de-escalation and should influence the choice of an appropriate strategy (Bercovitch 1984). If the conflict has been maintained for a long time, it may have become so institutionalized that the vested interests for its continuance are great. The original issues in contention may have become submerged so that the conflict persists based in part on the dynamics internal to each party, on misunderstandings and on mutual dehumanization. For example, the Israeli-Palestinian struggle's intractability has been enhanced by such developments.

De-escalation efforts are especially likely when a conflict has rapidly escalated and violence has broken out (Bercovitch 1984; Stein 1989). For example, United Nations (U.N.) intervention is most likely to occur at a time of crisis or when a conflict is intense. This likelihood is illustrated in the chapters by Juergen Dedring and Indar Rikhye. The success rate of efforts at such times, however, is probably lower than for efforts undertaken when the conflict has become stalemated at a high level of antagonism. Often, after a long-term stalemate, mutual accommodation and mutual acceptance of the status quo gradually emerge. To a significant degree, that happened to the Cold War in Europe (Kriesberg 1989). That accommodation became the basis for the fundamental transformation of Eastern Europe in the late 1980s.

Effective de-escalation is more likely between adversaries with a history of cooperation than among adversaries lacking such a history. For example, consider the U.S. and Soviet governments, which were once allied in a war against a common enemy, and the Israeli and Syrian governments, which were not. It is easier to restore a mutually accommodative relationship than to create it.

Partisans in a fight often assert that the relative strength of the adversaries is critical for de-escalation moves (Touval 1982; Zartman 1977). Each side seems more ready to undertake de-escalation initiatives when it believes it is stronger than its adversary compared to when it believes that it is relatively weak but expects to gain strength in the future. If one party is much stronger, however, it often raises its demands rather than offering to de-escalate the fight. Consequently, de-escalation moves from intense and stable antagonism are more likely to occur when the adversaries experience parity than when one adversary is much stronger than the other. Parity, however, must be considered relative to the issue about which de-escalation is being considered. The chapter by I. William Zartman and Johannes Aurik contributes particularly to our understanding of such matters.

The prospective power balance is as important as the current power balance. The party that believes it will gain relative strength in the future tends to resist making concessions in the present, hoping for better terms of settlement later. An adversary that thinks it is winning may keep raising its demands, frequently overextending itself. The wise policy often is to settle for half a loaf rather than to hold out for the whole and gain only a crumb.

Relative power is only one dimension of relations between adversaries. The level of cooperative exchanges and potential exchanges and the degree of shared interests and values are other significant dimensions. Thus the accommodative transformations in Soviet foreign policy and reciprocation by the United States are the result of more than changes or stalemates in relative military power. The transformations in part have been generated by earlier cooperative relations between the Soviet Union and Western Europe as well as the United States. The prospect of positive benefits is also significant in the timing of de-escalation moves.

Domestic Circumstances

Domestic conditions may change and generate pressure for a government to initiate efforts to reduce conflict behavior, but they may also inhibit or constrain leaders from making such efforts. Officials also may be influenced by the domestic conditions in the adversarial country. The constituency of the adversary's officials may be viewed as likely supporters or antagonists of a de-escalation effort. Whether domestic circumstances are generally conducive to de-escalation initiative moves is not clear. Jo Husbands, in her contribution to this volume, surveys the relevant research and infers that domestic pressure generally is not supportive of accommodative moves toward an adversary. It is indeed easy to note how public pressure has encouraged government leaders to assert demands against adversaries that handicap de-escalation. It is also possible, however, to point out how domestic pressure encourages accommodation in the long run or propels government leaders to make what are at least plausible de-escalation proposals to their adversaries. In this introduction, I outline the ways domestic circumstances may support explicit de-escalation as well as inhibit such de-escalation efforts.

For example, in the early years of the Reagan administration, the nuclear freeze campaign in the United States grew extremely rapidly and had an important impact on Congress (Waller 1987; Solo 1988). The Reagan administration was compelled to present a plausible bargaining position in negotiations on strategic nuclear weapons and intermediate-range nuclear weapons at the Strategic Arms Reduction Talks (START) and the Intermediate-range Nuclear Forces (INF) talks (Talbott 1984). The latter is examined in the chapter by Richard Haass.

Domestic factors in allied and in adversarial countries have indirect consequences as well. For example, during the negotiations on the INF Treaty, demonstrations against the planned deployment in Europe of U.S. Pershing II and cruise missiles became massive and very intense, especially in the Netherlands and West Germany. The possibility that deployment would not be politically feasible in those countries may have encouraged Paul Nitze (heading the U.S. INF delegation) to seek an agreement with the Soviets while the bargaining chip was still available. He and Yuli Kvitsinsky (heading the Soviet INF delegation) indeed reached an agreement in their walks in the Geneva woods. Their agreement, however, was not accepted by either government. The demonstrations may have led the Soviets to believe that the new missiles could not be deployed.

Domestic support for reducing antagonism can facilitate official de-escalation initiatives and moves in other ways. A government may appeal for support from its adversary's domestic population. Or if the adversary undertakes a de-escalation effort, it is more likely to be regarded as serious and, therefore, reciprocated when it seems to be supported by that adversary's constituents. The absence of constituents backing for de-escalation may make the initiative seem implausible or unstable to the other conflict party.

Perhaps, however, domestic pressure in one party leads the adversary to believe that it can hold out for better terms and, consequently, reduces the chances of an actual de-escalation move. This may have been the case with the Soviet unwillingness to settle for the walk-in-the-woods formula during the INF negotiations in 1982.

Domestic conditions certainly include more than popular opinion or mass demonstrations. Governmental representatives have many constituencies who have to be taken into account. Some of those constituencies have a vested interest in particular matters to which the government representatives give lower priority. The government representatives in international negotiations, then, find that they cannot trade off certain matters to win an agreement that they themselves might regard as worthwhile. Such constituencies include ethnic groups, business organizations, and military bureaucracies.

The government leadership itself may have a vested interest in pursuing policies it has favored in the past, even if it is not advancing the goals that it purports to serve. Changes in government leadership appear to be conducive to de-escalation initiatives, both by the new leadership and by the external adversaries. New leaders often are relatively free to undertake fresh initiatives, and, furthermore, they are likely to be perceived to be relatively freer by the leaders of the adversarial countries. In addition, the prospect of a change in leadership is a stimulus for concluding a de-escalatory agreement that had been initiated earlier and has progressed slowly. The prospect of a new government that might require starting over can be an incentive for concluding the agreement if it seems at all in reach.

The profound de-escalatory changes in the East-West relations in the 1980s were significantly affected by domestic developments not only in the Soviet Union but also in European countries and in the United States. In the Soviet Union, economic difficulties were certainly aggravated by the drain of military expenditures. Those burdens became increasingly heavier as popular demands for improved consumer goods and services grew, partly as a result of increasing familiarity with the West. In the Western countries, military-based security was no longer consensually supported. The Cold War consensus of the 1950s and early 1960s was ruptured so that even when Ronald Reagan was president, strong opposition to his anti-Soviet policies arose.

International Context

Terrence Hopmann's chapter in this volume analyzes the impact of the international context on a particular set of negotiations, for example, between the U.S. and Soviet governments. He focuses on the international context in terms of the relations between the negotiating partners external to the particular negotiations in which they are engaged. The international context, however, is broader. It includes each primary adversary's cooperative pattern and conflicts with other parties as well as the network of governmental and nongovernmental international organizations within which these adversaries function.

The world is full of conflicts, and they are interlocked in many ways. As one becomes salient, others become less so and more amenable to de-escalation (Kriesberg 1980). Consequently, one fundamental way in which the international context affects the appropriateness of de-escalation efforts is the relative salience of the conflict among the many others in which the adversaries are engaged. For example, the rise of detente in U.S.-Soviet relations was undoubtedly made possible by the intensification of the Soviet-Chinese conflict and the persistence of the U.S.–North Vietnamese war (Garthoff 1985).

Major conflicts are linked in other ways as well. One important connection is that people draw lessons from past conflicts, and those lessons then affect their readiness to escalate or de-escalate a future conflict (Neustadt and May 1986). Many of these lessons are learned by members of the society engaged in the conflict; for example, people in the United States have drawn various lessons from their involvement in the Vietnam War. But there is also a more general diffusion of some inferences. For example, the disastrous consequences of appeasing Nazi Germany became widely diffused and extrapolated to many other conflicts in the world. The horrors of nazism and fascism and their total defeat had another effect. They gave violence and the glorification of war a bad reputation. This result has made peacemaking appeals particularly attractive in the contemporary world and especially in Europe.

Another major aspect of the international context that is conducive to de-escalation efforts and moves in a conflict is the readiness of governmental and nongovernmental actors to serve as intermediaries in the conflict. International governmental and nongovernmental actors are varyingly available for initiating and facilitating de-escalation efforts for different conflicts. For example, from the outset of the Israeli-Arab conflict, the United Nations was involved and has often sought to perform various mediating services.

Combinations of Adversary Relations, Domestic Circumstances, and International Context

The impact of each condition for de-escalation depends in part on the other conditions. Thus, domestic pressure for an improvement in living conditions can be conducive to de-escalation but not necessarily. It can also propel government leaders toward an aggressive international venture in order to divert attention from domestic hardships.

The likelihood of government heads seeking a de-escalation movement in response to such domestic pressures will be increased if they believe that a mutually satisfactory agreement with a principal adversary is attainable. Thus the Soviet leadership's belief in the late 1980s that domestic economic improvements were needed could have been acted upon in more than one way. The leaders chose policies of accommodation with the West rather than antagonism that might help mobilize the population because past détente and U.S. domestic constraints on President Reagan made accommodation seem possible and useful.

What is crucial for propitious timing is the convergence of interest among two or more major adversaries. Domestic pressures and changes in the international context affect such timing. For example, the 1988 agreement between the Nicaraguan Sandinistas and Contras was partly a response to constituency considerations in the United States and in Nicaragua and to changes in external Soviet support for the Sandinistas.

A long-standing, low level of antagonism does not in itself constitute a propitious time for tension-reducing moves. In combination with certain changes in domestic conditions or international context, however, the time may become ripe. Thus, the antagonism between West Germany and the Soviet Union endured with little change during the mid-1960s. Gradually changing opinions among West Germans and the 1969 electoral triumph of the Social Democratic party and of Willy Brandt's *Ostpolitik* transformed the circumstances. Similarly, U.S.-Soviet relations during the mid-1960s had also changed little. The intensification of the U.S. involvement in the war in Vietnam, however, combined with domestic U.S. pressure against American involvement in that war made the early 1970s a propitious time for accommodative initiatives by the U.S. government.

STRATEGIES OF DE-ESCALATION

Giving much attention to timing for de-escalation might seem to encourage passivity for those who would want to move toward the settlement of a dispute and more cooperative relations. A strategic perspective goes beyond that view. Conditions are never entirely fixed; various actors can modify many of them. Even when certain conditions are not malleable for a party within a given time frame, they may be propitious for long-term de-escalation strategies. Furthermore, the conditions may not be conducive for one party but may be for another. These variations demonstrate the usefulness of considering alternative strategies to reduce antagonism.

Strategies should be considered in terms of the various actors who might be seeking to de-escalate a conflict. The actor may be the president of the United States, the U.N. secretary general, the head of a U.S.-based corporation, a church leader, a political party official, or a trade union president. Such actors may be from one of the primary adversaries, from an ally of one of them, or from a country or organization that purports not to be aligned in the conflict. Actors also differ greatly in the resources available to them to pursue their strategies and in the time frame within which they are operating.

Actors may seek to modify time itself as it pertains to the opportunity to de-escalate. They may try to set deadlines by which accommodation efforts must be undertaken. They may try to affect the other parties' views about the prospect of conditions conducive to a particular settlement improving or deteriorating soon. The efforts may be persuasive, urging new interpretations, or they may be manipulative, altering the reality.

Within a long-term perspective, some actors can pursue strategies that seek to mobilize support for accommodation. This mobilization may include efforts directed at domestic elites and significant elements of the attentive public (Saunders 1985). It may even be directed at marshaling support from other governments or international organizations. Of course, different actors may be constrained by different time frames. For example, in the United States, the presidential term of office has been cited as a major constraint in foreign policy making (Quandt 1986).

Whoever is undertaking to reduce antagonism must pursue a strategy that entails deciding which parties should be part of the de-escalation effort, which issues should be subject to the effort, and what inducements should be included. How those choices are made is critical in the basic task of helping to create the right conditions for de-escalation. Fundamentally, the strategies are directed at transforming an intractable conflict into a negotiable one or reframing a conflict so that it appears to be a shared problem with a possible solution.

Parties

Several choices about the parties to be included in the de-escalation effort must be made. One choice pertains to the number of primary adversaries to be included. Conflicts are often viewed as if there were simply two sides and, therefore, two parties. However, this is never the case; there are always many pairs of opponents and, hence, alternative overlapping pairings. For example, in the U.S.-Soviet conflict, the parties may be NATO versus Warsaw Pact, the Free World versus the Communist World, or the imperialist bloc versus the Socialist camp. In addition, other cleavages may crosscut those pairs: for example, nuclear powers versus nonnuclear powers and advanced industrialized countries versus economically developing countries.

Another choice is whether or not intermediaries participate in the de-escalation effort. Intermediaries include actors, such as governments of countries not primarily engaged in the conflict; for example, the U.S. government often has played a mediating role in Israeli-Arab de-escalation efforts. Many international governmental and nongovernmental organizations have played such roles formally and informally; the list includes the U.N. secretary general and the Dartmouth Conference (Bendahmane 1987). Such intermediaries are themselves critical in exploring which sets of parties should be participants in negotiations. This is an important aspect of the prenegotiation stage of a de-escalation sequence.

When the relations between the adversaries are almost entirely hostile, involving intermediaries is likely to help initiate movement toward effective negotiation. For example, in the period of relatively intense U.S.-Soviet antagonism, during the Cold War, effective negotiations in U.S.-Soviet relations included governments not aligned with either country (Kriesberg 1987; 1992). The contributions of nonadversary governments may be illustrated by negotiations producing the 1959 Antarctica Treaty, signed by twelve countries in addition to the United States and the Soviet Union. Only in later years, when some accommodative agreements already had been reached, were formal bilateral treaties achieved, including the Antiballistic Missile (ABM) and Strategic Arms Limitation Treaty (SALT I) agreements in 1972.

Finally, a choice must be made regarding the level and official character of the parties to be involved in the efforts. Initiatives may be conducted by heads of government, nonofficial personages, high-level official diplomats, or many others. The same is true for negotiations or other de-escalation moves. Initial probes can be speedily and often effectively conducted by nonofficials and later pursued by official government representatives.

Recently, attention to the role of nongovernmental actors in peacemaking efforts has increased. One avenue nongovernmental actors have followed is that of Track Two diplomacy (Berman and Johnson 1977). Participants in Track Two diplomacy range from private persons serving at the request of officials to sound out representatives of adversarial governments to self-appointed intermediaries acting at variance with their own governments' policies.

Ralph Earle and John McDonald, in their chapters, examine the varieties and possible contributions of nonofficial diplomacy. They note the limitations of such diplomacy and agree that private citizens may be relatively useful in the preliminary stages of de-escalation efforts.

Nonofficial diplomacy may help create the conditions that lead adversary officials to believe a mutually satisfactory solution to their conflict is possible, or they may themselves engage in prenegotiation explorations about the possible agenda and format for negotiations. Nongovernmental actors may be well-established entities, such as church organizations, or they may be individuals with no formal constituency (Kriesberg 1972). They may be serving on a short-term, single mission, or they may be involved in long-standing transnational organizations, such as the Pugwash movement (Pentz and Slovo 1981).

The earlier discussion of the conditions that are propitious for beginning serious negotiations has implications for the strategic choices about the possible parties for initiating de-escalation. Thus for an intermediary or the leader of one of the adversaries, the search for negotiating partners can be guided by taking into account the domestic conditions or constituency pressure of the potential partners. Similarly, the internal context for one or more of the adversaries may change when a new conflict becomes salient for the adversary. This constitutes an opportunity to de-escalate the old conflict. For example, the 1969 border skirmishes between the Soviet and Chinese military forces signaled that the U.S. government had an opportunity to reduce the confrontation level between itself and both the Soviet and the Chinese governments.

Inducements

A strategy also entails choices about the use of inducements by one party to the other; the inducements are various mixtures of persuasion and of positive and negative sanctions. The package of inducements used is critical in the fundamental aspect of creating the right time to attempt de-escalation. Government officials often argue that their adversaries only understand strength, suggesting, therefore, that their own threats are necessary to bring about de-escalation. Sometimes the same officials, assuming their own virtues and the adversaries' vices, argue that their adversaries must offer significant concessions in order to begin to move toward de-escalation. Whatever the rhetorical use of claims about various kinds of inducements may be, choices must actually be made about the combinations and sequences of carrots and sticks and of persuasive communications.

An often-cited idea in the literature on international conflict resolution and peacemaking was formulated by Charles E. Osgood (1962). He proposed that to initiate de-escalation moves a conciliatory concession that does not weaken the initiator's security should be announced and reciprocation not specifically requested. Further concessions should be consistently made so that eventually reciprocation would follow. This strategy of gradual reciprocal initiatives in tension reduction is known by its acronym, GRIT.

The effectiveness of this strategy under different circumstances should be seriously assessed. Because it has not yet been employed fully in any situation, it is necessary to systematically compare the effectiveness of varying forms and magnitudes of its major components: announcements and conciliatory gestures. Another strategy emphasizes the use of both coercion and concession, of carrots and sticks on a tit-for-tat basis (Axelrod 1984). One party seeks a cooperative relationship by initiating a conciliatory move but thereafter only reciprocates what its adversary does—whether coercive or conciliatory.

Although these ideas have been discussed for many years, relatively little systematic research has been conducted to assess these strategies in practice. The steps leading to the Limited Nuclear Test Ban have been considered in this light as have more recent negotiations in U.S.-Soviet and Arab-Israeli negotiations (Etzioni 1967; Kriesberg 1981). These ideas may be effectively applied under some circumstances but are not universally applicable. The time must be right for various formulations of them.

The analysis of the role of persuasion in de-escalation strategies has been relatively neglected. The current interest in discourse analysis may contribute some needed insight in this area. The circumstances discussed earlier in this introduction could be given different interpretations by partisans in a conflict. If they can persuade others to accept their interpretations, the bases for de-escalation moves might be found.

A major influence in bringing about de-escalation is the prospect that the alternatives now and in the future will be worse if the conflict continues unabated. Each party then seeks to convince the other that time is on its side. For example, one party may try to convince the other that its subsequent leaders will be less accommodative than the current ones.

A change in the definition of the relationship between adversaries and of their conflict may enable de-escalation to occur. This often means that the conflict is reframed; the interpretative schema that partisans use to organize and understand their conflict changes (Schon 1983; Goffman 1972). A conflict framed as zero-sum may be reframed to have possible outcomes with mutually beneficial, win-win payoffs. Redefinitions or reconceptualizations of the conflict may come about when it is viewed in a new context, as when a new superordinate shared goal is found (Sherif 1966). Defeating a common enemy or avoiding a common loss (such as a mutually suicidal war) are such goals. In chapter 5, Roger

Hurwitz illuminates some aspects of such changes, arguing that there was a transformation in U.S.-Soviet thinking following the 1962 Cuban Missile Crisis. Shifts in issues of contention and in who the adversaries are may be part of such redefinitions.

De-escalation is fostered by reconceptualizations of a conflict and how it is to be waged. Such reconceptualizations give coherence and meaning to peacemaking efforts and can help mobilize support for them. The "new thinking" articulated by Mikhail S. Gorbachev in the late 1980s is illustrative. Rather than saying the Soviets were making concessions, especially out of relative weakness, President Gorbachev argued that reducing Soviet military forces would enhance Soviet security. He drew from some of the ideas created by peace researchers of West Germany and other European countries. (Dragsdahl 1989). The researchers argued for example, that one's security would be enhanced not by threatening the security of others but by developing mutual or common security.

In another approach to reframing a conflict, facilitators help adversaries discover what their basic needs or underlying interests are (Burton 1987; Fisher and Ury 1981). Disputes about hardened positions may thus be overcome as the adversaries discover ways by which each side's underlying needs or interests can be satisfied without denying the other side's satisfaction of its needs or interests. Among the cases examined in this book, such reframing and conflict resolution is not evident in sudden shifts; however, partial settlements and incremental peacemaking do occur.

Inducements should be carefully targeted, taking into account appeals to the adversary's constituency. Thus threats can be counterproductive, as when they consolidate constituency support for a nonaccommodative posture by the leaders.

When considering the inducements that can be part of a strategy to de-escalate a conflict, taking into account the international context is important. The international system and other actors in it can provide resources that expand the pie so that the adversaries do not have to gain only at the expense of each other. This is most apparent in the way large, relatively prosperous countries can supplement and compensate small powers for the loss that a de-escalation agreement may entail (Carnevale 1986).

Issues

International conflicts are always about many matters of contention. De-escalation strategies must focus on particular issues, giving lower priority to some and higher priority to others. The issues vary in content, including human rights, boundaries, arms control, trade, fishing rights, and agreements about influence in areas of contention. The issues vary also in perceived importance—from vital to peripheral matters. Finally, a strategy may seek to isolate one or two issues or to link many in a package (Fisher 1964).

It appears that in the long course of an international conflict relationship, effective de-escalation at the early stages of accommodation is achieved more often in peripheral issues than vital ones. Once some accommodative agreements have been reached, more significant ones can be attained; for example, the 1972 ABM Treaty followed agreements in 1959 about Antarctica and the 1971 prohibition of weapons of mass destruction placed on the seabeds. Linkage among many issues seems to work better after the overall intensity of a conflict has been reduced. At the outset, dealing with issues in relative isolation usually is conducive to reaching de-escalation agreements; for example, the complex negotiations of détente followed relatively isolated agreements.

Issues also vary in the extent to which the adversaries have relevant equality in strength and in the extent to which the issues are changing in ways that are adverse to the primary opponents. For example, particular weapons systems become technologically feasible at specific times. Agreements about controlling weapon systems are differentially attainable depending on the stage and nature of the weapons' development.

Whatever the set of issues addressed in a de-escalation strategy, the possible terms of a settlement of those issues must be considered. Everyone is for peace but not on just any terms. When considering whether to undertake de-escalation negotiations, each party takes into account what the outcome of the negotiations is likely to be. This calculation underlies partisan insistence upon preconditions for entering negotiations or undertaking de-escalation initiatives; the preconditions ensure minimal terms for the outcome. Prenegotiations always include some agenda setting: which issues are included and which excluded.

Negotiations, once entered, do have a dynamic of their own. Often, public expectations that an agreement will be reached rise and are expressed as pressure to conclude one. For example, the Peace Now movement emerged in Israel only after President Sadat had visited Israel and negotiations for a peace treaty had begun. Furthermore, the act of carrying on negotiations may weaken the resolve to sustain or to reinvigorate a high level of hostility against the adversary. So there are risks to each party in beginning a negotiating journey unless the likely destinations are acceptable to the major negotiating parties.

Implementation

De-escalation strategies combine choices about parties, issues and inducements. Different sets of combinations are available to different actors, whether they are individuals or large organizations, officials or nonofficials, and partisans or intermediaries. Different combinations are appropriate depending not only on the conditions but on the time frame in which the strategy is to be implemented.

To illustrate, the reframing of U.S.-Soviet relations in 1963 was not merely a response to the Cuban Missile Crisis. Conditions within each society had shifted to support some mutual accommodation, following long-run trends. The strategy of selecting one easily managed issue, nuclear weapons testing in the atmosphere, was appropriate to begin a de-escalation movement.

POLICY IMPLICATIONS

The review of elements of de-escalation strategies and of conditions relevant to their timing has implications for implementing a particular strategy within a given set of conditions. The variety of possible strategies suggests that an effective one might be developed for almost any set of existing conditions. Such a strategy, however, may be effective for a settlement that is not wanted by anyone in a position to implement the strategy.

In this work, the authors often presume the desirability of de-escalation, assuming that the alternative is likely to be continuing suffering and the prospect of even more loss. Finding a way to cut the losses and yet achieve a mutually acceptable settlement among the primary antagonists is often preferred. This may mean accommodation to the status quo. Yet for many of us, for particular conflicts, that is not good enough.

Policy implications are discussed here in terms of possible errors and risks: first, the risks of *trying* to de-escalate when the time is *not* right (for a particular effort); and second, the risks of *failing* to try when the time *is* right. Because I do not assume that all de-escalations are good, I will also consider some of the risks of trying and succeeding when the time is right. Finally, I will discuss the risks of not trying when the time is not right.

The basic argument is that the time is never simply right or wrong for de-escalation. Rather, the time may be right for one conflict settlement but not another and, hence, for one strategy but not for another. Therefore, the failure to move effectively into de-escalation negotiations does not necessarily mean that the time was not right: it may mean that the wrong goal and strategy were pursued.

Of course, there are reasons for persons to have acted as they did, and in retrospect what happened often seems inevitable. Reflecting on past conduct, however, may bring to light implications that can improve one's choices in the future. For example, President John F. Kennedy read Barbara Tuchman's *The Guns of August*, about the outbreak of World War I, shortly before the 1962 Cuban Missile Crisis (Schlesinger 1965). He sought to avoid the steps that he believed had generated the escalation in August 1914 that led to the First World War.

The times are never right or wrong for any and all strategies. Possible errors of trying or not trying particular strategies under specific historical conditions should be considered. Consequently, alternative strategies for particular situations will be discussed.

Trying at the Wrong Time

Parties who might try to de-escalate a conflict often fail to do so. They may fear, perhaps with good reason, that if they try and the time is not right, they will fail and have to deal with the consequences of that failure. One consequence is that the party making the attempt might then appear inept or foolish. To avert that interpretation, parties undertaking a de-escalation effort often assert that the chances of success are slight, but an effort must be made. That disclaimer enhances a success, if it comes, and minimizes the political damage of a failure, if that occurs.

These considerations are particularly important for representatives of one of the adversaries. Although of lesser significance for mediators, their judgment may be questioned for trying when the time is not right. Of course, if mediators are not acting on the basis of their own judgment, but at the instructions of others, that problem is obviated. This often is the case, for example, when the U.N. secretary general acts on the instructions of the Security Council.

There is another danger, not only to the person making a de-escalation proposal but to the proposal itself. Perhaps, once made and rejected the proposal becomes tainted. The proposal may seem less credible than it would have been if offered freshly at a more propitious time. This seems like reasonable folk wisdom, but no one has systematic evidence that this actually occurs. Again, nonofficial explorations can reduce what risks there are of such failure.

Finally, there are costs of failing to de-escalate associated with the conflict itself. Trying and failing to de-escalate a conflict may contribute to the partisans' view of the conflict as intractable. Not only is the party making the effort and the effort itself tainted but any other effort is likely to be regarded as hopeless. Such views, generating despair, may be self-fulfilling. For example, the failed de-escalation initiatives of Anwar el-Sadat and of Moshe Dayan in 1971 and 1972 convinced President Sadat that the conflict with Israel would have to be escalated before progress could be made toward an acceptable de-escalation settlement (Stein 1989, 204).

Consider the complex case of President Jimmy Carter's mediating efforts for peace in the Middle East. When he became president, he sought a comprehensive peace through the vehicle of an international peace conference cochaired by the U.S. and Soviet governments. Clearly, President Anwar el-Sadat did not regard that as the right strategy at that time, and he went to Jerusalem himself. President Sadat's strategy of involving the U.S. government as a full partner in negotiations with Israel proved to fit the circumstances and resulted in a partial settlement.

President Carter generally is not faulted in the West for trying to bring about a peace settlement at the wrong time or with the wrong strategy. The successes of his mediation at Camp David and in the final negotiations of an Israeli-Egyptian peace treaty overwhelm the earlier failure. However, the Arab governments and the Soviet government, for many years, did criticize the U.S. government for fostering a separate peace, splitting the Arab front, and excluding the Soviet Union.

Not Trying When the Time Is Right

The risks of not trying when the time is ripe are parallel to the ones discussed. Failing to seize an opportunity may not be immediately apparent, but later it may become clear that is what happened. The persons in the position to have made the effort and who failed to do so may be charged by opponents among their constituencies with having lost a chance for peace. But the argument that an effort would have been worthwhile *if tried* is more difficult to sustain than the argument that an effort that was tried had failed.

In addition, the de-escalation that would have been achieved had the effort been made obviously is not attained. Presuming that it would have been a beneficial outcome for many parties, the failure to reach it is a loss. It may be that the loss is forever because circumstances may not be right for that settlement again. For example, a settlement between the Arab governments and Israel based on the 1949 armistice lines might have been achievable before the June 1967 war; it no longer is.

Furthermore, the time available to reach an agreement may be limited and, if not fully exploited, may cause a very long delay. For example, an agreement about strategic offensive weapons was signed on November 24, 1974, in Vladivostok by President Ford and General Secretary Brezhnev. It might be argued that a de-escalation effort, including greater concessions, should have been pursued with greater urgency by both sides to conclude a treaty before the November 1976 U.S. presidential elections. When they failed to do so, the SALT II Treaty was not signed until June 1979, by which time Senate ratification was not possible.

Finally, not trying when the opportunity is present, enables the conflict to persist, perhaps to escalate. As it endures, the hostilities may become institutionalized, making a settlement more difficult later. All this argues for serious, ongoing de-escalation efforts. An active search for the appropriate strategy under the circumstances often should be made.

The Israeli-Arab conflict can provide many examples of opportunities for de-escalation efforts by the U.S. government that were not taken. For example, in the summer of 1981, Philip Habib, representing the U.S. government, did mediate, through intermediaries, a cease-fire agreement across the Lebanese-Israeli frontier between the Palestine Liberation Organization (PLO) and the Israeli government (Khouri 1985; Young 1987). During the ensuing months no incremental steps were taken to build on that agreement: for example, by fostering the Israeli-Egyptian talks regarding autonomy for Palestinians or by involving other Arab governments in that process.

The strategy seemed, instead, to support or not discourage those government leaders in Israel who envisaged an escalation of the conflict and a defeat of the PLO in Lebanon. This was viewed by high U.S. officials in the context of a general strategy to reduce Soviet influence in Lebanon and the Middle East. The consequences were a monumental failure for the U.S. government in Lebanon and for an accommodation between Israel and its Arab neighbors.

Trying When the Time Is Right

Undertaking a de-escalation effort when the time is right might seem to be no error; it is the essence of peacemaking efforts. There should be no risks in such peacemaking, but there are. Whatever effort is made involves the choice of some parties, issues, and inducements. When an agreement results, critics might argue that the wrong strategy was followed, and, hence, a poor settlement was reached.

It may be that reaching an agreement reduces the support for a more comprehensive settlement, which is then not reached. This argument has been made about the Limited Nuclear Test Ban Agreement of 1963. A similar argument might be made about the mediating role that the U.S. government played in the Camp David negotiations and the ensuing peace treaty between the Egyptian and Israeli governments. Certainly, many Arab leaders condemned President Sadat for signing a separate peace treaty with Israel.

In general, a comprehensive reconciliation among adversaries engaged in a long, harsh struggle cannot be brought about suddenly. Incremental steps are necessary. Even President Sadat's extraordinary journey to Jerusalem in November 1977 followed two separate negotiated settlements involving partial Israeli withdrawals from the Sinai. These were mediated by Secretary of State Henry Kissinger in 1974 and 1975. This argues for seizing the opportunity, even for a partial agreement; holding out for the correct, just, and comprehensive agreement entails the greater dangers.

Not Trying When the Time Is Not Right

It would seem reasonable that not trying to de-escalate when the time is not right for de-escalation is no mistake and is risk-free. But there are risks here too. Not trying means that what would have been tried was not developed and tested. Something is learned by making a proposal, even if it fails. A probe can help provide information for a better effort at a later time and some support for the proposal might be developed that would be in place for a more propitious effort. Furthermore, when the window of opportunity opens, it is often necessary to move fast before it closes. If the adversaries have negotiated for a long time, they know what agreements are possible and can quickly conclude them. For example, this was the case for the INF Treaty and the Limited Nuclear Test Ban Agreement (Seaborg 1981).

In addition, trying to de-escalate even when the time is not opportune is a way of demonstrating an interest in peace. This effort can be useful in mobilizing support from allies and constituencies. Despite the frequent reference to the "rally 'round the flag" phenomenon, popular approval for presidents who engage in peacemaking efforts occurs as well as approval based on international confrontations (Borker, Kriesberg, and Abdul-Quader 1985).

The unfortunate consequences of not trying to de-escalate, even if the time is not propitious, can be illustrated by many instances. For example, immediately after the establishment of the State of Israel, negotiations about the borders and the Palestinian refugees were conducted, largely through U.N. auspices. In the later 1960s and even after the 1967 war when the problem intensified, relatively little effort was exerted by partisans or by intermediaries to de-escalate the Arab-Israeli conflict, at least as it pertained to the Palestinians (Forsythe 1972; Berger 1965). If such efforts had been made, one of the major sources for the intractable nature of the Israeli-Arab war might have been reduced.

The situation in Europe in the 1950s and 1960s is also illustrative. A great deal of attention was given to disarmament and then to arms control, particularly to limiting nuclear weapons. The political and social issues of contention in Europe were not substantially addressed. It is true that General Secretary Khrushchev did raise some of these issues, particularly about Berlin. The Soviet leadership, however, pursued a strategy in that regard that relied on mixing severe threats with the proposals, and this was counterproductive.

CONCLUSION

Three inferences can be drawn from this discussion. First, the prevailing conditions must be seriously considered when deciding whether to undertake a de-escalation effort but more importantly on deciding which strategy to pursue. The times are not always propitious for peacemaking, at least not for the peace settlement that is desired. Officials' assertions about the time being right or wrong for de-escalation or peacemaking efforts are often rhetorical arguments to gain support for a particular proposed course of action or inaction. That observation does not negate the relevance of prevailing conditions nor does it signify that the conditions have terminal effects.

Second, although constituency factors, adversary relations, and the international context constrain de-escalation moves, the variety of possible strategies to initiate de-escalation reveals opportunities for de-escalation over a wide range of times. A long-term strategy may be pursued to help create the conditions so that the time becomes propitious for a short-term strategy. Whether the time is ripe depends greatly on who is considering undertaking a de-escalation effort. This is true because different parties have different resources and time perspectives, making some conditions malleable or unalterable. The strategy chosen, to be effective, must be appropriate for particular parties.

Finally, the process of de-escalating is not value-free. The efforts to de-escalate a conflict are not morally neutral and do not have the same implications for all the partisans. Deciding whether or not to try to de-escalate a conflict and which strategy to pursue, necessarily involves value preferences regarding an acceptable outcome.

PART ONE

CONTEXT FOR DE-ESCALATION

CONTEXT FOR DE-ESCALATION

SUSAN FRENCH and LOUIS KRIESBERG

As NOTED IN THE INTRODUCTION, the appropriate timing for the de-escalation of international conflicts is shaped by both the potential de-escalator and environmental constraints. In this section of the book we explore some aspects of the setting that may influence the de-escalation effort.

A context exists around every conflict. For international conflicts, both the larger global system and the relations between conflicting nations must be considered. Within the global system, differential levels of power, development, wealth, and political stability affect the emergence of primary and secondary conflicts among nations. This, in turn, contributes to the ebb and flow of conflicts that may often facilitate de-escalation—whether an ebb has caused a cessation of hostilities suitable to the initiation of de-escalation moves and negotiations or a flow has brought about a mutually hurting stalemate, which provides the incentive for two governments to enter a process of de-escalation and negotiation.

Terrence Hopmann examines the international context more specifically, noting the interplay between external events and the course of negotiations to improve relations between two or more countries in a conflict. According to Hopmann, the outcome of international negotiations at least partially depends upon events occurring in the larger relationship between the contending parties, including economic, environmental, and political matters.

Another perspective for viewing the context for de-escalation entails considering possible intermediaries. Several types of parties may play this role or provide mediating services. These can include one or more governmental or nongovernmental, national or international organizations—whether members of an adversarial party or a nonaligned party. In Indar Jit Rikhye's chapter, timing for de-escalation is considered from the perspective of the secretary general of the United Nations. Rikhye's discussion of the various roles played by the secretary general in facilitating de-escalation covers many of the variables that must be taken into account in any mediating intervention. These include acquiring an appropriate entrée into the negotiating or dialogue process, maintaining the support of one's own constituency (in this case, the Security Council and the General Assembly), and constructing or facilitating a workable solution, given the position of each party to the conflict. Beyond the very important element of timing, the secretary general must also correctly determine the appropriate speed, direction, and force with which to intervene in a conflict.

These considerations are important ones, as both the secretary general's role and relationships with various governments are ongoing, and so must be handled in a manner that conforms to rules interpreted by many governments. The secretary general's position is different from that of most potential intermediaries: Involvement in any conflict stems from the normative goal of the United Nations— to stop armed hostilities and promote peace among nations. This is a motivating influence that is not as likely to be presented by an intervening government.

Rikhye claims that it is because of this lack of partisanship that the good offices of the secretary general may be employed to help create a situation where the timing is right for de-escalation. Although the secretary general must work in accord with both the Security Council and the General Assembly, the Secretary's influence alone has tended to be one of the most effective direct actions the United Nations has taken to achieve its peace enhancement mission.

The secretary generals may help to bring about a situation in which the timing is right for de-escalation through the nonintrusive nature of their role. The secretaries most often work with governments that have requested their involvement, although they may occasionally offer their services as intermediaries. Rikhye believes this open door policy enhances opportunities for de-escalation. If the time is right for one country to de-escalate, the involvement of the secretary general may facilitate the second country's entry into negotiations. Juergen Dedring discusses the role of another U.N. organization, the Security Council. It is even more circumscribed than that of the secretary general. The U.S.-Soviet cold war dynamic has prevented agreement by the Security Council on several de-escalation proposals.

The process of bringing about negotiations presents one set of variables, conditions, and strategies, whereas the successful conclusion of the negotiations themselves presents a different type of endeavor. Richard Haass discusses the conditions that led to the successful outcome of negotiations on U.S. and Soviet intermediate-range nuclear weapons.

When examining Haass's thesis, it is useful to note the ways in which protracted and stylized arms negotiations may differ from, or resemble, those between countries at war, or those between governments confronting a short-term crisis. In each case, the degree to which other aspects of the nations' relationship affect negotiations is different, as is the amount of tension and hostility that exists between the parties.

In the fourth chapter in part 1 Jo Husbands explores another aspect of the context of de-escalation, the constituency of one of the adversaries. Husbands discusses the relationship between various types of domestic factors, the conditions necessary for de-escalation, and the strategies employed by different publics. In an area that previously has been insufficiently researched, Husbands offers fresh insight into the impact of three different domestic factors on international relations: the basic political process and electoral cycle, public opinion, and the influence of elites and interest groups.

Although her discussion is most appropriate to the United States, the questions she raises and the variables she explores are valid to some degree for every country. A further step in understanding the domestic context in de-escalation would entail thoughtful consideration of the conditions in each country involved. One of the elements that Husbands discusses within the context of public opinion may have far more influence in de-escalation than is immediately evident in a U.S. context. The public sentiment of one country toward that of the parties with which it is in conflict may be a significant variable in assessing the appropriate timing of a de-escalation initiative. This aspect is clear in the Middle East and in Northern Ireland today, where the hatred and fear between two groups have been reproduced over generations. An attempt at de-escalation that does not take such an important aspect of the conflict into account is not likely to succeed.

The primary purpose in this section of the book is to explore the context of international conflicts and how they constrain and also provide opportunities for de-escalation. In addition to examining the aspects of the settings here, readers must move one step further and include additional information in their analyses. The actor's goal, for example, is critical to understanding de-escalation and timing as a part of it in examining the relationship between action and outcome.

U.N. interventions are usually predicated upon the belief that war and armed hostility are to be avoided in favor of nonviolent relations among countries, and it is upon this basis that actions are formulated and initiated. When a national government acts as an intermediary in the de-escalation of a conflict, the primary objective may be similar to that of the United Nations, or it may involve the government's self-interest in acquiring or retaining power in the international system, increased influence with one or both of the conflict parties, or cessation of the negative impacts of the conflict. It is certain that many other goals could exist for such an intervention. Likewise, any country that, as a party to a conflict, enters into a process of de-escalation will also have its own set of objectives based upon its desire for a positive outcome and minimized losses.

The importance of this distinction becomes clear when one attempts to examine the notion of timing and beyond that, of success, in de-escalating international conflicts. That which comprises ideal timing and success for one party may connote loss and disaster to another. This larger understanding of the context of de-escalation will allow the analyst to understand more fully the dynamics of the successes and failures of de-escalation efforts.

1

THE CHANGING INTERNATIONAL ENVIRONMENT AND THE RESOLUTION OF INTERNATIONAL CONFLICTS

Negotiations on Security and Arms Control in Europe

P. TERRENCE HOPMANN

THIS CHAPTER starts from the premise that international negotiations constitute a subsystem of the larger international system and that the employment of the negotiation process to resolve international conflicts depends very much on the state of relations among parties in the international environment. The appropriate timing for seeking negotiated resolution of international conflicts depends at least in part on the overall state of international relations. This state refers both to the general conditions within the international system, including the relations between parties to a conflict and outsiders, and to the specific relationship among the parties to a dispute. The international environment must not only be "ripe" for formal negotiations to open, but even more importantly, it must be ripe for those negotiations to proceed productively in the process of conflict resolution.

This analysis, therefore, focuses on those conditions within the international environment that may create ripe opportunities for resolving long-standing conflicts through negotiation or for bringing long-stalemated negotiations to successful conclusions. This subject can be approached in many ways. One is to look at changes in the global political system, as suggested by Kriesberg in his Introduction to this volume. This approach could examine changes in the overall distribution of resources and in capabilities to exert influence within the inter-

31

national system as a whole; for example, the achievement of military parity by the Soviet Union vis-à-vis the United States largely made strategic arms limitation agreements both possible and critically necessary. Alternatively, this approach could be confined to changes in the relationship between parties involved in a conflict and third parties. Thus, for example, the Paris peace talks between the United States and Vietnam to end the war in Southeast Asia depended not only on the nature of the conflict between these two states but also on their joint relationships with other key states such as the Soviet Union.

Still another approach is to examine changes in the overall relationship among parties to a dispute and to examine linkages between their overall relations—political, strategic, economic, ideological, and so forth—and their behavior within more specific negotiating fora. In this instance, the focus will be on the overall adversary relationship rather than on the global environment within which their interactions occur, and we treat specific negotiations as subprocesses within that adversary relationship that may be affected directly by the larger pattern of interaction. In a relationship between two states like the United States and the Soviet Union characterized by complex interdependence, negotiations on issues such as arms control are very much affected by the overall state of relations among the disputing parties themselves. This latter focus will be the emphasis of the present chapter.

When looking at linkages between the external environment and internal negotiating behaviors, however, several perspectives are possible. First, one may argue that changes in the overall state of relations among parties to a conflict is a *necessary* condition for progress in negotiations. For example, President Reagan and his advisors long maintained that no real progress was possible in arms control negotiations until the more fundamental conflicts between the superpower adversaries were resolved. Second, many analysts argue that changes in the international environment merely facilitate conditions for the resolution of specific conflicts; therefore, Soviet-American détente may create conditions that are ripe for progress in arms control, even though limited agreements that are clearly in the interests of both parties, such as the prevention of the horizontal proliferation of nuclear weapons, may be achieved in spite of substantial tensions between the two superpowers. Third, an element of circularity may be present in this process: that is, success in negotiations may, in turn, affect the changing state of political relations in the international environment. Thus improved Soviet-American relations may make progress in arms control negotiations possible, and successful agreements may reinforce progress in other areas of the relationship, such as in trade or in scientific and cultural cooperation. The latter was particularly evident in the series of summits in 1985–87 between President Reagan and General Secretary Gorbachev. As Richard Haass suggests in his chapter, a modest improvement in relations made the INF Treaty possible, and that was followed by a Soviet withdrawal from Afghanistan and the significant broadening of economic, scientific, and cultural ties between the two countries.

All three of these relationships suggest that the timing of de-escalatory moves by governments participating in ongoing negotiations may be affected by changing external events. Although the actors themselves may influence the state of their overall relationship, this normally can be done only over some time. Furthermore, national leaders can be on the lookout for significant de-escalatory moves, such as those initiated by General Secretary Gorbachev soon after he came to power in the Soviet Union. These changes are not likely to appear overnight, but they should become evident over the course of many months or at least over several years. It is also clear, however, that such fortuitous changes in the international environment do not occur very frequently, and the astute national leader must be vigilant to seize the opportunity for making progress in negotiations when the conditions are ripe.

It is also useful to note that these linkages may be both intentional or largely coincidental. That is, linkages may be created deliberately by national leaders to achieve specific negotiating ends, as when the United States "plays the China card" to try to influence Soviet negotiating behavior. In this instance, this relationship would seem to fall more appropriately under the heading of strategy than of the international context. On the other hand, many changes occur owing to other domestic or international conditions, and these changes may create opportunities or obstacles for agreement in negotiations. Linkage may also be mediated by domestic politics: whether or not U.S. political leaders wish to link Soviet actions in Africa, the Caribbean, or Central America with arms control negotiations, these linkages are likely to exist within domestic public opinion, thereby indirectly constricting the latitude of decision makers charged with managing the superpower relationship. These kinds of linkages are treated in the chapter by Jo Husbands.

In this chapter, I survey the behavioral science literature as it relates to the impact of the international environment upon the timing of moves to resolve international conflicts. On the basis of that literature review, some tentative hypotheses about possible environmental effects will be identified. Finally, these hypotheses will be evaluated to determine their plausibility in the light of recent negotiating experience on issues of security and arms control in Europe.

BEHAVIORAL SCIENCE RESEARCH ON THE IMPACT OF THE INTERNATIONAL ENVIRONMENT ON NEGOTIATIONS

A number of empirical studies of negotiation have suggested that the negotiation process directly mirrors what is occurring in the overall political relationships among the parties so that breakthroughs in negotiations may depend on a general improvement in the political relationships among adversaries. In arms control negotiations, this approach has been characterized by Singer (1962) as the "tensions-first" hypothesis, which asserts that political differences among adversaries must be resolved before negotiating on disarmament. The armaments are seen by proponents of this view as being largely symptoms of the underlying political conflict, and the arms may not be removed as long as the basic differences remain unresolved.

An alternative view holds that armaments may be in part a consequence of preexisting political conflicts but that they also reinforce those conflicts in a vicious cycle. As Claude (1963, 298) has observed, "The truth is that this is a circular problem, in which causes and effects, policies and instruments of policy, revolve in a cycle of interaction and are blurred into indistinguishability." Therefore, the negotiation process and the external international environment may change more or less in tandem.

There are several plausible political explanations for this relationship. Many negotiators have observed that the "atmospherics" of negotiations are influenced by the state of external tensions among the parties. In conditions of relative détente, the negotiators are more relaxed and open with one another, the situation is much more likely to permit a problem-solving rather than a confrontational bargaining style, and agreement may be viewed as part of a developing process. By contrast, when tensions are high, negotiators tend to be cautious, unwilling to explore novel options, or to risk being taken advantage of if they initiate new proposals or make concessions.

Similarly, the state of the international relationship may significantly influence the constraints under which negotiators operate, especially from their counterparts in their own governments. The more relaxed the state of relations with their negotiating partner, the more support they may see for reaching agreement from within their own governments and even from the public at large. Conversely, at times of high tension, they risk being accused of seeking agreement at any price with an untrustworthy enemy, which undermines their ability to negotiate freely and constructively with other parties. Under such conditions, they are likely to shun agreement, even if it were attainable.

Beyond the political explanation for this relationship also lies a plausible psychological explanation, namely, the effects of stress projected onto the negotiators from the international environment. A large experimental literature suggests the hypothesis that stress-related effects are likely to have a significant impact on negotiating behavior. Stress in this context refers to the way individuals interpret a situation, especially situations in which they perceive that they have little control over events. Typical effects of stress reported in the experimental research include oversimplified perceptions, reduced tolerance for ambiguity, cognitive rigidity, less efficient problem solving, and increased hostility or aggressive behavior (see Hopmann and Walcott [1977] and Druckman [1973] for reviews). The psychological literature is quite clear about the conditions that tend to produce stress, namely, a lack of information about the future, which leads to feelings of uncertainty (Lazarus and Folkman 1984; Levine and Ursin 1980).

In addition to sources of tension that may originate within the negotiation, tensions may be projected onto the negotiations from the international environment. Druckman (1973) has emphasized the dysfunctions of high levels of tension (i.e., they lead to overreactions to provocations) and the functions of low levels of tension (i.e., they lead to underreactions to another state's provocations). These hypotheses contrast to an approach often taken by policy makers that emphasizes the advantages of external tensions: tensions may be increased to reinforce threats and commitments; armaments may be procured and deployed as bargaining chips to induce the opponent to make concessions.

This relationship between external events and internal negotiating behaviors has been the subject of several empirical studies of arms control negotiations, especially of the negotiations leading to the Partial Nuclear Test Ban Treaty of 1963. Hopmann and King (1976) and Hopmann and Smith (1978) analyzed responsiveness to internal and external factors in the 1962–63 rounds of the partial nuclear test ban negotiations. Both of these studies examined interactions among the United States, United Kingdom, and Soviet Union outside and inside the negotiations. Outside interactions were coded along dimensions of cooperation and competition as defined by Corson (1970) from chronologies of events in the *New York Times* (for the United States), *Keesing's Contemporary Archives* (for the United Kingdom), and the *New Times* (for the Soviet Union). Internal interactions were coded using the categories of a content analysis system known as "bargaining process analysis" (Walcott and Hopmann 1978). These codes were combined into categories of "soft" and "hard" bargaining and aggregated on a monthly basis. The primary difference between the studies was the mode of analysis: Hopmann and King used correlational methods to test a modified stimulus-response model, whereas Hopmann and Smith examined alternative regression equations derived from Richardson's work on arms races (see, inter alia, Rapoport [1960] for a discussion of the Richardson process model).

Hopmann and King's (1976, 132–34) correlations showed a continuous sequence of mutual interactions among the nations inside and outside the negotiations. Symmetrical behaviors were reflected in high levels of reciprocation of cooperative (soft) or conflictual (hard) responses. Consistent behaviors were reflected in a high correspondence between interactions outside (either conflictual or cooperative) and inside (either hard or soft bargaining) the negotiation. The negotiators reacted in similar ways to both the internal and external actions taken by their opponents. More interesting, however, is the relative impact of the internal and external "stimuli" on the perceptions and responses of each state. The United States responded primarily to external events in the previous month, whereas the British and Soviet negotiators responded primarily to the other's negotiating behavior in the same or previous rounds.

Regression analysis enabled the researchers to estimate the relative importance of external compared to internal variables. The Hopmann and Smith (1978, 171–74) results largely confirmed the findings obtained by Hopmann and King: U.S. negotiating behavior, in hard or soft postures, was influenced by the actions taken by the Soviets toward the United States outside the negotiation. However, Soviet negotiating behavior was not affected by U.S. actions toward the Soviet Union outside the negotiations; the Soviets were influenced more by their own past negotiating behavior.

But going beyond the issue of evaluating the size of impacts, Hopmann and Smith also examined the role of perceptions in mediating between one party's behavior and the other's response. They found, for example, that when the American negotiators perceived the Soviet actions as being "softer," they became "tougher" in their negotiating behavior. Thus there were some exceptions to the complete "mirror" model, in that conciliatory gestures were sometimes exploited rather than reciprocated. Unfortunately, the present literature offers few clues about the conditions under which one or the other of these responses will appear following a more positive set of international interactions.

Most research would tend to suggest, however, that this relationship may be reciprocal, producing either vicious or benign cycles. High or low levels of international tension may affect whether negotiations lead toward or away from agreements; these negotiating outcomes may, in turn, affect the level of tension in the international system. Such cyclical processes were demonstrated in simulation results obtained by Hopmann and Walcott (1977, 310–13).

The Hopmann and Walcott research compared analyses conducted in the laboratory with the parallel studies by Hopmann and King (1976) and Hopmann and Smith (1978). Results obtained from twenty-four runs of a simulation of the partial nuclear test ban talks (1962–63) were buttressed by analyses of the actual discussions among the delegates from the three nuclear states that participated in these negotiations. Three environments were created in the laboratory: a malign condition (a news bulletin announcing the onset of a crisis), a benign condition (a bulletin announcing a tension-reducing agreement on nondisarmament matters), and a neutral condition in which no intervention occurred. Differences among the conditions showed the expected effects on several indices of negotiating behaviors and perceptions: the malign condition (compared to both the benign and neutral conditions) produced more hostility in mutual perceptions, more hard relative to soft tactics, more commitments, more negative relative to positive effect, a higher ratio of disagreements to agreements on substantive issues, and fewer overall agreements; no significant differences were found between the benign and neutral conditions. These results suggested that high-stress environments hinder performance but that low-stress environments do not necessarily enhance performance (compared to a neutral-control condition). Tension reduction was not a necessary precondition for agreements in the simulation runs; it was more often simply a facilitative condition for more cooperative bargaining strategies and higher levels of agreement.

Several results from the Hopmann and King (1976) study reinforced the simulation findings. Coded levels of tension in external interactions correlated significantly in the hypothesized direction with indices of negotiating behavior and perceptions. Unlike the laboratory results, however, lower levels of tension (compared to the benign condition) were related to more positive perceptions and softer bargaining tactics (for the Western nations); this relationship became stronger as they approached the agreement. Thus, as expected, the Cuban Missile Crisis of October 1962 exerted a dampening effect on the test ban negotiations in the short run. However, when President Kennedy in his address at American University on June 10, 1963, announced a coordinated set of measures to reduce tensions, a positive cycle of reduced tensions and greater cooperation within the test ban negotiations followed immediately thereafter.

Moreover, these analyses demonstrated reciprocal effects. Harder bargaining tactics taken by the negotiators in an earlier month were followed by increased external tension in their interactions during the next period. Such spiraling effects suggested similar patterns for interactions inside and outside the negotiations. Further work is needed to explore the threshold problem, that is, the amount of tension required to produce negative effects on negotiation tension. This level may depend, at least in part, on the relative importance of the negotiations to the countries involved.

Although stress is generally dysfunctional, under some conditions it may have positive consequences for the performance of individuals in negotiations. Below some critical threshold, stress may actually motivate negotiators to work harder to solve problems and to overcome obstacles to agreement. Many analysts have suggested that the long-term impact of the Cuban Missile Crisis on the test ban negotiations was to produce just this sort of stress (Hopmann and King 1980, 183–86).

Spiraling effects of internal and external tension have implications for breakdowns of negotiations. From the practitioner's standpoint, it would be useful to monitor tension levels for warnings of the conditions that lead to crises. To do this effectively, however, may require a statistical approach that differs from the regression/correlation analyses used in the studies reviewed. In this regard, statistical techniques that depend less on patterns from the past and more on the conditions that signal an abrupt departure from normal activities would be appropriate. One such technique is stochastic modeling. Duncan and Job (1980) demonstrate the value of this approach for ascertaining characteristics of an interaction process that shift a system from one state (minor tension) to another (major tension). Their calculated transition probabilities enabled analysts to fine-tune their estimates of tension in Israeli-Syrian interactions and of stability in the Southern Rhodesia–Zimbabwe situation. Taking this process a step further, it would be useful to join the monitoring of external conditions to internal negotiating stages; this approach would enable analysts to warn of conditions that might lead to stalemate or to identify ripe conditions that might provide opportunities to break through prior impasses.

HYPOTHESES ABOUT THE RELATIONSHIP BETWEEN THE INTERNATIONAL ENVIRONMENT AND NEGOTIATING BEHAVIOR

Evidence from previous research supports several hypotheses about the relationship between the international environment and the negotiating process: (1) increases in international tensions frequently hinder the bargaining process in international negotiations or create stalemates both through their political effects on the governments and publics of participating states and through their psychological effects on the negotiators themselves; (2) relaxation of international tensions, although not a sufficient condition for an improved bargaining process, frequently facilitates the negotiation process and enhances the ripeness of international disputes for negotiated settlement.

Before proceeding, several exceptions and qualifications to these hypotheses must be noted. At least two exceptions may be suggested to hypothesis 1. First, there may be some situations of extreme conflict or tension that are so severe that they produce an overwhelming incentive to resolve a conflict. This may have been the case with the impact of the Cuban Missile Crisis on the partial nuclear test ban negotiations. Many analysts of that crisis, such as Hilsman (1967), have noted that it dramatically affected both Kennedy's and Khrushchev's perceptions of the dangers of a nuclear war, thereby encouraging them to make the necessary concessions to reach agreement in the long-stalemated test ban negotiations. Hopmann and King (1980, 183–86), in an empirical study of the impact of the Cuban Missile Crisis, have noted that it had some short-term deleterious effects on the test ban negotiations, but over the long run it represented not only a turning point in those negotiations but in the entire pattern of U.S.-Soviet relations between the preceding and the subsequent decade.

Second, Touval and Zartman (1985, 16) have identified another aspect of external tensions that may turn out to be functional for making breakthroughs in negotiations, namely, the "hurting stalemate." In this instance, they suggest that long periods of pain and suffering may finally lead parties in a dispute to realize that neither can benefit from continuation of the conflict and that both have no choice but to reach a negotiated accommodation. Up to a point, of course, mutual suffering usually just makes the parties to a dispute dig in their heels more firmly; however, beyond some point, the parties may become so desperate that they are prepared to negotiate seriously in spite of the risk of having to give up on important and long-defended interests. Such may have been the case between Israel and Egypt prior to the Camp David Accords. Similarly, in Nicaragua, six years of war without any apparent victory in sight plus a deepening economic crisis may have led the Contras and Sandinistas into a ceasefire in March 1988, leading to negotiations to permit free multiparty elections, achieved more out of the desperation and suffering of both parties than out of any belief in an external improvement in mutual relations.

Both of these exceptions to hypothesis 1 have one common element, namely, that they both suggest a curvilinear relationship between external tensions and ripeness for dispute resolution. To a point, external tension detracts from the ability to negotiate a resolution to the conflict; but once the conflict itself becomes so intense or so enduring that it clearly has become more costly than any plausible negotiated agreement, the external conflict may actually contribute positively to conflict resolution. Of course, the threshold beyond which the relationship changes will differ in every case, and some parties to conflicts have demonstrated what seems like an endless ability to endure suffering with little or no prospect of gain. Certainly this was the case for most of the conflict on the Western front during World War I, and it also appears to have been applicable for many years to the Iran-Iraq war. In other words, the threshold for a "hurting stalemate" (Touval and Zartman 1985) clearly depends upon the relative ability of state leaders to withstand pain. But, as Blainey (1973, 245) has suggested, peace becomes possible when all parties to a conflict believe that they will "gain more by negotiating than by fighting."

Hypothesis 2 also needs to be qualified. This hypothesis clearly states that improved external relationships merely facilitate rather than necessitate a set of ripe conditions for achieving agreement. In some cases, of course, there may be a substantive connection between the changing external events and the issues under negotiation. In this way, the external events may remove substantive obstacles that were previously hindering agreement. On the other hand, the hypothesis does not necessarily assume a direct connection between issues; it suggests that external events will be mirrored in negotiating processes even if the relationship is largely coincidental owing to the improved "atmospherics" and political receptivity to agreement. In this instance, however, a mere improvement in coincidental relationships does not necessarily imply that substantive differences will somehow automatically be overcome. Insofar as negotiations were blocked due to tensions, mistrust, and misperceptions, the improved international environment may break down some of those obstacles to agreement. But it will not necessarily solve the substantive problems themselves; the most that can be expected is for improved external relations to facilitate agreement by making the process more open, more task oriented, and potentially more creative.

One final consideration involves the deliberate manipulation of the external environment by the decision makers in one state to affect the negotiation process, commonly referred to as *linkage*. In this case, one state's negotiators may make their acceptance of an agreement contingent upon some change in the behavior of the other parties toward issues having no direct bearing on the negotiations. Thus, for example, Henry Kissinger made progress in the SALT I negotiations partly contingent upon the Soviets pressuring the North Vietnamese to negotiate more seriously for an end to the Vietnam war. Kissinger clearly believed strongly in the wisdom of manipulating international events to enhance the prospects for negotiating solutions to various disputes.

It is, of course, correct that a deliberate policy of linkage can facilitate agreement by changing the relative costs and benefits for the parties associated with agreement compared to their next best alternative to a negotiated agreement. On the other hand, such deliberate linkage may also create fears of being manipulated that may engender resentment and a desire to avoid being pressured. If the linkage process produces this kind of psychological response by the other parties, then it may turn out to be dysfunctional to overcoming impasses. Therefore, the hypotheses presented would seem to apply only to the relationship between more or less coincidental changes in the international environment and the internal behaviors within negotiations, and such deliberate linkage may have very different effects depending upon the subtlety with which it is presented and the way in which it is perceived by its intended target.

The Case of Security and Arms Control in Europe

Five arms control negotiations dealing with European security have taken place over the period from 1973 through 1988. I will consider four issues, but one issue—Intermediate-range Nuclear Forces—was effectively divided into two separate negotiations. Three of these issues led to relatively successful outcomes represented by agreements, and two others ended in stalemate. The three negotiations that produced agreement include the following:

1. The Conference on Security and Cooperation in Europe (CSCE), 1973–75, which produced the Helsinki Accords in July 1975

2. The Conference on Disarmament in Europe (CDE), 1984–86, which resulted in the Stockholm Agreement on confidence and security-building measures in September 1986

3. The Intermediate-range Nuclear Forces negotiations, phase two (INF/2), 1985–1987, which led to the signing of the INF Treaty at the Washington summit in December 1987

The two stalemated negotiations include:

1. Mutual and Balanced Force Reductions (MBFR), 1973–1988, which were suspended at the end of 1988 and recreated in a new forum on Conventional Forces in Europe (CFE) in early 1989 (Although this latter negotiation eventually produced an agreement in 1990, it will not be considered as part of this study.)

2. The Intermediate-range Nuclear Forces negotiations, phase one (INF/1), 1981–83, which ended when the Soviet Union walked out to protest the decision by the West German Bundestag to accept the actual deployment of U.S. Pershing II and ground-launched cruise missiles in November 1983

It is impossible in a short chapter to give a full accounting of each of these negotiations and to describe in detail how they were affected by the external environment; this is the subject of a much longer work (Hopmann, forthcoming). All that can be done at present is to suggest the plausibility of some significant relationships by looking at the general trends in East-West relations during the sixteen-year period, 1973–87 and then examine each of the five cases briefly in light of these criteria.

Ideally, it would be desirable to have systematic measures of the changes in East-West conflict and détente throughout the entire period; unfortunately, I have such data available only for the period 1973–79, although additional data will eventually be added. I will, therefore, present only impressionistic observations about the course of East-West relations throughout this period, although most observers probably would concur with the following categorization:

    1. Period 1, 1973–75. *The height of détente.* This period came in the aftermath of the SALT I agreement and the Paris Accords leading to U.S. military withdrawal from Vietnam; Soviet-U.S. cooperation was expanding in every area, including science (e.g., the Apollo-Soyuz space mission), culture, trade, and so forth.

    2. Period 2, 1975–79. *The slow decline of détente.* During this period, the cooperation that had been evident earlier in the decade gradually began to decline.[1] Tensions increased over alleged Soviet violations of human rights, especially after Jimmy Carter entered the White House, as well as over the slow progress of the SALT II negotiations and rising opposition to SALT in the U.S. Congress, and over Soviet involvement in the Third World in places such as Angola, Ethiopia, and eventually Nicaragua. The period ended with the Soviet military intervention in Afghanistan in December 1979.

    3. Period 3, 1980–84. *The renewal of the Cold War.* This period was characterized by stepped-up political conflict over issues such as Soviet involvement in Afghanistan, the suppression of the Solidarity Union movement in Poland, stepped-up competition in the Third World, and the U.S. grain and Olympic boycotts. Relations further deteriorated following Ronald Reagan's entrance into the White House and his "evil empire" speech, the U.S. military buildup, Reagan's announcement of his decision to embark upon a major program for strategic defenses, the deployment of the INF missiles in Europe, and the breakup of both the INF and START negotiations in Geneva.

    4. Period 4, 1985–88. *Renewed thaw.* This period largely coincides with Gorbachev's rise to power and his redirection of Soviet policy toward restructuring its domestic economy and society, which gave him an incentive to cut back on the extension of Soviet power abroad (see Haass's and Husbands's chaps.). East-West relations began to thaw with the reopening of the tripartite arms control negotiations on START,

INF, and space-based weapons, the beginning of annual summit conferences between Reagan and Gorbachev, and the eventual signing of the INF Treaty in December 1987.

With these broad trends in external relations in mind, the discussion now turns to a brief overview of the five arms control negotiations on European security during this period. Two negotiations ended in stalemate.

Mutual and Balanced Force Reductions (MBFR), 1973–88. The MBFR negotiations opened in October 1973 at the very height of détente, and they represent the only negotiation to endure throughout the entire sixteen-year period under consideration. These negotiations came about largely at the insistence of NATO, which wanted to redress what it perceived to be an imbalance in conventional forces facing one another in the center of Europe. Thus although the negotiations were open to all members of NATO and the Warsaw Pact, they focused on the area of the two Germanies and neighboring countries on both sides of the East-West divide (i.e., Poland and Czechoslovakia in the East; Belgium, the Netherlands, and Luxembourg in the West). All countries with forces in those countries were the principal participants, and the objective was to negotiate a mutual reduction of those conventional forces nearest to a possible "front line."

Almost from the beginning, MBFR was deadlocked by very different perceptions in the East and West of the fundamental requirements for security in Central Europe. Essentially, the Warsaw Pact states perceived an approximate equality in the "correlation of forces" in Europe so that the objective of negotiations was to retain the same ratio of forces at lower levels. Conversely, the NATO states perceived that the Warsaw Pact possessed significant conventional advantages, especially in certain categories of armaments, so that the negotiations should strive to attain a more stable balance at any level of force. Additional complexities were introduced by a geographical asymmetry in which Soviet forces could be withdrawn from the region just 1,000 kilometers or so to the east, whereas U.S. forces would have to be withdrawn across the Atlantic. Furthermore, among the countries actually located in the reductions region, the Federal Republic of Germany had the largest forces, comprising over 40 percent of the NATO forces in the region; by contrast, U.S. forces in Western Europe comprised a much smaller percentage of NATO forces than was the case for Soviet forces stationed in Eastern Europe. Therefore, the main Soviet combat elements on the eastern side would only have had to be withdrawn, whereas the main

West German combat elements on the western side would actually have had to be dismantled. It was largely for this reason that the West Germans insisted that NATO oppose armament reductions, thereby restricting reductions to troops alone. This was a curious position for NATO to adopt, however, because by most NATO estimates the force differences between NATO and the Warsaw Pact were far more significant in certain weapons categories, especially main battle tanks, than in troops.

These substantive issues were certainly sufficient to make the MBFR negotiations extremely complex, inviting stalemate. These differences were further exacerbated by the difficulties of arriving at a common negotiation position within NATO. From the outset, the Federal Republic of Germany took a very hard line on MBFR. Two of NATO's major proposals were largely dictated by the Germans against the preferences of most other alliance members: (1) the insistence that reductions be restricted to uniformed personnel rather than including armaments; and (2) the opposition to national subceilings on forces, requiring that force ceilings apply only to each alliance as a whole. Furthermore, neither of these positions was acceptable to the Soviets, which reduced the space for bargaining. The British were mildly supportive of these negotiations when the Labour government was in office, especially when David Owen was foreign minister, but their attitude turned to hostility as soon as the Conservative government of Margaret Thatcher took over in London. In the United States, attitudes varied over time, but the negotiations never received high priority in Washington relative to other arms control issues. What little interest in an agreement may have been evident in the United States in the 1970s disappeared effectively by 1980 (Dean 1983). Although most other NATO countries were genuinely interested in reaching an agreement, they had little influence in shaping NATO's negotiating positions. Therefore, domestic and intraalliance politics also preserved the stalemate in Vienna.

Furthermore, on those few occasions when one country or another within the alliance became interested in overcoming the impasse, others generally tried to block progress. For example, the West Germans tried hard, but unsuccessfully, to block a NATO initiative in 1975 to introduce a trade of NATO tactical nuclear weapons for Warsaw Pact tanks as a mechanism to overcome the stalemate. The Soviets, however, were slow to react to this proposal when it was advanced, and their eventual reaction demonstrated some lack of serious intent on their part. Although this and other initiatives between 1975 and 1977 made it possible to agree in principle upon a common ceiling of nine hundred thousand men in the reductions zone (with a common subceiling of seven hundred thousand ground troops), the negotiations became bogged down in disagreements about data on the size of present Warsaw Pact forces in the zone. Neither side showed much interest in taking the initiative to overcome this dispute about data.

NATO also pushed to overcome the stalemate in MBFR in 1979 with an offer to agree upon a first-phase reduction of U.S. and Soviet forces to be followed by further negotiations to reduce indigenous forces. At that time, NATO also proposed a package of verification and confidence-building measures, and they announced their willingness to withdraw one thousand tactical nuclear weapons from Western Europe as a "unilateral initiative" to try to overcome the negotiating impasse. These new initiatives were unveiled in December 1979 to provide a "sweetener" to offset the "bitter pill" contained in the simultaneous "double track" decision to prepare for deployment of 572 new Pershing II and ground-launched cruise missiles in Western Europe. The Warsaw Pact, however, saw only the bitter pill and rejected the NATO proposals.

After December 1979, MBFR went more or less into the deep freeze. In 1982, the West Germans began advocating some new initiatives to try to overcome the impasse and to reduce the pressure that they came under as a result of the upcoming deployment of the INF missiles. They essentially favored an agreement to reduce forces first and then verify afterward to determine if the forces had been reduced to the specified levels, rather than agreeing upon data in advance as NATO had advocated up to that point. The United States, however, managed to convert the verification requirements of this proposal into such stringent measures that the Soviets clearly found them unacceptable. Once again, the principal NATO allies found themselves out of synchronization when it came to efforts to break the impasse in MBFR. The domestic requirements for moving forward were never ripe in all of the principal countries at the same moment, which condemned this complicated multilateral negotiation to failure.

The major findings from quantitative data collected about the relationship between the international environment and bargaining within MBFR for the first seven years or nineteen rounds of MBFR, from 1973 through 1979 (Hopmann 1981) are as follows:

> 1. During the first seven rounds, from October 1973 through December 1975, there were strong positive correlations between Warsaw Pact external actions toward NATO and NATO's behaviors within the negotiations (r = .91,

$p = .002$), and between NATO external actions toward the Warsaw Pact and the Warsaw Pact's moves in MBFR ($r = .73, p = .03$). Thus through the end of 1975, the negotiations largely mirrored and responded to the state of East-West relations.

2. During the next twelve rounds (rounds 8–19, 1976–79), these positive correlations largely faded away. NATO's behavior within the negotiations was weakly correlated with Warsaw Pact external actions toward it ($r = .7, p = .12$), and Warsaw Pact bargaining behaviors were inversely related to NATO's external actions toward the East ($r = -.45, p = .07$).

In other words, during period 1, at the height of détente, the MBFR negotiations seemed to be moving forward in correspondence with the generally positive state of external relations, very much along the same lines as the findings reported earlier for the negotiations on the Partial Nuclear Test Ban Treaty. However, this responsive pattern disappeared during period 2, when détente itself also began to fade. From 1976 through 1979, MBFR seemed to be operating more or less in isolation from the international environment, driven more by the vagaries of domestic policies and alliance politics than by the dynamics of East-West interactions.

Unfortunately, I do not have similar quantitative data on the last two periods in this study. However, MBFR definitely became locked in a stalemate pattern and was regarded by almost all parties with a certain cynicism through at least 1986. When the Conference on Disarmament in Europe reached a successful agreement in 1986, with thirty-five rather than twenty-two participants and covering Europe from the Atlantic to the Urals, rather than just a Central European zone, it became apparent that MBFR was dead. At the end of 1988 it came to a close. A new forum was created, however, under the framework of the CSCE, with participation of all NATO and Warsaw Pact countries and with the neutral and nonaligned states maintaining an observer's status. Furthermore, these negotiations on Conventional Forces in Europe (CFE) covered forces stationed on the entire European continent from the Atlantic to the Urals. This new forum reflected the spirit of post-INF Europe, and it adopted a far more ambitious program, eventually producing an agreement signed at the Paris Summit in November 1990.

The Intermediate-range Nuclear Forces (INF) negotiations, phase 1, 1981–83. The first phase of the INF negotiations took place during the period of greatest East-West tension covered in this study, and they seemed to have been very much affected by that hostile international environment.

The proposal for negotiations originated with NATO's "double track" decision of December 1979. At that time, the alliance decided to deploy 572 new U.S. missiles in five West European countries beginning in 1983 but only if negotiations to eliminate this category of weapons had been tried and failed in the period between the decision and the actual deployment date. However, no sooner was the deployment decision made than the Soviet intervention in Afghanistan and the acrid debate over SALT II combined to sour the atmosphere for all arms control negotiations. Thus no negotiations began during the 1980 election campaign in the United States.

When Ronald Reagan emerged victorious and entered the White House in 1981, he made clear his opposition to the "negotiations track" of the double track decision. He preferred to negotiate "from a position of strength," which implied that the missiles should be deployed before opening negotiations. After much protest from West European leaders, especially West German Chancellor Helmut Schmidt, Reagan did agree to open INF negotiations in Geneva in November 1981. However, the proposals advanced by both sides in these negotiations might cynically be interpreted as having been designed to guarantee rejection by the other. The United States proposed its so-called "zero option," which prohibited both countries from deploying any INFs in Europe. In other words, the United States was prepared to scrap its deployment of 572 new missiles if the Soviets were prepared to dismantle about 370 missiles with 640 warheads. The United States also insisted that the Soviets be limited to 100 SS-20 missiles in the Asian parts of the Soviet Union. In other words, the Soviets would have to eliminate a large quantity of new weapons in exchange for the United States' promise to tear up a piece of paper that was a mere commitment to deploy, a deployment that the Soviets apparently believed might be forestalled through political action emanating from the public in several West European countries.

On the other side, the Soviets proposed a freeze at current levels of deployment; that is, they would cease replacing old SS-4s and SS-5s with the newer SS-20, and British and French forces on NATO's side along with U.S. forward-based aircraft and nuclear submarines committed to NATO would counterbalance these Soviet forces. Neither side really viewed the other's proposal as a sincere basis for negotiation, and the exercise seemed caught in futility. An effort to bargain privately between U.S. Ambassador Paul Nitze and Soviet Ambassador Yuli Kvitsinsky in the so-called "walk in the woods" seemed to yield a plausible agreement that was greeted enthusiastically in Europe, but the conditions for accepting such an agreement were not present in either superpower capital (see Haass's chap. for an explanation of the "walk"). As the deployment date approached, hostility between the two superpowers reached a high point, and last-minute efforts to find a solution in Geneva yielded no positive results. Thus on November 22, 1983, the Bundestag voted to accept the INF missiles definitely; on the next day, the first nine Pershing IIs arrived in West Germany, and the Soviets walked out of the negotiations in Geneva.

In this instance, there were no serious substantive obstacles to an agreement. Indeed, most of the essential terms of the treaty eventually negotiated in 1987 were on the table throughout the phase one negotiations. There were, of course, serious domestic obstacles to agreement in both countries throughout this period. In Washington, the Reagan administration was deeply divided over the INF negotiations, and the opponents of all arms control were at the height of their power in the administration (Talbott 1984). In Moscow, the period was one of immobility, which included the illness and death of General Secretary Brezhnev and then the short reign and rapid death of his successor, Yuri Andropov. During such transitional periods, the Soviets are generally reluctant to undertake major foreign policy initiatives.

But this was also the time of the greatest tension in U.S.-Soviet relations, at least since the 1960–62 period, spanning the U-2 incident, the Berlin crisis, and the Cuban Missile Crisis. The emergence of a team of arms control opponents in the highest levels of the U.S. government not only immobilized U.S. negotiators but also added to Soviet mistrust and cynicism about American motives in the negotiations. Thus the atmosphere of the first-phase INF negotiations was tense and conflictual, and the result was a breakdown of the negotiations.

Three negotiations on European security issues during this period yielded concrete agreements.

The Conference on Security and Cooperation in Europe (CSCE) 1973–75. The CSCE was primarily oriented toward solving a number of the issues involving the post–World War II settlement in Europe, especially the division of the continent in two. Its participants included all of the states of Europe—NATO/EEC, Warsaw Pact, and neutral and non-aligned—as well as the United States and Canada. Its mandate went far beyond arms control. The Soviet Union had originally been the prime advocate of this conference, and the United States and its NATO allies had subscribed to it only reluctantly. However, as the negotiation unfolded in Geneva it became evident that the states of Eastern and Western Europe were most interested in the outcome of this negotiation, and both superpowers came to regard it with some caution. During this period, the two superpowers seemed to regard the status quo in Europe as essentially benign, and they both tried hard to avoid anything that might undermine that stability. By contrast, most of their European allies as well as the neutrals and nonaligned viewed this attitude as indicative of a "Soviet-American condominium" that was trying to dominate Europe. As a result, throughout the negotiations the European states generally sought to expand the scope of the conference, whereas the two superpowers tried to keep it well confined.

The primary arms control measures on the agenda of the CSCE involved so-called "confidence-building measures" (CBMs), procedures designed to provide mutual reassurance that neither side was planning to launch a surprise attack upon the other. The negotiators quickly agreed that this could best be accomplished through a series of measures to enhance the openness or transparency of military activities on each side of the divide between the two halves of Europe. Particular attention was directed toward military maneuvers, which could provide a cover for preparations for an attack. Therefore, the primary agreement involved the preannouncement of such maneuvers and the voluntary invitation of observers to such maneuvers to provide assurance that they were not being used to disguise attack preparations. Although most European states wanted a series of obligatory measures that would apply at a very low threshold, the two superpowers agreed together to restrict the provisions to the voluntary announcement of maneuvers involving more than twenty-five thousand men and the possibility of inviting observers. Despite this limitation, the Helsinki Accords did set a precedent for on-site inspection by military experts from each alliance on the territory of the other during such preannounced maneuvers.

In the spirit of détente and relative mutual trust that characterized this period, no one seemed to object very much to the voluntary nature of these provisions. Certainly, other issues in the negotiations, such as the statement of principles about human rights and about the inviolability of current borders in Europe, caused greater dissension than the issues about CBMs. Therefore, in spite of the complex multilateral nature of these negotiations as well as the breadth and complexity of the issues under consideration, the CSCE was able to move forward fairly consistently throughout the two-year period of negotiation. The external environment provided a context that was ripe for a large range of East-West agreements reflecting common needs to enhance mutual security, especially in Central Europe. The signing ceremony involving the heads of thirty-five states in Helsinki on July 31–August 1, 1975, is often marked as the apogee of East-West détente in Europe. It was, thus, both a product of détente and a further stimulus for détente on the continent of Europe.

The Conference on Disarmament in Europe (CDE), 1984–86. The CDE was in many ways an outgrowth of the CSCE. Originally, the CSCE set up a series of review conferences intended to expand the various provisions of the Helsinki Accords. Both the review conferences in Belgrade (1977–78) and in Madrid (1980–83) became stalemated over Western insistence upon a "balanced" implementation of the Helsinki provisions, by which they meant that no further confidence-building measures could be negotiated until progress was made on the issue of human rights. Between these two conferences, however, French President Giscard d'Estaing had proposed the creation of a European Disarmament Conference to cover the region, in de Gaulle's phrase, "from the Atlantic to the Urals" (in Couve de Murville 1965, 8). At Madrid, this conference was created as a stepchild of the CSCE but where confidence- and security-building measures could be discussed without automatic linkage to progress on human rights. This effort to de-link these two issues was essential to the success of the CDE.

The CDE opened its negotiations in Stockholm in January 1984, and it began considering a broad range of CBMs as well as additional measures that might serve as constraints on military activities on the European continent. Initially, the major interest in the negotiations stemmed from the states of Central Europe, especially the neutrals and nonaligned, with the two superpowers looking on with some degree of skepticism. Initial U.S. and Soviet positions on these negotiations were far apart, as would be expected in 1984 when CDE and MBFR remained the only fora in which the two superpowers were involved in direct negotiations on security issues.

Specifically, NATO called for announcement of all "out of garrison" activities involving one division or more, obligatory as opposed to voluntary observation of these activities, obligatory rights to inspect activities that were not announced but which were suspected of exceeding the threshold, and the exchange of annual forecasts of these activities. The Warsaw Pact, by contrast, wanted to reduce the Helsinki threshold from twenty-five thousand to twenty thousand troops, applying only to maneuvers and major force movements into or out of Europe; they also proposed a treaty on the nonuse of force, "no-first-use" of nuclear weapons, the creation of a mechanism for crisis consultation, a mutual freeze of military budgets, establishment of nuclear weapons free zones, and a ban on chemical weapons in Europe (Dean 1987, 191–93).

Progress in these negotiations was very slow throughout all of 1984 and 1985. Indeed, it was only in 1986, and especially in the last few weeks of the negotiations in September, that much progress was actually made. By this time, Gorbachev was clearly in control in Moscow and firmly committed to the program of *perestroika*. Almost one year had passed since the first Reagan-Gorbachev summit in Geneva in November 1985. The result was a substantial set of Soviet concessions at the last minute that enabled the negotiators to break the stalemate. Specifically, the Soviets essentially accepted the Western proposals for an annual calendar of military activities, for constraints against holding large maneuvers that were not preannounced several years in advance, for a threshold for announcement of all major maneuvers and troop movements involving more than ten thousand soldiers, for obligatory exchanges of observers at these activities, and most surprisingly, for up to three annual, obligatory inspections of suspected unannounced activities, all of which would be "politically binding." In exchange, the West effectively accepted only the provision for the nonuse of force to resolve political disputes from the Soviet menu of proposals, an essentially innocuous concession.

In many ways, the Stockholm Agreement did not appear to be so much a product of a renewed détente as a first sign of the developing thaw. The success of the agreement reflected the change in leadership and direction of the Soviet Union under Mikhail Gorbachev. Although Gorbachev's goals were primarily domestic, a necessary condition for the attainment of these goals was a renewal of détente. Not only would this reduce the pressure for such heavy expenses upon military hardware that drain the civilian economy but it also represented a need to open relations with the West, especially with Western Europe, to gain access to the technology upon which Soviet long-range economic development clearly depends. In this light, Gorbachev may have made the concessions necessary to consummate an agreement in Stockholm not necessarily because he believed that an agreement on confidence- and security-building measures was all that intrinsically valuable or desirable but because it would reduce tensions and create a climate that would promote greater contact and trade with the West. In this sense, the CDE agreement may have been more of a stimulus to détente rather than a consequence of it. In short, this issue became ripe for settlement largely because of changes in the overall direction of Soviet foreign policy, which resulted in turn from a shift in domestic leadership and internal priorities.

Intermediate-range Nuclear Forces (INF) negotiations, phase 2, 1985–87. After a hiatus of over one year, the INF negotiations resumed in Geneva in March 1985, this time under the umbrella of a tripartite negotiation including strategic arms reductions and space-based weapons in which all three issues were to be considered in their interrelationship. By this time, U.S. deployments of Pershing IIs and GLCMs were well underway in the Federal Republic of Germany, the United Kingdom, and Italy. As the negotiations opened, the two sides still seemed to be divided by the same old issues, including:

1. The United States wanted both sides to reduce to zero launchers (and if not that, to 140 launchers on each side), whereas the Soviets agreed to reduce to French and British levels if the United States would eliminate all of its newly deployed missiles. The United States refused to acknowledge the relevance of British and French missiles to the negotiations because they were "independent" deterrents and thus not under U.S. control.

2. The United States wanted the limits to apply worldwide, whereas the Soviets wanted the limits restricted to the European area, that is, west of the Ural mountains within the Soviet Union.

To these old differences, however, was added a new one, namely, that the Soviet Union insisted upon the interrelationship among the three issues being discussed in Geneva: in this instance, an INF agreement would be contingent upon a U.S. commitment to forego development of its Strategic Defense Initiative (SDI) and to abide by a strict interpretation of the SALT I ABM Treaty.

One other significant event also coincided with the opening of the new round of INF negotiations in March 1985, namely, the death of Yuri Andropov and the emergence of Mikhail Gorbachev as general secretary within the Soviet Union. Less than one month later, Gorbachev publicly announced a unilateral initiative, namely, a freeze on the further deployment of Soviet SS-20s, and he urged the United States to freeze INF deployments, an offer the U.S. quickly rejected. Although this proposal and subsequent action did not immediately affect the negotiations, it clearly signaled a seriousness of purpose that had not been present before.

Clearly, the level of participation was raised in this second round of INF negotiations because substantial progress had been made at each of the three summit meetings between the two heads of state. In Geneva in November 1985, the Soviets appeared to accept the principle of some U.S. INF deployments, but little actual progress was made. This stalemate was reversed, however, at Reykjavík, Iceland, in October 1986, when the Soviets began to move toward the United States' position. Throughout the next year, Soviet concessions on INF flowed in rapid succession. They dropped the linkage between INF and an agreement on SDI; they then dropped insistence on counting British and French systems in an agreement; they agreed to worldwide limits rather than to European constraints alone; finally, they accepted the zero-option principle for INF missiles of both superpowers.

In short, the Soviets throughout 1987 largely accepted all of the terms of the U.S. position put forward at the outset of the negotiations in 1981, which everyone had believed were nonnegotiable at that time. As negotiations moved on, the United States also toughened several aspects of its position. The American negotiators insisted on eliminating short-range as well as intermediate-range missiles, a so-called "double zero option." To the surprise of many, the Soviets also accepted this proposal. The United States also developed more specific and tough requirements for verification, including on-site inspections of the destruction of missiles and continuous monitoring of missile production facilities. Once again, the Soviets accepted the U.S. proposal, causing some concerns in the West that the U.S. proposals might provide too much access for Soviets within the United States.

The INF Treaty signed in Washington in December 1987 was thus the result of an extremely one-sided set of concessions by the Soviet Union. Indeed, some Reagan administration officials reportedly found themselves trapped by their own positions, which they had assumed would never come to fruition owing to inevitable Soviet opposition. But once the Soviets accepted the U.S. negotiating position almost in its entirety, there was little that the United States could do to avoid accepting the final agreement.

Why was an INF agreement possible in 1987 on terms that had been available since 1981? The answer seems to lie partly in the changing international environment between the two superpowers, which was in turn largely a reflection of some major internal changes, especially in the Soviet Union (see Haass's chap.). In Washington there was a notable moderation of the second Reagan administration in comparison with the first. Some of the president's most hard-line advisors departed the administration during its second term, and other observers noted that the president became more conscious of his "place in history" as well. With few enduring foreign policy accomplishments to mark his administration, Reagan needed a breakthrough in arms control.

But the major impetus for an INF agreement, just as for a CDE agreement, seems to have emerged from the dramatic political changes taking place in the Soviet Union since the ascent to preeminence of Mikhail Gorbachev in March 1985. Gorbachev recognized that the major challenges to the security of the Soviet Union lay within its borders, not outside. The necessity to increase industrial and agricultural efficiency and productivity, to improve health, to reduce alcoholism, to deal with discontent among minority nationalities and ethnic groups, and to modernize the Soviet system were all apparent to him. None of these objectives could be fulfilled in an international environment characterized by tension and external threats to Soviet security. Thus détente was largely a means for Gorbachev not an end in itself. But it was a vital means to his conception of Soviet security.

Within this framework, an easing of tensions with the United States was extremely important, and arms control is necessary to achieve this. But even more important was bringing an end to European fears of Soviet power so that the Soviets could achieve much greater access to technology and management skills available in Western Europe. Therefore, arms control was essential not only because it freed military resources that could be allocated to the civilian sector but even more importantly because it would enable the Soviets to build new bridges with Western Europe, which they viewed as a more reliable partner for their long-term development needs than the United States. In this task, it is not surprising that arms control in Europe received an even higher priority for Soviet leaders and that they have been more willing to make concessions to the West to achieve it than was the United States. In this sense, an extremely conciliatory set of Soviet negotiating behaviors in phase two of the INF negotiations was probably intended largely as a lever to affect the attitudes of European publics and leaders, and this was perhaps a higher Soviet priority in these negotiations even than achieving a new military stability with the United States. Although one cannot easily dismiss the reinforcing cycle between negotiations and the international environment, in this instance it appears that negotiating initiatives were intended more to change the international environment than they were to reflect prior changes in that environment (see Husbands's chap. for a description of the use of initiatives as a strategy rather than as a condition).

CONCLUSION

The relationship between the international environment and negotiations is clearly a complex one, with influences operating in both directions. Furthermore, the effects of the environment on the negotiation process cannot be separated from other influences, such as domestic factors, the substantive issues in dispute, the presence or absence of intermediaries, bargaining strategies and tactics, and the psychology of group dynamics within negotiations. All of these considerations must be taken into account to have an adequate model of the negotiation process, especially one that will help to identify the crucial difference between conditions that facilitate agreement and those that impede agreement. Further research will be necessary to develop such an integrated model of the negotiation process, including systematic quantitative and focused case studies of the many different factors that affect the likelihood that negotiations can achieve agreements to de-escalate or resolve international conflicts.

In light of the treatment of the impact of the international environment in this chapter, however, several specific suggestions of a more practical, policy-oriented nature may be proposed.

1. In general, the promotion of international tensions, such as by threatening other parties to a dispute, undertaking hostile actions against them, procuring "bargaining chips," and linking other contentious issues to a dispute, is likely to be dysfunctional for the success of negotiations.

2. Negotiators should pay careful attention to changes in the external relationship with the other party and look for signs of greater cooperation, which may be indicated by actions such as unilateral initiatives, the settlement of related issues under dispute, the cessation of various hostile actions, and the promotion of new areas of cooperation. All of these actions may indicate that the environment has become ripe for the resolution of the conflict.

3. Negotiators wishing to overcome stalemates should consider making unilateral initiatives or other cooperative gestures outside of the negotiations to communicate a consistent desire to resolve outstanding disputes.

4. Finally, negotiators should look for ways in which negotiated agreements may be used to promote a cycle of reciprocal conflict resolution in overall relations with other parties while also seeking ways to break out of vicious cycles of external hostility and negotiating stalemate.

In the end, international negotiations are but one subset of the overall state of the international relationships within which they are imbedded. Negotiators who want to resolve conflicts through negotiations must carefully monitor the relationship of their own countries with other countries in the negotiation to look for signs that the conditions in the environment are ripe for progress while also being aware of ways in which the negotiations themselves may be used to generate more constructive overall relationships.

NOTE

1. The events data used here suggest that the correlation between conflict and time increased slowly but steadily throughout this period. The correlation between time and increased conflict for NATO actions toward the Warsaw Pact was .60; for the Warsaw Pact toward NATO, .54; for the United States toward the Soviet Union, .59; and for the Soviet Union toward the United States, .68 (Hopmann 1981, table 1).

2

CRITICAL ELEMENTS IN DETERMINING THE SUITABILITY OF CONFLICT SETTLEMENT EFFORTS BY THE UNITED NATIONS SECRETARY GENERAL

INDAR JIT RIKHYE

> People engaged in good offices must have the gift of good timing
> and a flawless sense of balance.
> —de Soto 1989

INTRODUCTION

AN EXAMINATION OF THE ELEMENTS determining when or whether the United Nations secretary general should become involved personally in efforts to resolve a given conflict or to attempt its de-escalation requires an understanding of the context within which the secretary general works. Hence this chapter is divided into four parts:

    1. A discussion of the United Nations' organs for the peaceful settlement of disputes and their relationship to the office of the secretary general;

    2. An examination of the development of the institution of the secretary general's good offices, with illustrations from several cases;

    3. A case study of the secretary general's role in the Cuban Missile Crisis;

    4. Conclusions.

UNITED NATIONS DISPUTE SETTLEMENT MECHANISM

Governments of major powers, and especially the superpowers, as a rule, prefer bilateral negotiations because they permit greater control over the negotiation process, whereas multilateral negotiations broaden the negotiation process, increasing the risks of control over it by the parties concerned. Therefore, great powers, more than others, prefer to deal with their conflicts through bilateral negotiations, which enable them to maximize their influence and resort to the multilateral process only when necessary. On the other hand, smaller states, unless they are involved in alliances with one or more big powers, turn to the international process as the best safeguard for their interests. Thus the need of the states for multilateral resolution efforts increases inversely with their ability to influence negotiations.

Multilateral settlement of disputes may involve international government agencies other than the United Nations. Numerous nongovernmental organizations participate in some form of international dispute settlement, for example, disaster relief agencies that operate in areas where there is rampant insurgency. In crisis situations, governments tend to explore limited measures and to overlook multilateral diplomacy. The United States, with a legacy of power and unparalleled influence, has sought unilateral solutions to international conflicts and has avoided intervention by the United Nations in many instances. In a multipolarized world, it has become more difficult for any one nation to exert its preeminence to influence negotiations, and, therefore, international dispute settlement offers more creative moves.

The founders of the United Nations, determined to avoid another global war, decided to create a structured international system for international conflict management to replace the League of Nations, which had proven inadequate for the task. The new organization, representing the world community, would determine and condemn breaches of international peace and decide upon appropriate measures to deal with them. The founders, the victorious allies, who had brought World War II to a successful conclusion, had hoped that international decision making was possible and, therefore, could provide a precedent for an international system of dispute settlement. The United Nations required international behavior by law and in practice, which was uncommon at the time the charter was signed and even less common later. The Cold War made it worse. The United Nations has had many successes and at least as many failures. The successes are usually forgotten but the failures remain more indelible in human memory. The world organization has fallen short of the hopes and the expectations of its founders and the people who put their faith in its ability to maintain international peace and security.

The Charter established three main pillars for dispute settlement, namely, the Security Council, the General Assembly, and the International Court of Justice. It established a secretariat with a secretary general as the chief executive officer of the organization. In its early years, the Security Council was successful in dealing with the situation in the Balkans in 1946, which was a consequence of the civil war in Greece; with fighting between the Arabs and Israelis after the emergence of the Jewish state; with the conflict in Kashmir; and with the independence of Indonesia. Thereafter, the Security Council was unable to function effectively owing to the frequent use of the veto in the 1950s and the beginning of the Cold War. The decision by the council to take military action against North Korea after its forces crossed the 38th parallel, made possible by a Soviet delegation walkout over a technicality, became the only example of collective international enforcement action. Thereafter, the council had limited success in halting fighting, was mostly unable to resolve conflicts, and met little success in conflict avoidance.

The start of the Cold War and frequent use of the veto by the Soviets led the United States and its Western allies to turn to the General Assembly, where they enjoyed a majority. The Uniting for Peace Resolution of 1950 enabled the assembly to deal with critical issues when the council was hamstrung by a veto or a threat of a veto. The Soviet bloc was never reconciled to this move. When the Suez War broke out in 1956 and the Security Council was blocked by British and French vetoes, it was the assembly meeting under the Uniting for Peace Resolution that called for a cease-fire and established a peacekeeping force, the first ever, to end the fighting. A decade after the emergence of the assembly as an effective organ for the maintenance of peace and security, a large increase in its membership by the admission of newly independent countries changed the voting pattern to the disadvantage of the West, reducing their interest in the organization. The effectiveness of the organization declined to its lowest ebb. In spite of such developments, the assembly has often been the preferred venue for international dispute settlement. In dealing with the invasions of Cambodia by Vietnam and Afghanistan by the Soviets, the member states turned to the assembly rather than to the council, where a veto was certain to make any action impossible.

A number of considerations influence the choice between the council and the assembly. In the council, one or more of the veto powers should support the proposed action. The approval of the council requires that if support by one or more of the veto powers is lacking, at least their tacit support should be ensured. Another important requirement is the support of the maximum number of nonpermanent members of the council. A total of nine votes without a veto is essential to council action. The assembly meets yearly, beginning on the third Tuesday of September and generally concludes its session by mid-December. When this is not possible, it may meet in a resumed session in the new year. The assembly decides on meetings of special sessions to discuss a limited agenda, for example, disarmament. To deal with critical issues, the assembly can meet in an emergency session under the Uniting for Peace Resolution. Such sessions were called to deal with the 1956 Suez and the June 1967 wars. The members generally vote in blocs in the assembly, although there is some movement within the blocs. The assembly requires a two-thirds vote for approval.

Only recently have attempts to revive the organization's effectiveness for international dispute settlement been noticeable. The war in the Persian Gulf has involved the great powers and other interested states besides the states in the Gulf. Only the United Nations provided a suitable forum for international negotiations. Similarly, solutions to the war in Afghanistan were sought in the United Nations, and the use of U.N. peacekeeping machinery is under consideration to resolve the conflict in Cambodia. Even the implementation of the Arias Peace Plan for the Central American conflict required the United Nations to help establish an impartial monitoring system.

The history of the International Court of Justice as a useful third pillar of international dispute settlement has proved far less impressive than that of the council or assembly. Recent attempts by Nicaragua to take up the case of the mining of its harbor by the United States and the latter's refusal to accept the authority of the court was a reminder of the court's impotency in international dispute settlement.

Mindful of the deficiencies of the United Nations' system of dispute settlement from its inception because of the failure of the great powers to cooperate, member states have attempted to improve it over the last decade (U.N. 1979, 1980, 1981). In what has become known as the Manila Declaration on Peaceful Settlement of Disputes Between States (U.N. General Assembly 1982a), it is emphasized that all states should settle their international disputes exclusively by peaceful means in such a manner that international peace, security, and justice are not endangered. It declared that states should seek in good faith and in the spirit of cooperation an early and equitable settlement of their international disputes by any of the following means: negotiations, inquiry, mediation, conciliation, arbitration, judicial settlement, resort to regional agencies or arrangements, or other peaceful means of their choice, including good offices.

The Manila Declaration reaffirmed the important roles of the United Nations' three main organs for dispute settlement and called for strengthening the role of the Security Council by making greater use of the potential to review disputes or situations that were likely to endanger international peace and security, including the use of its fact-finding capability. The Security Council has addressed these issues, which were also raised in the *Report of the Secretary-General on the Work of the Organization* (U.N. General Assembly 1982b): The results of these discussions have not been made public, but it is generally known that no conclusions were reached.

GOOD OFFICES OF THE SECRETARY GENERAL

The weaknesses of the three pillars in the conflict settlement system of the United Nations has brought to the foreground an important role of the secretary general, generally known as the good offices of the secretary general. This chapter focuses on this aspect, with particular emphasis on consideration of timing as the secretary general seeks to resolve or to de-escalate conflicts. The secretary general has used his good offices in all phases of de-escalation: initiation, reciprocation, negotiation, and reaching agreements.

As the chief executive officer of the organization (U.N. Charter XV 97), the secretary general and the staff arrange and organize meetings. The secretary general is to act in that capacity in all meetings of the organs (including the Security Council and the General Assembly, which deal with conflicts), and will perform such other functions as are entrusted to that office. The secretary general will report annually on the work of the organization to the General Assembly (U.N. Charter XV 98), giving the secretary general another exclusive responsibility that has been judiciously used to draw the attention of the member states to critical issues as well. Lastly, and most importantly, the secretary general may bring to the attention of the Security Council any matter that may threaten international peace and security (U.N. Charter XV 99).

The good offices of the secretary general have evolved over the years by the performances of five Secretaries General in the tasks enumerated. Each of them brought a personal style and yet individually added to the practice and precedent of the office. Hardly a day passes in which the secretary general does not have to use good offices in the performance of normal responsibilities in the functioning of the main organs of the United Nations or when acting independently. However, many of those tasks originate when the General Assembly and the Security Council request action in pursuance of their resolutions. Such tasks include fact finding, observing, inquiry, and a large responsibility for peacekeeping operations. All these tasks facilitate the de-escalation of crises, provided that the secretary general chooses carefully the timing for situations.

The Greek Frontier Commission (U.N. Security Council 1946) first laid down the principles and guidelines for dispatching investigators, fact finding, good offices, and conciliation bodies. Following the outbreak of fighting between the Arabs and Israelis, the General Assembly (U.N. 1948), in a momentous decision, appointed a mediator for Palestine, setting another precedent for the future. Although an independent post, the support responsibilities for this position were added to the secretary general's office, and when the mediator, Count Bernadotte, was assassinated and Ralph Bunche, a United Nations staff member, was appointed acting mediator, the secretary general had to play a more active role in support of his efforts. This precedent enhanced the stature of the office with regard to conflict settlement.

The development of the conciliatory functions of the secretary general has continued through the years, even apart from activities undertaken at the explicit request of the General Assembly and the Security Council. It is the least known and potentially the most useful form of United Nations activity. The rules and procedures followed by the secretary general acquire legitimacy from recognized principles of the charter and on precedent. Respect for sovereign equality of all states, noninterference in domestic matters (U.N. Charter I 2), and the right of the states to demand assistance by procedure freely agreed to in settling disputes are inherent in the use of the good offices of the secretary general. Whereas the General Assembly recommends (U.N. Charter IV 13) actions, the Security Council's decisions are mandatory (U.N. Charter IV 15). The first provides a framework for negotiations, the other a definite mandate.

The secretary general and the senior staff maintain a constant watch over international developments. They are in touch with the member states through their missions to the United Nations, the heads of the United Nations agencies or their representatives in New York, and the global United Nations network, including many missions that report to the Secretary General. Thus the secretary general is one of the most informed persons in the world. Unlike heads of government or cabinet ministers, who rank among the most well informed and who have been known to use their knowledge to gain power in domestic bureaucratic battles or in disputes with their allies, the secretary general is called upon to use personal knowledge for the betterment of the international community and to strengthen global peace and security. This wealth of information and the interaction of the mix of nationalities that make up the staff enable the secretary general to make an objective and realistic appraisal of the attitudes and goals influencing the parties to the dispute. Thus the secretary general is in a unique position to select both the timing and the process of de-escalation.

The secretary general undertakes routine exploratory consultations in the conduct of political responsibilities. Representatives of countries and heads of states and governments as well as foreign ministers call on the office. The secretary general often meets with distinguished personalities to share their ideas and to consider the degree to which timing is propitious for the de-escalation of specific conflicts. When there are matters already under consideration by the organs of the United Nations, the secretary general, acting under the mandate given to the position, explores ways to advance the negotiations. On occasion the secretary general is asked by member states or nongovernmental organizations to act. Caution is needed when deciding the timing: Does the request deserve to be followed up by further consultation or inquiry? or Should the secretary general frankly inform the party or parties that made the request that no action will be taken because such efforts would be objected to, would lack support, or would not be productive for some other reason? The secretary general may take the initiative, especially when opportunities arise to stop fighting and de-escalate a heightening crisis. Such situations should include, besides the secretary general, parties to the conflict, other states with interests, and the United Nations' organs.

One of the earliest exercises of the good offices of the secretary general was by Dag Hammarskjold in 1955 to obtain the release of eleven American airmen held prisoner by the People's Republic of China during the war in Korea. The United States decided to employ the United Nations to obtain the release of the airmen because the peace negotiations to end the war had been stalled. The General Assembly requested that the secretary general try to obtain the release of the airmen. The People's Republic of China was not a member of the U.N. because its seat was occupied by the Republic of China (based in Formosa). With the exception of one state, the Afro-Asian group abstained in voting, and Sweden voted for the resolution after expressing its misgivings against using the assembly. An analysis of these attitudes led Hammarskjold to decide that the time was right for him to handle this mission in his own capacity as the secretary general. He was able to obtain the release of the American prisoners, help de-escalation, and deal with this complex situation by taking into consideration the interests of the main parties. His success provided the basis for the greatly enhanced role of the secretary general at the time of the Suez crisis, and the slogan in the halls of the tall glass building on the East River was "Leave it to Dag."

In situations where parties are willing to accept the good offices of the secretary general, the initiative generally comes from them. U Thant's role in resolving the crisis over the future of Bahrain took shape over several months during 1969–70. He had exploratory talks with the parties, Iran and the United Kingdom, on the possibility of exercising his good offices, which he eventually told them he was willing to provide. Upon receiving a letter from the Iranians containing such a request with their suggestions for terms of reference, he sent a copy of the letter to the permanent representative of the United Kingdom to the United Nations. The British agreed, and U Thant advised both governments of his willingness to become involved and to agree to the terms of reference. Thus, the secretary general held consultations with the parties, received a request from the parties to intervene, and then conveyed his acceptance to the agreed terms of reference. These three elements are essential for the secretary general to enter negotiations. If these elements are present, the situation is probably ripe for serious negotiations.

The idea of providing assistance may originate with the secretary general, but the request for the secretary general's good offices could be initiated by one or more other parties. For example, Secretary General U Thant was concerned about the war in Yemen in 1962–63 and himself initiated the good offices of the secretary general to facilitate the de-escalation that led to a cease-fire. Following a pro-Nasser army coup against the traditional ruler of Yemen, Egypt (then the United Arab Republic) provided sizable military assistance. Saudi Arabia was involved in the fighting that at times spread across the Saudi borders. U Thant's consultations with the parties to the fighting and other powers including the United States, which were concerned because the escalation in fighting had spread into Saudi territory, led to an agreement (U.N. Security Council 1963).

On occasion, the initiative may come from a third state or states, which may be too myopically concerned with its own interests to give sufficient consideration to timing. The June 1967 war resulted in the closing of the Suez Canal, blocking ships of a number of countries. Several attempts to extricate the ships were aborted. States with ships in the Suez approached the secretary general to request that he intervene, and he negotiated with Egypt to get the boats out but had little success. The secretary general may take the initiative even when it is not requested by any party. However, the timing of such intervention must be chosen carefully.

Under ARTICLE 99, the secretary general may bring to the attention of the Security Council any matter that in the secretary general's opinion may threaten the maintenance of international peace and security (U.N. Charter XV 99). This provision was used only once by Hammarskjold, and its timing was chosen with care, when civil war broke out in the Congo (Zaire) immediately after its independence, and Belgian troops intervened. Bunche, representing the secretary general at the independence celebrations, was asked by President Joseph Kasavubu and Prime Minister Patrice Lumumba for advice and assistance. Consequently, Bunche cabled the Congolese request to Hammarskjold, who brought the situation to the attention of the council. International constitutional experts will agree that Hammarskjold acted under ARTICLE 99, but an official communication from the Congolese government forwarded by Bunche on an official mission to Léopoldville (Kinshasa) had to be transmitted to the council, in any case.

Why did Hammarskjold turn to the ARTICLE 99 procedure at that time, and why have he and others who followed him not employed it since? The answer rests with the circumstances of the conflict and the climate created by the Cold War. The effectiveness of the good offices of the secretary general could be damaged if the attempt to draw the attention of the council to act is faced with a certain veto. In fact, it would also greatly prejudice the secretary general's overall performance. The occasion and timing for the use of this diplomatic tool has to be so chosen that its acceptance is certain.

In the Congo, the Cold War had already made inroads by the time the country gained its independence. Belgium was a Western ally, had retained military bases through a treaty with the young state, and had an enormous economic stake that was linked to similar Western interests. Lumumba and other Congolese leaders of his party had established links with Afro-Asian leaders who opposed many Western policies and enjoyed the support of the Soviet bloc on anticolonial issues. Deeply sympathetic to the difficulties of the newly emerged states in Africa, Hammarskjold probably chose the dramatic use of ARTICLE 99 on this occasion to rally universal support for aid to the Congo and succeeded in doing so.

As the Cold War widened the rift among the great powers in the aftermath of the Congo operation by the United Nations and the Cuban Missile Crisis, to mention only two examples, the secretary general had to walk a tightrope. The Soviets opposed Hammarskjold, and the difficulties caused by the United Nations' military operations in Katanga had weakened his support from France, the United Kingdom, and even the United States. Had he lived, the rules by which he had played his role would have had to change. His successor certainly had to be assured of the support of the member states, especially the great powers. The office of the secretary general had survived the Soviet attempt to replace it with a troika. During the election of U Thant, the Soviet attempt to have the secretary general commit himself to consult eight under secretaries general, five representing the permanent powers and three from the rest of the world, was also rejected. The signal from the Soviets was clear—the secretary general's authority must be held in check. The West was never far from this view, although it did not openly express it. Nonetheless, Western behavior during the last days of Hammarskjold and its attempts to influence the secretary general by every type of pressure were obvious although it never reached the demonstrative stage shown by Khrushchev's shoe banging during his condemnation of Hammarskjold before the assembly in 1960.

When he took over the office of secretary general, first as acting secretary general to complete Hammarskjold's term and later after he was elected, U Thant was fully aware of the requirements of his role. He had spent years as the permanent representative of Burma to the United Nations and later served as the chairman of the Congo Conciliation Committee. He recognized that the secretary general had a vital role to fulfill, which he could only perform by remaining effective. His effectiveness, in turn, depended upon his ability to choose when to become involved. This awareness notwithstanding, he felt that when there were great risks to international peace and security—for example, the threat of nuclear holocaust—the secretary general should act audaciously. Accordingly, he chose to act during the Cuban Missile Crisis and offered his good offices to resolve the conflict. He was willing to take high risks as the crisis threatened to generate a war between the two superpowers. Because much of the information on U Thant's role in the missile crisis has escaped public notice, it is discussed in detail in the third part of this chapter. U Thant also tried, in vain, to become involved personally in ending the war in Vietnam.

U Thant's efforts regarding the mounting civil unrest in East Pakistan that was threatening to break out in war on the subcontinent were not successful. Concerned over the huge influx of refugees from East Pakistan into West Bengal and the border incidents between India and East Pakistan, he attempted to bring the situation to the attention of the Security Council by addressing a memorandum to its president. Pakistan was opposed to any United Nations intervention in its internal affairs. Although the flight of millions of refugees and incidents on the border were not solely internal matters, the United States agreed with Pakistan. The president of the council went no further in his consultations to bring the matter to a meeting. In spite of this negative response, U Thant went ahead with his humanitarian initiatives and dispatched a relief coordinator to Dhaka.

U Thant's memorandum fell short of his ability to act under ARTICLE 99 because he did not ask for a meeting of the Security Council. Obviously, he intended to test the climate in the council, and it did not take him long to learn that East-West lines were drawn, with the United States favoring the position of Pakistan; the United Kingdom as the former imperial power attempting to keep an even hand, with a tilt toward Pakistan; the French sympathizing with India because of the refugee problem; and the Soviets backing India. The nonpermanent members were divided over the issue. There was no hope for an attempt at U.N. preventative action at that stage of the conflict. The timing was all wrong. As U Thant explained his action, "The political aspects of this matter are of such far-reaching importance that the secretary general is not in a position to suggest precise courses of action before members of the Security Council have taken note of the problem." He then went on to state that the United Nations, with its experience in peacekeeping and with its varied resources for conciliation and persuasion, should play a more forthright role in dealing with the human tragedy and the deteriorating situation (*U.N. Monthly Chronicle* 1971).

This attempt to explain his action is an interesting contrast to his attempts to clarify his actions related to the withdrawal of the United Nations Emergency Force from the Sinai, which led to the June 1967 war. His critics claimed that U Thant's interpretation of Hammarskjold's agreement with the Egyptians about how to determine when the task of this force had been completed did not conform to a memorandum that Hammarskjold had kept in his personal papers, copies of which were in the possession of others. This document stated that the General Assembly was the ultimate authority to decide when the task of the United Nations was completed. U Thant and Bunche, who was with Hammarskjold at the time, disclaimed this interpretation as nonofficial. General E. L. M. Burns of Canada, the United Nations commander of the troops at the time, had accompanied Hammarskjold to Cairo for the negotiations; a copy of the conclusions of this meeting was in his official files and was seen by the author when the general assumed command of the force. U Thant was correct in stating that Hammarskjold's paper was not an official document, and, in fact, Nasser refused Hammarskjold's efforts to give the General Assembly the right to decide when the task of the force was done because that was a right that Egypt intended to retain as a sovereign state, one which could withdraw its consent for the peacekeeping force to remain.

The contrast between these two actions by U Thant in the Sinai and in East Pakistan was that in the latter, U Thant placed the responsibility for dealing with the rising conflict on the Security Council. In the Sinai, other than resting his case on international law and precedent, he remained silent and was made a scapegoat by some member states, particularly Israel and its friends, and, surprisingly, by Egypt after it lost the war, for failing to prevent a war that after a decade of relative peace again threatened the existence of the young Jewish state. U Thant was unsuccessful in de-escalating the crisis, which led to the 1967 war.

What U Thant never said in public was that the responsibility for the war lay elsewhere. Lulled by the success of the United Nations peacekeeping force, which had brought normalcy to life in the area of its operations, the incentive to continue the process of peacebuilding went nowhere. The parties to the conflict and the great powers were, therefore, responsible for allowing themselves to be lulled into inaction. As the years rolled by, the Arab nations failed to alleviate the conditions of the Palestinian refugees, and their hope for statehood was no nearer. From this arose a determination for self-action. The Palestinians formed a liberation organization with a military wing—Al Fatah. Once formed, raiding started from the adjoining Arab states. Only Egypt disallowed it, attributing its action to the presence of the United Nations peacekeeping force. As the border incidents increased, tensions mounted. It was no longer possible for Egypt to remain on the sidelines and for Nasser to allow the leadership of the Arabs to slip into other hands. Because the United Nations peacekeeping force remained in the way, it had to be removed.

The record shows that the members of the Security Council failed to face up to their responsibilities as the situation between Israel and frontline Arab states worsened. Canada and Denmark attempted to move the council to action without avail. The General Assembly lacked consensus to meet in an emergency special session. Now only the secretary general remained. He was aware that the Soviet Union and a majority of the Third World, including troop-contributing countries, in supporting the right of consent for the deployment of peacekeeping forces, would support the Egyptian stand (Rikhye 1978)[1] Therefore, if he was to force a debate in the council by invoking ARTICLE 99, the timing would be wrong because nothing substantive could be achieved, and in fact, the inevitable ugly exchanges between the two power blocs could hinder quiet diplomacy and new efforts to keep the peace or, if war did break out, to end it. Furthermore, if he took the ARTICLE 99 route, his position in any future negotiations would be greatly compromised.

A number of other opportunities have added to the good offices of the secretary general. The secretary general has been requested to intervene by governments and nongovernmental organizations to dampen conflicts and remedy grievances and by minority groups to protect their interests. On humanitarian issues, the secretary general has been able to co-opt other United Nations agencies, for example, the High Commissioner for Refugees and the International Committee of the Red Cross. As in Nigeria and Bangladesh, the secretary general assumed the duties of the coordinator, appointing a representative in the field. The secretary general assisted the release of the hijacked hostages of the El Al plane to Algeria and the TWA plane to Damascus. He assisted the release of several leading personalities of Guinea, who had to land in the Ivory Coast owing to bad weather and were detained there, causing tensions between the two governments. Innumerable other examples of this kind led to de-escalation.

Every secretary general has attempted to do everything possible to perform the tasks to the extent circumstances permitted. Kurt Waldheim's period of duty was marked by a revival of U.N. peacekeeping responsibilities after the October 1973 Arab-Israeli war. The modalities for these operations were somewhat different from those in past practice because negotiations leading to their establishment were conducted by Henry Kissinger, and the secretary general dealt with the operational aspect thereafter.

However, the United Nations peacekeeping operation in South Lebanon was handled by the secretary general. It began on a U.S. initiative; it later lost its impetus and, thereby, its effectiveness because of Israeli objections. The inability of the United Nations to maintain its peacekeeping operation in the Sinai after the Camp David Accord because of Arab objections and the certainty of a Soviet veto in the Security Council, in addition to the failure of the United Nations to fully implement the mandate of its peacekeeping force in south Lebanon, cost the international organization most of its gains in its ability to maintain peace and security. All this further reduced the ability of the secretary general to perform the duties of the position. Waldheim's valiant effort to help in the Iran hostage crisis, which had little hope for success, did not add to the status of the good offices of the secretary general. Thus timing does not always assure success, but it is almost always related to de-escalation efforts.

The secretary general, Javier Perez de Cuellar, was able to enter the negotiations in the Falkand/Malvinas crisis at a critical stage. In the Iran-Iraq war, he had a major role until the acceptance by both sides of the U.N. Security Council Resolution 598 on July 17, 1988, and the end of the fighting. The negotiations on Cyprus have gone on for twenty-five years. Yet there has been no change in the political will of the parties to resolve the conflict. However, the negotiations on ending the war in Afghanistan, first started by Perez de Cuellar as the special representative of the secretary general and taken over by Diego Cordovez in the same position, succeeded because of a major Soviet foreign policy change.

Generally, the five secretaries general have avoided creating waves and have operated within political realities of the time. Each has had opportunities for action, but situations and their environments were different. Trygve Lie, a labor union leader and former cabinet member in Norway, and Dag Hammarskjold, an economist, former civil servant, and minister in Sweden, were the two Scandanavians who could be said to have been more assertive in their personal interventions. In 1946, Lie upset the West by publicly favoring the Soviets in the dispute over the presence of their troops in Azerbaijan. Lie maintained his independence in spite of an acrimonious exchange with the United States representative and later criticized regional military pacts, such as the North Atlantic Treaty Alliance. Lie also campaigned for the seating of the People's Republic of China. In June 1950, when he condemned the invasion of South Korea by North Korea, he annoyed the Soviets, who declared him persona non grata, and he won back the support of the West. Lie resigned in 1953.

Enough has been said about Hammarskjold in this chapter. He was even more of an activist than Lie and was bold to take advantage of timing to de-escalate conflicts or to end fighting. He emerged through his early years in the office with a heightened reputation and trust. The Congo operation led to the greatest crisis in the life of the United Nations and its secretary general. When Lumumba's government fell from a Western-sponsored military coup, Hammarskjold was vilified by the Soviet Union, and when the United Nations troops, acting under orders, exceeded his instruction to end the secession of Katanga, he lost the support of France and the United Kingdom. This, in turn, so reduced support from the Kennedy administration, which was and would continue later to be a tower of strength, that it weakened the secretary general's political capacity and the United Nations troops were unable to properly defend themselves in the field.

U Thant, Waldheim, and Perez de Cuellar, have been more passive. All have been cautious in their timing and initiatives. Their roles have been less dramatic than those of Lie and Hammarskjold, but each has made significant contributions to peace and security. There is a time and place in history for each of them. They all have added to the role of the good offices of the secretary general. Given the opportunity, Perez de Cuellar is in a position to make a significant contribution to peace and security.

THE SECRETARY GENERAL AND THE CUBAN MISSILE CRISIS

The Cuban crisis had been building for some time, leading to an invasion on April 15, 1962, of Cochinos Bay by Cuban exiles with the support of the United States. The battle, popularly known as the Bay of Pigs Operation, ended in disaster for the invaders, and the survivors were captured. The Security Council met to consider the Cuban complaint of an invasion by the United States. The fighting, however, was over in three days, and thereafter, the two parties dealt with each other through several official and nonofficial channels. U Thant was involved.

It was soon evident that the Cubans had turned to the Soviets for greater assistance. The reasons for the Soviet decision to send missiles together with fighters and bombers and about twenty thousand ground forces were not entirely clear. Fearing invasion, Cuba desired extra defense against the United States. Cuba also desired that Russia should be held accountable for having chosen a defensive system that had offensive capability against the United States, including nuclear weapons. But this security could probably have been afforded by extending guarantees under the Warsaw Pact to Cuba, or more explicitly, by Khrushchev declaring war in case of aggression against the Soviet ally. Yet for the Soviets, the installation of say, sixty missiles,[2] some with a range of 1,000 miles, a few with ranges of 1,500 to 2,000 miles, would, in fact, have doubled the capacity of Russia to strike the United States (Thomas 1971). The Soviets would have gained two other advantages:

missiles on Cuban soil would outflank the North American missile defense system which was directed entirely against an attack from the north, and Cuba would provide a base for operation in Latin America.

In the United States, during August, information from agents inside Cuba and air reconnaissance gave evidence that ground-to-air missiles (SAMs) had reached the island. If SAMs had arrived, the oft-asked question in the Kennedy administration but not given much credence was, "Were they protecting intercontinental and medium-range missiles?" By August 23, the United States had sufficient intelligence to confirm the presence of SAMs but insufficient information about the missiles. On September 7, Kennedy formally asked for congressional approval to mobilize one hundred fifty thousand reserves. In mid-September, Khrushchev sent Kennedy a letter, assuring him that no missiles had been sent to Cuba (Kennedy 1968). At about this time, two large Russian freighters, used for carrying heavy timber, reached Cuba, and much activity was reported in the San Cristobal area. U-2 flights during the first week of October provided no evidence, but air force flights on October 14 in areas not covered by the U-2s, confirmed mobile, medium-range sites at San Cristobal. The die was cast.

Of the two choices available to Kennedy—invading Cuba or putting into effect a blockade—he chose the latter. For reasons of secrecy, the administration did not consult or share this information with its allies, the Organization of American States, or the United Nations. The American forces were ordered to establish a "quarantine"—the administration thought this to be a milder term than blockade—to be ready for an invasion, and to be on the alert to defend an attack by air or missiles.

A full account of events leading up to and during the missile crisis is not intended here. But essential information is included to illustrate the attitudes of the parties concerned, their objectives, and the framework in which negotiations could be developed, and thereby, to provide the context in which the good offices of the secretary general were exercised, especially in respect to timing and de-escalation.

U Thant had met Khrushchev at the end of August in Yalta and had the impression that he did not desire a showdown with the United States. The newspapers were busy reporting the Soviet responses to the Berlin crisis and were not concerned about Cuba. The United States had managed to keep the information regarding the Soviet buildup a well-guarded secret, with the exception of warnings by one or two politicians about the Soviet role in Cuba.

On Saturday, October 20, U Thant's U.N. military adviser, Maj. Gen. Indar Jit Rikhye, received a telephone call from the military adviser to Adlai Stevenson, Adm. John McCain, who said that the U.S. government had definite proof of the presence of the Soviet missiles in Cuba. The military adviser expected to bring the aerial photographs with him to show on Monday, October 22. Rikhye immediately informed U Thant. On Monday, McCain told Rikhye that the president was about to make an important announcement and that he had fully briefed Stevenson. This information was passed on to U Thant, and he was urged to send for Stevenson for further consultation. Stevenson arrived at 4:30 P.M. and confirmed what U Thant already knew. Meanwhile, a White House statement had further confirmed the news about the presence of Soviet missiles and announced that the president would address the nation that evening.

While instructions were sent to the United States representatives at the Organization of American States and the United Nations Security Council to gain support for the U.S. actions, in an address to the nation, Kennedy spoke of the presence of Soviet missiles in Cuba and of the grave threat to U.S. security.

In his speech, Kennedy said offensive missile sites were prepared in Cuba, an area with special, historic ties to the United States. These sites had altered the international balance of power and were not acceptable to the United States. The long-range missiles threatened the area between the Hudson Bay and Lima. Although the United States was opposed to nuclear war, it would not shrink from it when need be. A quarantine was ordered to prevent a further supply of offensive materials. Finally, Kennedy called on Khrushchev to withdraw the bombers and missiles and abandon the establishment of their launching sites.

Kennedy's speech and the opening of the missile crisis debate in the council brought a stream of callers to U Thant. He received them in his office adjacent to the council chamber and in the main office on the thirty-eighth floor. The majority expressed shock and concern because the world was too close to a nuclear war. The big powers were divided by ideology, but not all of the western group agreed with the Kennedy strategy, notably France. In a wise move, Kennedy had, for the time being, avoided recourse to immediate war. Thus the expected explosive event would be the confrontation between the convoy of twenty-five Soviet cargo ships escorted by their naval surface fleet and submarines. Therefore, without hesitation, U Thant decided to act immediately to de-escalate, concentrating all his efforts to prevent an armed confrontation that could lead to war.

Late that evening, Adlai Stevenson, the permanent representative of the United States, called on U Thant and requested an emergency meeting of the Security Council. The Soviet permanent representative, Valerian Zorin, came thereafter and requested an immediate examination of the question of violation of the charter and threat to peace by the United States. Zorin, president of the council by monthly rotation, properly chose the secretary general to call a meeting of the council to avoid controversy from his role as a party to the crisis. Zorin's request for a council meeting was based on the Soviet objection to the quarantine ordered by Kennedy. Although the Organization of American States permits such action, under the United Nations Charter, authorization of the Security Council was required. Later, Cuba came with its request for a council meeting to consider the act of war unilaterally committed by the United States.

Dean Rusk addressed the Organization of American States, and a stunned membership readily endorsed the measures proposed, including the quarantine, a step permissible under their charter. The debate in the Security Council was dramatic and acrimonious, made even more so by the use of maps and enlarged aerial photographs of the missile site by Stevenson. In submitting a draft resolution on behalf of the United States, Stevenson called for the dismantling of the offending sites, the removal of missiles and aircraft, and the establishment of United Nations observers to supervise and monitor their withdrawal. The Soviet permanent representative, Zorin, was caught by surprise and denied the presence of the offensive weapons in the face of hard evidence exhibited by the U.S. representative. Apparently Anatoly Dobrynin, the Soviet ambassador in Washington, was faced with a similar dilemma, and earlier in September in a meeting with Kennedy on the Berlin crisis, Foreign Minister Gromyko had insisted that only defensive weapons were brought to Cuba.

In between the heavy traffic of ambassadors, U Thant learned of the latest developments in Cuba. In an atmosphere of trust established by the secretary general, his immediate advisers had built excellent working and personal relations with their counterparts. During the worst crisis since World War II, members of the U.S. delegation, their military staff, and the State Department could turn to the secretary general and his personal advisers and trust them with highly sensitive security information of immense national importance. Their faith in the office of the secretary general was vital, as was proven by the timely information given to U Thant's military adviser by his American counterpart from midnight on. The United States estimated that about thirty missiles had reached Cuba and that they perhaps were capable of striking any part of the United States. But they were not yet operational and could only be activated by additional supplies, which presumably were en route in the Soviet ships approaching Cuban waters. At least the missiles were not ready for launching, but whether the Soviet air force was operational and whether they had nuclear weapons was not clear. The likely answer to both questions was "probably not," but there was no evidence in either direction. Thus the main danger apparently was from a confrontation on the high seas on the approaches to Cuba, which had to be prevented.

U Thant had decided that he must intervene at once to de-escalate. He prepared a statement to the council and an appeal to Kennedy and Khrushchev, which he intended to make at the council meeting the next day. His decision to play a role to control the crisis was reinforced when 45 permanent members of the organization out of 110 urged him to intervene to avert the oncoming catastrophe. At the council meeting, charges were exchanged between the three parties, and the atmosphere was highly conflictive when U Thant took the floor. He called for urgent negotiations by the parties and said that he had addressed identical messages to Kennedy and Khrushchev with an urgent appeal for a moratorium of two or three weeks, involving, on the one hand, the voluntary suspension of all arms shipments to Cuba and, on the other, voluntary suspension of quarantine measures on the movement of Soviet shipping to Cuba. In a message to Castro, he requested him to suspend construction of military installations in Cuba during the period of negotiations. He called to offer his good offices. All these appeals could be characterized as efforts to initiate de-escalation.

In the afternoon, U Thant received Khrushchev's reply in agreement with the proposals. Later a reply was received from Kennedy, who said that Stevenson was ready to discuss promptly the suggested arrangements. Both sides feared that escalation would lead to nuclear holocaust, which they wished to avoid. U Thant immediately sent identical messages to Khrushchev and Kennedy conveying his gratitude and noting that he hoped to begin discussions with their respective permanent representatives. After the council meeting, U Thant sent messages to the heads of governments expressing his grave concern that the Soviet ships already on their way to Cuba might challenge the quarantine, thus destroying the possibility of the discussions proposed by him. Accordingly, he asked Khrushchev to instruct the Soviet ships to stay away from the confrontation area and requested Kennedy to do everything to avoid confrontations with the Russian ships. If he could have assurances of the cooperation of each side, he could convey that to the other, thereby gaining a breathing spell. Kennedy agreed, contingent on Soviet acceptance. Khrushchev also agreed, but stipulated that he could not keep ships immobilized on the high seas, therefore, his order was temporary. De-escalation had thus been successfully initiated.

U Thant sent a message to Castro informing him of the agreement by the U.S. President and the general secretary of the Soviet Union to his proposals and again requested his cooperation. Castro's reply was not encouraging. Although he was willing to resolve the crisis, he rejected the violation of his sovereignty caused by the quarantine and the presumption of the United States in deciding the type of weapons Cuba should take. However, he did invite the secretary general to come to Havana for discussions. U Thant accepted his invitation. Meanwhile, U Thant's office was deluged with cables from all parts of the world expressing their concern and encouraging him to continue with his efforts.

U Thant was aware of several private channels of communications between the Americans and the Russians, and he received several letters from Bertrand Russell, who was in correspondence with the two heads of state. On the high seas on October 25, the Americans allowed an East German passenger ship to pass without inspection. The Soviets had halted twelve other ships near the area of search. The following day, a Panamanian ship on its way to Cuba under Russian charter was searched and allowed to proceed because it was not carrying any weapons or munitions. The first part of U Thant's proposals was working as the parties reciprocated de-escalatory moves. According to U Thant's plan, there were not supposed to be any searches. However, the Americans did search the ships in a businesslike manner, carefully avoiding high-handedness, and the Russians avoided confrontation by halting ships with military hardware and only moving innocent cargo to Cuba.

In Washington on October 26, the Soviets contacted John Scali of ABC News through an embassy official, Aleksander Fomin, to test a proposal for compromise (Thomas 1971). Would the United States be interested in a promise not to invade Cuba in return for a Russian withdrawal of their missiles under United Nations inspection? Scali consulted Roger Hillsman, assistant secretary of state for intelligence, and later Dean Rusk, who saw some possibilities in the idea. Soon thereafter, Kennedy and U Thant received letters from Khrushchev with the proposal. In fact, Zorin personally brought Khrushchev's letter to U Thant accompanied by the Cuban ambassador, thereby indicating the support of the latter's government. The following day another letter arrived from Khrushchev for Kennedy suggesting that the Americans should remove their missiles in Turkey in exchange for the Russian removal of theirs from Cuba. He also assured Kennedy that the missiles in Cuba were under their exclusive control.

On October 27, the United States representative informed the secretary general of a letter sent by Kennedy to Khrushchev, indicating that according to the proposals, which were generally acceptable to the United States, the Soviet Union would agree to remove weapons from Cuba under appropriate United Nations observation and supervision and also undertake suitable safeguards to halt the further introduction of such weapons into Cuba. The United States on its part would agree to the establishment of adequate arrangements (by the United Nations) to insure the carrying out and continuation of these commitments, to remove promptly the quarantine measure, and to give ensurance against invasion of Cuba.

The level of negotiations and its pace had increased. Kennedy had sent John J. McCloy, former president of the World Bank, to help Stevenson. It was said that Stevenson was too soft in his debate in the council and had suggested the exchange of U.S. missiles in Turkey for the Soviet missiles in Cuba. An able and accomplished man, McCloy was a tough negotiator and certainly took harder stances in negotiations. The Soviets sent Vasily V. Kuznetsov, the first deputy foreign minister, a persuasive and charming man who was highly esteemed in the United Nations where he often came to represent his government.

U Thant had found Zorin somewhat dry and colorless and was not at ease with him. The U.S. and Soviet negotiating teams were by then actively engaged in direct negotiations under the good offices of the secretary general. The two teams were in telephone communication with their governments and made a valuable contribution to the direct exchanges in progress at the heads of state level.

On October 28, a U-2 flight over Cuba was shot down by a SAM. To establish that he was in command, Castro declared that the aircraft was shot down at his orders. Tensions were high that day. The debate in U Thant's private office between the two delegations was almost stifling. The U.S. side often spoke of invasion. It took all the tact at U Thant's command to keep the discussions under restraint. Because Kennedy had responded to Khrushchev's first proposal positively, on October 28, U Thant sent a message to Khrushchev acknowledging having received a copy of the message sent by him to Kennedy. U Thant said that he would consult with Kuznetsov and Castro to work out the modalities of establishing the United Nations observers, which would greatly facilitate de-escalation.

The Soviet response to observation of the withdrawal of the missiles, presumably because of Castro's objection to inspection, was that they preferred that it be done by the International Commission of the Red Cross. A telephone call by the secretary general to Geneva confirmed their willingness to undertake this responsibility. On October 30, U Thant, accompanied by Under Secretaries General Omar Loutfi of Egypt and Hernane Tavares de Sa of Brazil and by his military adviser, flew to Havana. In these meetings, Castro made it clear that he would not accept any observers whether they were from the United Nations or the International Commission of the Red Cross. Under the terms of the agreement, U Thant was obliged to observe and supervise the removal of the missiles, aircraft, and other offensive weapons. He invited several ambassadors who had good relations with the Cubans and was told that no one, not even Raul Castro, the chief of the Cuban armed forces, was allowed in the Soviet security area. The Soviets had their troops guarding their sites, which were wired, and had brought their own construction force. Thus, only the Russian ambassador could tell U Thant what had left the country, as only the Russians were permitted in the harbor area.

U Thant informed the Soviet ambassador that because he was not able to deploy his observers, he would need Soviet help to know when all the weapons had left the country. He also requested that the Soviet military commander meet with his military adviser on the withdrawal details. All missiles and aircraft were being removed within a two-day period. U Thant decided to return to New York the next day, after the departure of the Soviet missiles and aircraft.

Because the United Nations was not allowed to set up a mission, it could not use the cipher equipment that was brought. However, the United States had to be informed of U Thant's activities and his decision to return to New York. Only the telephone line was available, and the military adviser was asked to call U Thant's chef de cabinet, C. V. Narasimahn, a fellow Indian, and speak to him in Hindi. The conversation was not easy because most Indians from different regions of India speak to each other in English. In any case, the State Department had an intercept of this conversation with the faulty Hindi corrected.

Later, Narasimahn called back to inform the secretary general that the State Department did not want him to return until the observer system was in place. But further discussion on this subject with Castro was futile. After the Soviet ambassador informed the secretary general that all weapons had left, he decided to leave too. On arrival at Idlewild airport in New York, U Thant was met by Dean Rusk, who conveyed the annoyance of the administration at U Thant's inability to place observers and his return without completing his task. No amount of explanations appeared to change his expression of dissatisfaction. This argument continued for a day or so until the U.S. Navy reported that all known missiles had left the country. However, the argument as to what remained still surfaces occasionally.

To prevent escalation, U Thant started the process of bringing about an understanding between the parties on basic issues and the search for a solution. He worked out the formula to avoid confrontation and persuaded the superpowers to agree. He succeeded in persuading the two sides to meet in his private conference room. He chaired the meetings and provided food and refreshment, which permitted some relief in the tense negotiations and a haven where participants could talk to each other freely without media attention. It was here that the two sides worked out the details of the agreement reached by their leaders. When U Thant returned from Cuba without a United Nations inspection of withdrawal, the Kennedy administration was angry, and the American public was disappointed. His reward for his quiet diplomacy in helping the superpowers avert a war, perhaps a nuclear war, was to be forgotten despite the very important role he played.

CONCLUSION

Some general rules apply to the practice of good offices by the secretary general. Such efforts must conform to the charter. The secretary general must decide whether the timing of personal intervention is likely to be helpful, ineffective, or even harmful. In many of the problems, the prestige of a government is involved, and often a domestic political situation stands in the way of an agreement. The secretary must first strive to de-escalate. A leader has to tread carefully here, using quiet diplomacy, even while possibly under personal attack in public for ignoring the problem. The secretary has to avoid publicity even though the decision conflicts with letting the people know what the United Nations is doing. This is a dilemma because the exercise of good offices demands discretion when the public is being misinformed about the role of the world organization by interested parties. The secretary must always maintain the trust of the parties.

The growing role of the secretary general in the use of good offices has increased the ability of the United Nations to deal with many conflict situations with which its main organs are not able to cope. Although the fundamentals of the Charter remain, the situations change. U Thant said, "Things that were possible for one secretary general are no longer possible for his successor, and vice versa. There are some times when action, dynamism and innovation are in demand, and other times when governments shun them like the plague. This office is, of necessity, developed through trial and error and in response to the demands and challenges of the passing years. Each secretary general must build as best he can on the office as he inherited it. If he cannot hope to repeat all the successes of his predecessors, neither should he fear to try again where they failed" (Thant 1971).

Working within the Charter, the secretary general is operating in the framework of sovereign states. The new global trends have made nations more interdependent, which in turn demands reassertion of their nationalism. The secretary general has to work with idealism at one end of the spectrum and the pragmatic and selfish reality of sovereignty on the other. Some governments will ask the secretary to do more and others less. The Security Council and the General Assembly directives to the secretary general offer an area of consensus, yet it is the secretary who must understand the shades of differences in their implementation. The interpretation of each mandate has several variations, and it is the secretary general who must find the acceptable one within the Charter. Governments and the media have the liberty to pronounce judgments on a leader's actions, but the secretary cannot respond. Irrespective of personal views, secretaries general are obliged to work within the limits of the resolutions. They are not heads of governments but servants of the member states.

Secretaries general must take initiatives in all conflict situations regardless of the views of interested parties. But they should decide on the timing and the nature of their actions, including de-escalation, with a careful understanding of the conflict, the views of the parties concerned and other interested parties, and how best they can play effective roles. Both U Thant and Hammarskjold felt strongly that in the most critical situations, their own personal prestige and even the position of their office were expendable. Lastly, their independence (U.N. Charter XV 100), which gives secretaries general freedom to act, must be maintained. It is this independence that is essential to the long-term interests of peace and security in the world.

NOTES

1. Conversations with the author who had returned to New York after the withdrawal of the United Nations Force, of which he was the commander, to his post as the military adviser to U Thant, as well as special adviser for the Middle East.

2. About thirty, according to a later report by the United States.

3

RIPENESS, DE-ESCALATION, AND ARMS CONTROL
The Case of the INF

RICHARD N. HAASS

A GOOD DEAL of contemporary thinking and writing on negotiations concerns itself with matters of technique and approach. Questions of when to bluff and when to lie, when to use a single negotiating text and when to use two, when to negotiate directly and when to deploy a third party as mediator—these and similar issues fill the literature of negotiations and not a few memoirs.

A second area of great emphasis is less concerned with technique and approach per se than with substance. This area is more traditionally the province of the area or functional specialist. Thus countless articles and books suggest one formula or another formula for solving this regional dispute or that arms race.

Both of these areas of endeavor are necessary and often useful. Neither, however, is sufficient. They provide a good deal of insight into how an agreement was forged or how one might be. But they cannot and do not reveal everything or even the most important things about why some agreements prove possible and others do not. For this, one must turn to the concept of ripeness, by which is meant context and, more specifically, the presence or absence of certain conditions in which any negotiation takes place.

Such conditions are essentially of two types. Some of these apply to the substance of the matter at hand. They can thus be understood as *intrinsic*. In the area of arms control, for example, such intrinsic factors include the balance of arms being discussed and the investment each side has made in the arms in question.

A second set of conditions is *extrinsic* to the inner details of any accord, be it actual or possible. These factors reflect the larger negotiating context—the overall political relationship between the parties, the occurrence of crises, and, above all, the quality of the respective leaderships. Here, in this last category, two characteristics count most: the degree of commitment to reaching agreement—the perceived desirability of the accord—and the political capacity to negotiate and sustain compromise. Leaders must both want agreements and be able to bring their own polities with them.

In short, no negotiation takes place in a vacuum. No outcome is preordained by the existence of any particular balance or set of concerns. This is especially so in the case of arms control. In any arms control negotiation, one is dealing with but one dimension of the military balance, which in turn is but one dimension of the overall relationship between the parties. Agreements thus become possible only when leaders choose to make them and when leaders are sufficiently strong to see them through.

THE HISTORY OF THE NEGOTIATIONS

On December 8, 1987, Ronald Reagan and Mikhail Gorbachev met in Washington, D.C. to sign the Treaty Between the United States of America and the Union of Soviet Socialist Republics on the Elimination of Their Intermediate-range and Shorter-range Missiles. The treaty affects all U.S. and Soviet land-based missiles with ranges from 500–5,500 kilometers. Upon going into effect, it bans immediately all production and flight testing of existing INF missiles or "new types." It also eliminates all U.S. and Soviet INF ballistic and ground-launch cruise missiles, associated systems, and related facilities within three years. Finally, the treaty includes, as well, extensive provisions for verification of compliance, including detailed data exchanges and provisions for intrusive, on-site inspections of a range of INF-related facilities.

For obvious reasons, this agreement (often referred to as the Intermediate-range Nuclear Forces Treaty [INF]) raises a host of questions. Some of these are political. What will be the treaty's impact over time on NATO and U.S.-European relations? How will it affect the future of arms control and East-West relations? And, to choose the issue that most preoccupied many members of the U.S. Senate during the 1988 debate over the INF Treaty, can the treaty be adequately verified?

As interesting and important as these and similar questions are, however, they largely fall outside the purview of this study. What is most relevant here are questions concerning ripeness and de-escalation. What were the political and military factors and conditions comprising the negotiating context? Did these change over time, and if so, with what effect? In short, why were the United States and the Soviet Union able to reach agreement on an INF Treaty in 1987 and not before?

Answering this basic question requires a capsule review of the treaty's negotiating history. That said, it is difficult and somewhat arbitrary to choose a starting date for the history of the INF accord. One could go back to the early years of the Atlantic Alliance, for in significant ways the INF experience is but the most recent chapter in a story of U.S. and West European efforts to cope with the realities of extended deterrence. In important ways the INF Treaty resulted from Western deployment of U.S. nuclear systems designed to compensate for Soviet military improvements, part of a continuing struggle involving, on the one hand, Western efforts to make credible the U.S. pledge to extend its nuclear umbrella to cover its West European allies and, on the other hand, Soviet efforts to bring this same credibility into question.

It is perhaps more useful to begin in early 1977 with the initial Soviet deployment of the SS-20 missile, a mobile ballistic missile carrying three nuclear warheads but with a range (some 5,000 kilometers) that, although holding all Europe at risk, placed it below the threshold (5,500 kilometers) covered by the strategic arms limitation negotiations. West European leaders and, in particular, the then chancellor of the Federal Republic of Germany, Helmut Schmidt, were understandably concerned, especially because the new Soviet deployments came against a backdrop of more general concern about the strength of the United States and its commitment to Europe.

What ensued were several years of intense NATO consultations culminating in the December 1979 decision that the United States would deploy in Western Europe a new generation of intermediate-range nuclear missiles unless negotiations with the Soviet Union succeeded in creating a balance at the lowest possible level. NATO thus embarked upon what became known as the Track Two policy: a deployment track that, beginning in December 1983, would introduce 464 ground-launch Cruise missiles (to be distributed among five European countries) and 108 Pershing II ballistic missiles in West Germany and a negotiating track that would seek to limit these deployments or even make them unnecessary altogether.

The Soviets sought to head off NATO deployments even before the Track Two decision was formally adopted. In October 1979, General Secretary Leonid Brezhnev proposed a freeze on Soviet SS-20 deployments (then totaling some 130 missiles with 390 warheads) if NATO foreswore its counterdeployments, on the basis that a balance already existed. This gambit failed; nearly one year later, in July 1980, the Soviets agreed in principle to participate in formal INF negotiations, but an inability to agree on the specific focus of any talks together with the delay associated with the change in U.S. administrations (see Husbands's description of "electoral rhythms") combined to prevent the start of formal talks.

The real history of the INF negotiation begins in November 1981 (Talbott 1984; Talbott 1987, 18–30; U.S. Arms Control and Disarmament Agency 1987).[1] President Ronald Reagan proposed the so-called "zero option," offering to cancel the planned U.S. INF deployments in exchange for Soviet elimination of all their SS-4, SS-5, and SS-20 INF missiles. The position was adopted only after fierce debate in Washington. Advocates viewed the zero option as the best means to capture the public relations high ground in Europe, something seen as essential if West European governments (and especially those five slated for INF deployments) were able to fend off the powerful peace movements. The zero option was also seen as a major disarmament step, thereby distinguishing the Reagan administration from its predecessors. Opponents within the executive branch argued that the proposed deal was too unequal to be credible—that few in Western Europe would take seriously the U.S. offer not to deploy missiles in exchange for Soviet destruction of missiles already deployed—and that, as a result, support for deployments would evaporate in the face of certain Soviet rejection. In addition, there was concern related to the zero option itself; namely, that if the Soviets did accept the idea, it would not be in the interests of the West because the result would weaken the nuclear link that coupled the United States to Western Europe—a connection that lies at the heart of the Atlantic Alliance.

Within weeks, formal negotiations between the United States and the Soviet Union opened in Geneva. The U.S. side tabled the zero option; the Soviets responded with a proposal for equal ceilings of three hundred "medium-range" missiles and nuclear-capable aircraft, with the additional factor that British and French nuclear forces would be included in the U.S. count (given Soviet estimates of British and French systems, this addition left no room for new U.S. deployments). Months later, the Soviets sought to increase the attractiveness of their offer by announcing a moratorium on new SS-20 deployments. This bid for support mostly failed when it became clear that a good deal of work on SS-20 sites was continuing despite the so-called moratorium.

With the two sides far apart on the formal negotiations, the principal negotiators at the Geneva talks, Paul Nitze for the United States and Yuli Kvitsinksy for the Soviet Union, produced (after a "walk in the woods") an alternative package that would establish equal levels of INF missile launchers in Europe, preclude U.S. deployment of the Pershing II, and freeze Soviet SS-20 deployments in Asia. (The package would have allowed the Soviets 225 warheads on 75 SS-20s and the United States, 300 warheads divided among 75 ground-launched cruise missiles [GLCMs].) Neither government was happy with this attempt at de-escalation within the larger context of negotiations, in themselves a formal de-escalation effort; the Soviets were unwilling to accept the legitimacy of any Western INF deployments, the U.S. side believed a cruise missile–only deployment for the West would confer advantages upon the Soviet Union in that it would still be permitted ballistic missiles.

For all intents and purposes, the formal negotiating channel remained deadlocked. The Soviets opposed any U.S. deployment of new missiles and sought inclusion of British and French systems. The Soviets were not interested in negotiations per se but rather in using them to raise public opposition in Western Europe (and especially West Germany) to the deployments. The United States, which wanted equality of rights between the two superpowers, exclusion of third parties, and global limits, also sought to use the negotiations to win the hearts and minds of European publics and governments (see Husbands's discussion of playing to a third party). Toward this end, the United States (to demonstrate that it was not inflexibly tied to a zero option only position) introduced in March 1983 a proposal for an "interim agreement," which in effect would have established equal global levels of U.S. and Soviet warheads on INF launchers at any level.

This initial interim option was rejected by the Soviets as was a further version put forward in September 1983. The negotiations came to an end in November 1983, when the Soviet delegation walked out after the first deliveries of GLCM components arrived in Europe. The Soviet strategy to prevent Western deployments had failed, with the negotiating track ending in stalemate, the United States and its allies began to implement INF deployments.

Negotiations did not resume for over one year until in early 1985 the two sides agreed to establish a new comprehensive arms control framework that would discuss not only INF but also strategic offensive

forces along with defense and space issues. The first sign of real movement came that October when the new Soviet general secretary, Mikhail
Gorbachev, dropped Soviet insistence that all Western INF deployments
be canceled. Instead, the Soviets called for a freeze in Soviet and U.S.
INF deployments—to be followed by the "deepest possible" reductions.
Gorbachev also stated that the Soviets were phasing out their older SS-
4s. Although this proposal was unacceptable to the U.S. side—a freeze
would have made Soviet superiority permanent—President Reagan did
note its positive elements and outlined a modification of the U.S. position. He suggested that the two sides might want to consider an interim
agreement with equal ceilings of 140 launchers/420 warheads, something that would allow a Western mix heavily weighted towards GLCMs,
thereby implicitly moving toward meeting the Soviet concern over the
Pershing II.

INF was a prominent topic at the November 1985 summit in
Geneva after which Gorbachev wrote Reagan suggesting that all long-
range intermediate nuclear forces (LRINF) be eliminated from Europe
within five to eight years as part of an overall process of ridding the
world of nuclear weapons over a fifteen year period. (Around this time,
the negotiations began to focus as well on short range intermediate
nuclear forces, or SRINF, systems with a range of 500–1,000 kilometers.) Less than one year later at the October 1986 Reykjavík summit,
the two leaders agreed to no LRINF in Europe and to equal global
ceilings of one hundred LRINF warheads apiece: the Soviet warheads
were to be in Asia, the U.S. warheads in the United States. As they had
done since early 1985, however, the Soviets linked progress on INF to
resolution of U.S.-Soviet differences on what sort of testing would be
allowed under the 1972 ABM treaty.

Several months later, though, after it became clear that the Reagan
administration was both willing and able to hold firm to its refusal to
tie INF to strategic defense, the Soviets dropped this linkage, thereby
clearing the way to what became the final phase of the negotiating
history. In June 1987, the United States formally proposed that all
SRINF be eliminated as part of any INF treaty. This so-called double
zero—effectively eliminating all INF missiles with ranges between 500
and 5,500 kilometers—was accepted by the Soviet Union in July 1987.

Two issues still remained, however. The first was the status of the
seventy-two U.S. Pershing 1A nuclear warheads located in the Federal
Republic of Germany. Although these weapons fell within the SRINF
range and included U.S. warheads, they were unique in that the missiles
were West German. The United States refused to compromise on its

long-held position that third-party systems fell outside the scope of the negotiations; the Soviets refused to budge on their demand that the Pershing 1A systems be included. The issue was only resolved in August 1987 after German Chancellor Helmut Kohl announced his government's decision to dismantle their Pershing 1As and not to replace them with more modern missiles.

The second outstanding issue—verification—was scarcely a new one. Although elimination of the systems (as opposed to their limitation) eased verification challenges in that it is relatively less difficult to verify the absence of a system than it is to verify a specific number of systems (especially if they are mobile), the problems were significant, coming as they did against a backdrop of past compliance disputes and the ongoing START negotiations, for which the INFT would establish important precedents. What emerged in the end was a regime calling for highly detailed data exchange and a considerable degree of on-site, or intrusive, inspection.

INF IN HISTORICAL CONTEXT

Arms control constitutes a special form of negotiating enterprise because the goal is not to resolve a dispute per se but to delimit (or de-escalate) competition and thereby reduce both the risks and uncertainties unavoidable in a world characterized by the existence of large military arsenals in the possession of rival states. A number of agreements, including the principal modern inventory pacts up to and including the INF Treaty, do these things; other agreements such as the series of U.S.-Soviet agreements on confidence-building measures, focus on the reduction of risks and uncertainty alone.

The historical record of arms control negotiations and agreements suggests the centrality of several factors to the success of any de-escalation initiative.[2] Arms control agreements are concluded only when neither side has an appreciable advantage, that is, only when rough parity exists in the relevant forces in the two sides. Neither the United States nor the Soviet Union has been willing to enter a pact in which it would suffer enduring inferiority by any meaningful measure.

It is, for example, instructive to observe that no serious negotiations on strategic nuclear forces—offensive and defensive—even began until the end of the 1960s, by which time the Soviet Union had achieved rough parity with the United States. When the 1972 ABM Treaty was concluded—the treaty all but eliminates the deployment of antiballistic missile systems—neither side had a capacity (or even a potential one) for ballistic missile defense in which it could be confident. The absence of any clear, militarily significant inequality in either actual or near-term potential capability for defense against ballistic missiles appears as much as anything to have made agreement on the ABM Treaty possible.

Essential equivalence (although not identity of arsenals either quantitatively or qualitatively) of offensive strategic forces was one factor that made possible the 1972 SALT I Interim Agreement on offensive arms. The agreement itself set ceilings on land and submarine-based missiles (or, to be precise, missile launchers) of intercontinental range. SALT II also was negotiated in an environment of asymmetric strategic parity. The SALT II treaty's limits on nuclear weapon launchers (initially 2,400 each, to go down to 2,250 per side in the lifetime of the accord) reflected existing inventories; its several sublimits on systems with multiple independently targetable reentry vehicles (MIRVs) also reflected either existing or planned capabilities. Similarly, a nuclear arms accord along the lines discussed at Reykjavík and subsequently—one that would reduce U.S. and Soviet strategic arsenals by half to 6,000 warheads apiece with complementary limits on both launchers and the distribution of warheads—would also support the contention that parity is a precondition for success at the bargaining table.

One negotiating failure is also useful to cite in this context. The failure of the antisatellite negotiations (ASAT) during the Carter administration is in large part attributable to a fundamental discrepancy: the Soviet Union possessed a demonstrable if limited capacity to intercept and destroy some low-orbit U.S. satellites whereas the United States did not possess a capacity to do the same to corresponding Soviet systems. U.S. officials were largely uninterested in an accord that would preserve the Soviet advantage; Soviet officials were uninterested in an accord that would eliminate their advantage.

At first glance, the INF accord would appear to violate the parity requirement. A narrow "bean count" would suggest that at the time of the treaty signing in December 1987 the Soviet Union enjoyed a two-to-one advantage in warheads (1,667 to 429). Yet a more sophisticated assessment of the qualitative balance and the military significance of deployed systems—in particular the Pershing II's combination of short flight time and high accuracy, qualities that placed at risk valued targets in the Soviet Union—makes a strong case that the INF accord is fully consistent with the contention that rough parity is a prerequisite for progress.

It would also seem that this is how the Soviets viewed the situation. Negotiations were unsuccessful as long as the Soviet Union maintained a monopoly in modern INF missiles; indeed, the Soviet Union through the end of 1983 (when U.S. deployment was to commence) appeared mostly interested in using the negotiations to undermine Western consensus for deployment rather than to broker any compromise. A breakthrough in the talks was only achieved after deployment of U.S. cruise and Pershing II ballistic missiles was well underway in Europe.

In addition, arms control agreements instituting militarily significant restraints are unlikely to materialize in circumstances in which either party has tested the weapon in question or invested heavily in it. This explains why SALT II could ban land mobile launchers for heavy ballistic missiles, something neither signatory was interested in. It also helps explain why the SALT I Agreement did not include a ban on multiple warheads and why the SALT II Treaty dealt with cruise missiles in the protocol (due to expire before the missiles were to have been ready to deploy) rather than in the treaty itself.

A START accord that would call for 50-percent reductions would also constitute an exception to this principle in that it would require the parties to destroy systems in which each had invested a good deal. Yet the exception is more partial than full. The contemplated reductions would still allow considerable modernization of arsenals as well as retention of substantial numbers of existing systems. Moreover, it is significant that the major stumbling block to an accord—the Soviet desire to preserve the dominance of offensive systems by limiting U.S. development of antiballistic missile defenses—can be viewed as supporting the principle that parties are loathe to negotiate away areas of major investment. The Soviets seek to continue to benefit from their offensive strategic systems whereas the United States has resisted compromising in an area—strategic defense—in which it has both invested and tested.

Here the INF Treaty obviously constitutes an important exception to historical patterns. The United States and its European allies were willing to give up a new generation of weapons despite the considerable economic expense incurred in developing and producing the systems. (To this can be added the far from insignificant economic costs of verifying the treaty and carrying out the destruction of the missiles.) NATO was also willing to give up INF despite the major political costs already incurred in gaining public support for deployments. And the West was willing to forego both the military benefit of the missiles to Western security (and alliance cohesion) and to expose itself to the uncertainty of moving toward a less-nuclear environment.

Why this was the case is not immediately obvious. It can be argued that a full zero (and especially a double zero) was not in the interests of the United States and NATO given the inevitability that it would reinforce doubts about the viability of extended deterrence. Two factors explain why the Reagan administration plunged ahead despite this concern: the political desire of the president and some of his key advisors for an arms control (or, more accurately, disarmament) agreement and the determination (even by those uncomfortable with the possible political and military impact of the double zero and other aspects of the accord) that the potential adverse impact on the alliance of going ahead was outweighed by the risk of not going ahead at this point. It was simply too late for the United States to change course.

The Soviet Union also was willing to absorb major costs. The Soviets appear to have calculated that it was worth giving up their quantitative advantage in INF missiles that could strike Western Europe in exchange for the United States eliminating a smaller number of missiles that could reach the Soviet Union with great accuracy and, in the case of the Pershing II, great speed. The fact that other Soviet missiles not affected by the INF Treaty—for example, the SS-25—could still threaten Western Europe targets diluted the military significance of the Soviet decision. The Soviets may also have reasoned that the pact served their larger interests of reducing the role of nuclear weapons in Europe, something that would place a premium on conventional forces (an area of Soviet advantage) and weaken bonds between the United States and its European allies.

Beyond this calculation, however, it is increasingly apparent with hindsight that Gorbachev had concluded that his priorities—above all perestroika and the restructuring of Soviet society—required a reduction in international tension that in turn would reduce requirements for defense expenditure (thereby freeing scarce resources) and increase access to Western technology and economic assistance (see Husbands's discussion of domestic conditions influencing defense decisions). INF, and arms control more generally, was a means to these ends. Requirements for reform at home took precedence over any short-term foreign policy considerations.

Another characteristic of ripeness affecting arms control has nothing to do with the accord per se—that is, with either its content or the negotiating approach—but with the larger relationship between the parties. Arms control tends to be vulnerable to the general temperature of the U.S.-Soviet relationship. Both the 1977–1978 Indian Ocean naval arms limitation talks and the SALT II Treaty were undermined by U.S.-

Soviet differences stemming from their competition for influence in the Horn of Africa, the "discovery" of a Soviet brigade in Cuba, and (for the final blow) the December 1979 Soviet invasion of Afghanistan. Agreement at Reykjavík on INF or anything else was made more difficult by the controversy surrounding the Soviet arrest of an American journalist on espionage charges. It is this unintended intrusion of extrinsic political developments that, when linked by powerful domestic political forces, creates circumstances in which arms control cannot survive. Indeed, the power of unintended linkage can be sufficient to disrupt negotiations even where ripeness exists in the more narrow sense.

An earlier study of the prerequisites of ripeness (or de-escalation to use the language of this study) suggested that a number of factors or components can be identified (Haass 1988). All are relevant, and the absence of any one will pose an obstacle to successful negotiations. The most important is that there be a shared perception of the desirability of an accord. Parties must conclude that, in the absence of an agreement, time does not work in their favor and that they would be worse off in absolute terms, in relative terms, or both.

Thus, in the arms control realm, what is required is that, first, both parties conclude that an agreement does not prevent them from rectifying shortcomings (hence the refusal of weaker parties to sign agreements codifying their inferiority and the resistance of stronger parties toward signing agreements that undermine their advantage) and does not prevent them from exploring possible avenues of advantage (hence the U.S. refusal at Reykjavík). Agreements are possible, though, when parity exists, when no key attractive options are foreclosed (precluding exploitation of cruise missile technology for nonnuclear INF systems, which apparently was not sufficiently significant to block agreement to an INF treaty), and when some mutual benefit is anticipated. The INF Treaty falls squarely within this tradition.

Second, political leaders must either be sufficiently strong (because of popularity or force) to permit compromise or sufficiently weak so that compromise cannot be avoided. Leaders must either be able to agree or unable not to. It makes little difference whether leaders are strong or weak, but there cannot be a principal protagonist that falls in between—insufficiently strong to compromise but strong enough not to. By 1987, Mikhail Gorbachev had arrived at a plateau of sufficient strength to enable him to overcome any opposition to the INFT that might have existed in the Soviet military or elsewhere in the Soviet Union. Ronald Reagan, despite the approaching end of his presidency, remained sufficiently strong to be certain of overwhelming political support on this issue in the United States and Western Europe.

Third, short of situations of imposed peace such as those that followed World War II, there must be a formula that involves sufficient compromise on both sides for leaders to persuade their colleagues or publics that the national interest was protected. Such formulas or agreements are not all that difficult to come by except when some contested issue is truly considered nonnegotiable by key parties. Zero/zero fulfilled this requirement.

Fourth, there must be a mutually acceptable process. Parties can settle disputes themselves through the mediating offices of some third party or by resort to arbitration. Given that most protagonists need some assistance but are unwilling to accept arbitration, mediation is often a key element of reaching accord. Geneva and the well-established history of the U.S.-Soviet negotiations more than met this requirement.

Last, negotiations prosper most when no major diversion occurs. Events in the Horn of Africa, Cuba, and ultimately Afghanistan ruled out U.S. approval of the SALT II Treaty. The Soviet arrest of an American journalist on the eve of the Reykjavík summit did little to enhance the prospects for success on arms control. More important, the path to an accord was cleared when the Soviet Union dropped its insistence in the aftermath of the Reykjavík summit that progress on INF be tied to a settling of U.S.-Soviet differences over ABM Treaty interpretation and what sort of work on strategic defense would be deemed acceptable.

Modesty of scope can be an essential component of reaching an agreement. In the SALT I Interim Agreement, perhaps just as central to the accord's realization as the existence of essential equivalence was the decision to omit from the pact a number of militarily significant areas of asymmetry. These included multiple independently targetable reentry vehicles (MIRVs), bombers, warhead numbers, forward-based systems, and throwweight. Only long-range missile launchers were subject to limitations, and these limits were intended to apply for only five years. Modesty in scope was also a key factor leading to the Limited Test Ban Treaty; indeed, it was because the pact did little to constrain development of new weapons that made it acceptable—even if the price of doing so was to denude it of most of its nonpolitical significance.

At first glance, the INF Treaty, with its application to all land-based missiles with ranges between 500 and 5,500 kilometers, might appear to be an exception to the modesty principle. And to some extent it is, in that it covers both shorter-range and long-range INF missiles and its verification provisions extend not to all potential facilities but only to designated ones. But the treaty was achievable also because of what it did not include, namely, other nuclear forces ranging from aircraft to sea-based ballistic and cruise missiles of similar range and/or target coverage as that of INF missiles. Had negotiators sought a pact that banned these systems as well, they surely would have failed given the political and military questions such an accord would have raised.

All of this explains why an accord was possible in 1987. The confluence of essential parity, strong leadership in both capitals, a mutually acceptable formula, the absence of disruptive external events or conditions—these and related factors were the key (see Hopmann's discussion of environmental factors). But questions remain: Why not sooner? Why not in 1983? Or why not in 1985?

The key obstacle to successful de-escalation of the U.S.-Soviet INF competition before 1987 was the combination of inequality in strength, the absence of a mutually acceptable formula, and weak Soviet leadership. Most important, though, was the nature of the U.S. and Soviet approaches to and objectives for the negotiations.

Both sides approached the INF negotiations not as an exercise in de-escalation but as an exercise in political management. Washington and Moscow alike sought to use the INF negotiating process to win over Western publics and through them their governments. The key difference was the objective: the United States sought to demonstrate its good faith at the bargaining table and, by inference, the lack of Soviet interest in a fair outcome; the Soviets sought to demonstrate their nonthreatening intentions, the existence of an overall balance between East and West, and the resulting absence of any need or rationale to go ahead with Western deployments. To use the language of negotiations, both sides advanced positions at the negotiating table not to reach agreement but to shape attitudes in Europe that would in turn determine whether deployments would take place.

There is an important lesson here. Negotiations can constitute a confidence-building measure in and of themselves: the 1977–78 U.S.-Soviet Indian Ocean talks come to mind to the extent that exchanges persuaded the Soviet side that they did not face a U.S. strategic submarine threat in the Indian Ocean. Negotiations can also be a formal means to de-escalate competition or conflict. But negotiations are likely to serve these desirable ends only when the essential prerequisites, that is, ripeness, exist. Otherwise, and as was the case in the INF experience in the early 1980s, negotiations will at best be futile or even fuel the competition they are designed to moderate.

NOTES

1. This discussion also draws upon my experience serving in the Department of State between 1981 and 1985.

2. This study (Carnesale and Haass 1987) reaches conclusions based upon the Limited Test Ban Treaty, the Accidents Measures Agreement, the SALT I Interim Agreement and Antiballistic Missile (ABM) Treaty, SALT II, the antisatellite (ASAT) negotiations, the Nonproliferation Treaty, and the Biological Weapons Convention.

4

DOMESTIC FACTORS AND DE-ESCALATION INITIATIVES
Boundaries, Process, and Timing

JO L. HUSBANDS

INTRODUCTION

IN HIS INTRODUCTION TO THIS VOLUME, Kriesberg discusses three sets of questions necessary for understanding the timing of de-escalation efforts: questions about conditions, about strategies, and about policy. In this chapter, the relationship of domestic factors to the first two sets of questions is addressed, that is, how domestic factors serve as conditions affecting when and whether an initiative occurs and as potential parts of a strategy for attempting de-escalation. As Kriesberg notes, depending upon the focus of the moment, a particular factor may be considered as either a condition or an element in a strategy. "Domestic factors" are broadly defined to include basic political processes and cycles as well as public opinion and elites and interest groups with foreign policy agendas. These factors and their possible effects are illustrated with examples drawn from a variety of cases, most involving U.S.-Soviet nuclear relations.

Domestic factors commonly rank high in assessments of what affects the timing of efforts to de-escalate conflicts. Twenty-five years ago, in one of the first attempts to create a general framework for analyzing negotiations, Ikle (1964, 35–42) argued that, at least for negotiations for *innovation* (to create new relationships or arrangements), the mobilization of domestic political support provided one of

The views presented in this paper are those of the author and do not necessarily represent the views of the National Research Council or any of its constituent parts.

the most effective means for interested parties to induce reluctant actors to become involved in the negotiations. Kriesberg (1987, 8) lists domestic pressures as one of three fundamental conditions that can lead to conflict resolution. In his analysis of four postwar conflicts—Zimbabwe, Cyprus, the Panama Canal, and the Falklands—Zartman (1986) describes how conflicts may reach the stage at which settlement is possible. With his emphasis on process, Zartman does not rank particular causal factors. In each of the conflicts he describes, however, domestic politics play a significant positive or negative role. Accounts of particular initiatives, especially those involving the United States, usually consider the domestic context essential to understanding how options are defined, positions developed, and choices made (e.g., Quandt [1986]).

If the case materials are rich with examples of the impact of domestic factors on opportunities for de-escalation, the theoretical literature on international negotiation pays much less attention to such effects. De-escalation initiatives generally occur as part of the prenegotiation phase, a by and large underdeveloped area (Saunders 1984; Husbands 1979). More broadly, domestic factors receive only passing attention in most attempts to develop empirical theories of negotiation (see Druckman and Hopmann [1989] for a recent review of this literature). To be fair, this is part of a general neglect, until recently, of the context in which negotiations take place. This underdevelopment and neglect reflect both the way in which negotiation theory has developed within the social sciences and, I would argue, a fundamental ambivalence about the legitimacy of domestic factors' role in conflict resolution and international politics. This ambivalence, in turn, appears to be reflected in the bulk of attempts to analyze the role of domestic factors in international conflict. Taken together, the neglect and ambivalence present serious barriers to gaining a balanced view of how domestic factors may affect de-escalation initiatives.

BARRIERS TO UNDERSTANDING THE
IMPACT OF DOMESTIC FACTORS

The Role of Domestic Factors

There is a long and distinguished tradition of skepticism in the United States, from the founding fathers through Walter Lippman to the present, about whether domestic politics can have any positive impact on foreign and defense policy (Russett 1989; Nathan and Oliver 1983). When the question turns to public participation or the effects of public opinion on decision making, skepticism frequently becomes outright hostility. In the realm of foreign affairs, the American public is regarded as "uninformed, uninterested, unstable, acquiescent, and manipulable" (Kegley and Wittkopf 1987, 305). When the public's interest finally becomes aroused, reactions are expected to veer toward extremes. George Kennan, for example, wondered sadly whether "a democracy is . . . similar to one of those prehistoric monsters with a body as long as this room and the brain the size of the pin: he lies there in his comfortable primeval mud and pays little attention to his environment: he is slow to wrath—in fact you practically have to whack his tail off to make him aware that his interests are being disturbed; but, once he grasps this, he lays about him with such blind determination that he not only destroys his adversary but largely wrecks his native habitat" (Kennan 1950, 59). Issues of peace and war, especially those involving nuclear weapons policy, naturally reflect the greatest concern for the public's role. As Bruce Russett (1989, 175) neatly frames the issue, "Can something as vital to the life and independence of the nation safely be left to popular decision—and if something so central to individuals' lives cannot be subject to popular control, does 'democracy' any longer have much meaning?"

Specific concerns help differentiate the outlook from different parts of the political spectrum. Interestingly, there is a common perception that domestic factors have a significant impact; moreover, the effect is often considered undesirable. Conservatives are haunted by dark visions of democracy's inevitable unwillingness to face up to the challenge of totalitarianism with sufficient military preparedness and by its citizens' susceptibility to Communist propaganda and manipulation. "This [Communist support for 'peace'] is a particularly sound program because only democratic governments are easily influenced; they are the only ones exposed to whipsawing by their media and public opinion and responsible to their citizenry. In this area as in so many others, the congenital inequality of opportunity between democracy and totalitarianism shines forth" (Revel 1983, 147). This view could be called the "*Commentary* syndrome."

Frustrated progressives, on the other hand, point to the American public's deeply rooted anticommunism as the chief impediment to achieving their agenda. "The root of our problem in negotiating disarmament agreements is not the particular international framework or approach. . . . It is, in particular, the extraordinary strength and resiliency of anti-Soviet sentiment in this country. It's perfectly clear that this sentiment hampers the freedom of action of any administration . . . in getting the arms race under control" (James Leonard, quoted in Neidle 1982, 105). In spite of this mindset, progressives tend to be less antagonistic toward public participation than conservatives, perhaps because mass movements and popular mobilization play a greater role in their overall political strategies.

In between these positions are those who lament the shattering of the elite consensus, which until the Vietnam War provided a centrist ballast that avoided the worst fears of the left and the right (Holsti and Rosenau [1984] describe the phenomenon; Destler, Gelb, and Lake [1984] decry its impact). Realistically, whatever progress one makes in assessing the role of domestic factors, there is little likelihood of resolving the fundamental philosophical dispute about the proper role of the public in foreign and defense policy making that lies beneath.

Bargaining Models and the Real World

As already noted, although accounts of real international negotiations spend considerable time on the genesis of bargaining (Newhouse 1973; Sheehan 1976; Szulc 1974), and often find it as intriguing as the negotiations themselves, students of the bargaining process have generally ignored the prebargaining phase. One practical and one, more serious, theoretical problem may explain this neglect.

The practical explanation first: scholars choose the cases they analyze and may tend to select, post hoc, only genuine negotiating situations (although this may include cases that did not result in agreement). One must still identify "genuine" negotiations, but in spite of occasional charges of bad faith by one or more parties, consensus about which cases met the basic criteria usually exists after the fact. The process by which such negotiations become possible is of less interest. A researcher can also treat the entire development of a negotiation from the first appearance of a potential problem to its resolution as "bargaining" (Saunders 1984). This frequently occurs in analyses of continuing international conferences that, over time, may deal with many different issues (for example, Jensen [1968] and Husbands [1977] on the Geneva arms control talks). This approach may be appropriate for many research problems, but it does not help address the question of how issues become ripe for resolution in the first place.

A more fundamental problem is that the major empirical models of negotiation, whether game theoretic, economic, or sociopsychological, invariably begin with the assumption that a bargaining situation already exists (see Young 1975). From a theory-building perspective, assumptions of an existing bargaining situation may be a necessary sacrifice in the construction of manageable models. Without some basic limiting assumptions, which may be relaxed or stretched in practice, the hope for precisely specified relationships evaporates in the face of reality's massive uncertainties. Some parameters must be imposed to limit the real world to its salient features, but unfortunately, the standard parameters ignore important problems in actual negotiations. "It is largely for this reason that there has been a definite trend in the study of international negotiations away from formal models of bargaining, except as heuristic devices which may be useful in clarifying certain parameters and conditions of the negotiation problem. While most contemporary analysts acknowledge that bargaining is part of international negotiations, most would also insist on embedding their analysis within a broader framework that encompasses a variety of process, activities, and influences" (Druckman and Hopmann 1989, 92–93). Druckman and Hopmann acknowledge that in spite of this hopeful trend, considerations of the prenegotiation phase and of external influences, such as domestic factors, remain relatively neglected areas within negotiation analysis.

Relative neglect does not mean that researchers have completely ignored the problems of prenegotiation processes, particularly in social psychology. Reviews of the voluminous literature (Druckman 1973; Rubin and Brown 1975; Pruitt 1981; Druckman and Hopmann 1989) suggest that the emphasis has been on the effects of prenegotiation phases on subsequent bargaining rather than on the factors that determine whether or not a situation will be *negotiable.*

The two primary prenegotiation processes of interest to researchers have been (1) agenda formation, to ensure the existence of a basis for bargaining, and (2) caucusing within and between parties to formulate positions and to exchange information about them (Druckman 1973). Experiments with agenda formation have concentrated on the likelihood that negotiators will undertake "protective contracts" to ensure that each party bargains "in good faith." Studies of prenegotiation position formation have focused on the impact of communication on subsequent negotiations, including whether to focus on issues or underlying values (e.g., Druckman, Broome, and Korper [1988]). Former negotiators, perhaps not surprisingly, stress that those who will have to do the subsequent bargaining should be involved in these initial phases (Dean 1983; Leonard, in Neidle 1982). From this perspective, domestic factors are relevant to the extent that they impact on the basic prenegotiation processes.

For the purposes of this chapter, however, such a perspective is too narrow, although protective contracts could be part of a de-escalation strategy, and the forms and contents of communication in the process are certainly relevant. This chapter simply casts a wider net.

Domestic Factors and the Limits of Available Evidence

Anyone attempting to understand the impact of domestic factors on intrastate conflict quickly discovers that much of the literature emphasizes their negative effects. This is partially true for case studies and particularly true for quantitative analyses. The most comprehensive survey of attempts at U.S.-Soviet security cooperation, which assesses both successes and failures, includes domestic factors only as obstacles (George, Farley, and Dallin 1988). One explanation may be the ambivalence toward domestic politics already discussed, so that analysts may expect to find—and hence emphasize—negative consequences in their analyses. Another is that the sources of conflict, which in many cases do include domestic factors, may seem a more urgent subject of study than the conditions and strategies for conflict resolution. Whatever the reason, the result is an imbalance in the evidence available with considerably more information about the ways in which domestic factors may cause or exacerbate conflict, especially if one wants evidence that meets the criteria of good social science. Much of "peace science," for example, concentrates on the causes of war rather than the conditions for peace. In this chapter an attempt is made to strike more of a balance, although this sometimes entails only providing counterexamples or suggesting alternative explanations.

As discussed earlier, aspects of domestic politics may be treated as either more or less fixed conditions or as more or less manipulable elements in a strategy to bring about de-escalation, depending on the context and the focus of analysis. The lines are often blurred, and it is sometimes useful to move back and forth to compare how one perspective or the other affects one's analysis. Given this, the three broad sets of general domestic factors examined in this chapter—basic processes and cycles, public opinion, and elites and interest groups—are discussed in turn, with summary comments about domestic factors as conditions and as parts of a strategy left to the concluding section. Basic processes and cycles are discussed as fundamental conditions affecting de-escalation initiatives, whereas public opinion and elites and interest groups are evaluated as both conditions and strategic elements.

DOMESTIC POLITICAL PROCESSES AND CYCLES

"To busy giddy minds . . . ": The Scapegoat Hypothesis

One of the oldest propositions about the impact of domestic politics[1] is that political leaders will create or exacerbate conflicts abroad to rally support at home or to divert their publics from domestic problems (Levy 1989, 271–74). There is even a literary legacy: on his deathbed, Shakespeare's King Henry IV advises his son to undertake a crusade to the Holy Land to "busy giddy minds with thoughts of foreign quarrels" (Shakespeare 1901, 114).

This "scapegoat hypothesis" is central to much modern writing on the causes of international conflict.[2] If correct, it suggests that leaders may view moves to de-escalate conflict as less valuable politically, or even harmful, and that overall they will be more prone to heat up or prolong conflicts than to seek means to resolve them. The temptation is obviously not confined to democratic societies. An alternative hypothesis, that leaders with urgent domestic problems might seek to reduce or resolve foreign conflicts in order to concentrate on those priorities should be considered as well, however. Gorbachev's initiatives in arms control and his decision to withdraw Soviet troops from Afghanistan, for example, are frequently attributed to a desire to free resources for the pursuit of perestroika and other domestic economic reforms. Some of his acquiescence in the transformation of Eastern Europe can be seen as turning inward as well.

The actual evidence available about the links between domestic politics and international conflict is mixed. Scholars in quantitative international relations generally test the relationship between levels of internal and external conflict. By and large, these studies have found at best weak positive relationships (Stohl [1980] and Zinnes [1980] review this literature in considerable detail). Russett (1989) argues, however, that if the presumed relationships are carefully defined and specified, evidence emerges more clearly, although still not decisively. He cites two recent studies suggesting that states suffering domestic turmoil do appear more likely to engage in conflict (not necessarily war, however) and to escalate military disputes (Hagan 1986; James 1987).

Historical analyses and studies of particular wars frequently make a stronger case for the negative effects of domestic politics. Lebow (1981) and Stein (1989) find domestic factors a crucial element in understanding why deterrence failed or crises escalated in a series of historical cases. Lebow and Stein set out to study deterrence failures, however, so they did not examine cases in which conflicts did not occur or were resolved.[3]

Such broad generalizations are not especially helpful for predicting what may happen in particular cases. The scapegoat hypothesis nonetheless suggests that internal political conditions may tempt political leaders to escalate disputes. On the other hand, for states involved in an ongoing conflict, domestic conditions could help create the "mutually hurting stalemate" that Zartman (1986) argues is part of making a conflict ripe for resolution. Of the two cases of successful resolution he cites, domestic conditions seem to have been important in Zimbabwe but not in Panama. One can argue that domestic unrest was a prime force in bringing the United States to seek a negotiated settlement to the Indochina War in the 1970s. Domestic forces were not sufficient conditions to foster resolution in any of these cases, however.

Timing and the Democratic Process

Beyond the question of a fundamental relationship between domestic politics and international conflict, it is important to consider the degree to which the basic process of democratic societies—the electoral cycle—affects issues of timing. Are there points in the cycle at which it is easier or more difficult to initiate de-escalation moves? Is conciliatory or "tough" behavior more likely to be rewarded at the polls? Conventional wisdom, whether John F. Kennedy's famous remark that he could not withdraw from Vietnam until after the 1964 election (Gelb and Betts 1979, 195) or commentators' suggestions that Ronald Reagan's willingness to make arms control agreements with the Soviets stemmed from his desire to secure the legacy of his presidency in its waning days, suggests that the rhythm of democratic politics has a profound impact. Quandt (1986) begins his account of the Camp David process with a discussion of how the electoral cycle and natural course of presidential terms affect U.S. Middle East policy. As I will argue later in this chapter, conventional wisdom may itself have a significant effect on what political leaders believe is possible. The first step, however, is to examine the available evidence about the direct impact of electoral politics.

As with the "scapegoat hypothesis," the evidence about electoral cycles and timing is mixed. On a general level, Philip Tetlock's research on the rhetoric of U.S. presidents has found a significant decline in cognitive complexity in statements about the Soviet Union in election years and that such a decline is associated both with an increased likelihood of undertaking military interventions and a decreased likelihood of reaching international agreements (Suedfield and Tetlock 1977; Tetlock and McGuire 1985). Russett (1989) cites several studies that are essentially more focused analyses of the scapegoat hypothesis in which it is presumed that leaders who face potential punishment at the polls for domestic economic woes may try to divert attention and rally support through seeking quarrels abroad (e.g., Ostrom and Job [1986], and Stoll [1984]). Most of the empirical relationships are fairly weak, no doubt reflecting the immense complexity of the problem and the difficulty of isolating the effects in question.

There is considerable evidence that bellicose behavior or quick military actions may enhance the fortunes of political leaders. This is the well-known "rally 'round the flag" phenomenon in which presidential popularity ratings increase following a dramatic crisis or military action, regardless of whether the initiative was successful (Mueller 1973). The initial burst of support is short-lived, however (Kernell 1978), although presumably even a limited boost might be attractive in a close electoral contest. In 1980, for example, the Reagan campaign apparently feared an "October surprise" release of the American hostages in Iran, which would have aided Jimmy Carter's reelection campaign.

The rally 'round phenomenon is more complex than conventional wisdom suggests. Mueller's "rally points" include summit meetings between U.S. and Soviet leaders on the grounds that these engender a popular willingness to support the president, but these should not automatically be classed as confrontations. Kriesberg and his colleagues undertook a reanalysis of the rally phenomenon, extending the period covered and adding events that would clearly count as conciliation rather than confrontation—Nixon's diplomatic opening toward China and the Partial Test Ban Treaty, for example. They found that in general, "the American public tends to support U.S. involvement in conciliation events more than involvement in military confrontation" (Borker, Kriesberg, and Abdul-Quader 1985, 38). Other studies have also supported the argument that conciliatory initiatives may gain a quick reward in the polls (Ostrom and Simon 1985; Nincic 1988).

Finally, actually entering prolonged conflict can seriously hurt a political leader. One study of the electoral fate of American congressional and presidential candidates since the late 1800s, for example, found that "war has had a significant, detrimental, and independent effect on elected leaders of the 'war party' " (Cotton 1986, 632).

Electoral rhythms may also affect the behavior of one's adversary. If an election is approaching, leaders of an opposing nation naturally would be expected to calculate Ikle's classic threefold choice—accept the outcome currently available, break off negotiations, or keep bargaining in hopes of a better outcome—for both the administration in power and the one they may face after the election (Ikle 1964). Leaders may even be tempted to help or hinder the chances of a particular administration or political candidate by being more or less forthcoming. Behavior toward essential third parties may be affected as well. Both the United States and the Soviet Union played to Western European politics and elections throughout the attempts to resolve their conflict over deployments of intermediate-range nuclear missiles (Talbott 1984). Such attempts presumably require a certain subtlety, however, to avoid provoking a negative, nationalistic reaction from the public in the country one is trying to manipulate.

In summary, fundamental processes and rhythms of domestic politics serve as conditions affecting the opportunities for initiatives to de-escalate conflict. The results of many studies are not conclusive, which may reflect the limits of quantitative analysis when applied to complex issues. Much of the available evidence points toward these factors pressuring leaders to initiate or increase conflicts, provided they can keep them limited. Again, because many of these studies sought to test the scapegoat hypothesis, the lack of evidence about conciliatory behavior or initiatives toward conflict resolution may simply reflect a lack of attention to those phenomena. Several studies cited suggest that electoral rewards also await leaders who bring peace.[4] If current evidence suggests that domestic politics and electoral cycles may work to hinder attempts at de-escalation—although also the temptation to go to war—it also suggests that any attempt to identify timely moments for initiatives should be thoroughly grounded in the internal political dynamics of the parties in conflict.

PUBLIC OPINION

For all the masses of data on public knowledge and attitudes, how attitudes are formed and expressed beyond voting—where foreign and defense policy are generally considered less salient than domestic issues anyway—and how public opinion once formed affects actual policy decisions are not well understood (Cohen 1973; Page and Shapiro 1983). William Schneider argues that, "public opinion is reactive, not prescriptive; the operative relationship is one of support, not constraint. Policymakers do not look to the public for specific policy direction. But they must mobilize public support for the policies they want to pursue or at least preempt opposition to them. . . . The reason is that a policy without political support can be frustrated so easily in our system" (Schneider 1985, 31). Schneider's distinction between affecting particular policy choices and giving broad support suggests that it seems reasonable to expect that public opinion sets broad boundaries within which policy choices are made. As long as policy makers steer within these general limits, this "permissive consensus" (Key 1961) allows considerable day-to-day latitude. On the other hand, those boundaries can change either as the result of outside factors or, in some cases, through leaders' own efforts. When this happens, one would expect policy eventually to change as well.

Page and Shapiro (1984) found that popular presidents had some capacity to affect opinion, but "opinion leadership is not quick or easy; the public is not very malleable. . . . Intensive efforts over several months by highly popular presidents appear to bring about changes in opinion poll results of only some 5 or 10 percentage points, hardly a tidal wave. On few issues can presidents afford to invest even that much effort" (p. 639). Overall, in a study of the relationship in foreign and domestic policy over the period 1935–79, they found that policy outcomes generally followed public opinion in both areas (Page and Shapiro 1983).

This view that public opinion primarily sets boundaries within which political leaders operate raises two major issues for opportunities for de-escalation initiatives. One is how much the range of potential initiatives may be shaped by what is acceptable to public opinion. The other is how much and how readily boundaries can be changed by leaders' actions and external events or by domestic pressure groups and at what political cost.

Public Opinion as Boundaries

Until very recently, the boundaries set by public opinion in U.S.-Soviet relations were clear. On one side lay the strong anti-Communist sentiment lamented by James Leonard (quoted in Neidle 1982, 105). By and large the American public viewed the Soviets as dangerous adversaries who represented a system fundamentally opposed to American ideals and values (Public Agenda Foundation 1984, 22–23; WAND 1987). U.S. leaders could ill afford to appear "soft" on Communism, or they risked severe punishment at the polls. "Given the centrality of the Soviet Union to American security, mishandling of that relationship is a handy stick for an outsider to seize and try to beat the incumbent with, particularly if the latter appears not to hold a strong enough position against the Soviet Union. The years 1952, 1960, 1976, and 1980 followed that pattern" (Nye 1984, 7). To the extent that this was both valid and part of the conventional wisdom that guided American politicians, this basic anti-Communism would be expected to set limits on the kinds of initiatives leaders could undertake and certainly to condition the manner in which they were presented.

The other major and equally strong boundary was the American public's abiding fear of nuclear war. Americans believe that nuclear war would be suicidal, at least for the superpowers and probably for the planet (Public Agenda Foundation 1984, 21–22). They also believe that the superpowers' current nuclear arsenals represent massive and unnecessary "overkill" capabilities. Americans consistently support negotiations to reduce nuclear weapons, even though they may dislike specific arms control agreements and believe that both sides will cheat (WAND 1987). Policies that aroused the public's fear of nuclear war thus could also provoke a sharp political reaction. For example, "The Reagan Administration's nuclear weapons policies during its first fifteen months in office . . . reminded Americans that they lived in the shadow of the bomb and made the nuclear peace seem precarious. The Reagan policies suggested, if not a taste for war, at least a certain carelessness about the dangers of the nuclear age" (Mandelbaum 1983, 107). The nuclear freeze movement, a genuine grassroots movement, came in direct response to the fears these policies aroused.

These two fundamental aspects of American public opinion suggest that U.S. policymakers have probably tried to steer a course between appearing either too soft or too harsh in relations with the Soviet Union. Some level of communication was necessary to reassure Americans that the risk of nuclear war was being kept within bounds, but U.S. leaders also had to convince the public that they could keep America strong and protect its basic interests. A leader or a policy that appeared too accommodating toward the Soviets could expect a substantial negative response from the public.

The superpowers' arms control negotiations thus came to play a special role as a barometer of the overall state of their relationship. As long as the United States and the Soviets were talking, the American public was apparently reassured that relations could not be too bad or the risk of nuclear war unacceptably high. This reassurance was no guarantee that the public would support any particular agreement or initiative to reach one, but policy makers at least had to go through the motions of negotiation.

Public Opinion in De-escalation Strategies

Exploration for possible significant initiatives in U.S.-Soviet relations offers considerable evidence that public opinion—and, hence, the fundamental boundaries around U.S. policy—is changing. Over time, the American public has ceased to fear that the Soviet Union will undermine the United States through internal subversion (Smith 1983). The Reagan-Gorbachev summit in Reykjavík provided a similar breakthrough, although it has yet to yield concrete accomplishments. The discussions of deep reductions and even elimination of nuclear weapons opened new vistas for the public debate in the United States and made possible consideration of options that would have been deemed utopian before the two leaders met (National Academy of Sciences 1988).

The most profound effect on the traditional boundaries resulted from Mikhail Gorbachev's rise to power and the dramatic events in Eastern Europe. Americans' approval ratings for Gorbachev are astoundingly high for the leader of the primary U.S. adversary, reaching levels that many U.S. politicians would be delighted to enjoy. Changes in basic attitudes toward the Soviet Union are developing more slowly, but it is clear that most Americans now do not regard either the Soviet Union or nuclear war as a significant threat. "Only 18 months ago, most Americans responded with a military or foreign policy issue when they were asked to name the greatest threat to U.S. national security. Today a solid majority volunteer a non-military threat" (Americans Talk Security 1990, 5 [hereafter cited as ATS]). Of fourteen possible military and nonmilitary threats proposed in a survey in early 1990, Soviet nuclear weapons and Soviet aggression around the world ranked thirteenth and fourteenth (ATS 1990, 6). The fundamental fears may not yet have changed, but U.S. policy makers presumably have more latitude to offer initiatives in U.S.-Soviet relations than at any time in recent memory.

Exhortations to bold leadership have never held much appeal as policy prescriptions without at least some specification of the conditions under which such initiatives stand a chance of success. One piece of conventional wisdom holds that conservative U.S. presidents are better able to take such initiatives toward the Soviet Union because their anti-Communist credentials are presumably less open to question. Probably the most frequently cited example is Richard Nixon's dramatic diplomatic opening toward the People's Republic of China in 1972, which transformed that nation from a pariah to a strategic ally. Ronald Reagan was thus better situated than any president in recent memory to accomplish significant changes in U.S.-Soviet relations, and in Mikhail Gorbachev he found a Soviet leader interested in and capable of responding. When suggesting future policy choices, one should differentiate the objective reality of the fate of leaders from different parts of the political spectrum, who undertook tension reduction initiatives, from the subjective perception of political leaders that such a fate awaits them.

Adversaries may also seek to take advantage of public opinion as part of their de-escalation strategies. The importance of domestic support in persuading reluctant nations to take part in negotiations for innovation has already been mentioned (Ikle 1964, 35–42). As an example of a successful initiative, Stein (1989, 50) cites Anwar Sadat's offer to visit Jerusalem in 1977. "President Sadat spoke over the heads of Israel's leadership directly to Israel's public. With his flair for the dramatic, he created the psychological and political symbols which would mobilize public opinion to press their more cautious and restrained leaders. In so doing, he removed a constraint on Israel's leaders and created a political inducement to action." One famous failure to reach over leaders' heads was Woodrow Wilson's attempt to influence Italian opinion during the Versailles conference (Isaak 1975, 128). Such appeals require careful planning and an awareness of the domestic political realities for one's adversary and always carry the risk of sparking an adverse reaction. The existence of public opinion favoring de-escalation, even if one makes no direct appeals, may nonetheless help convince a leader to create an initiative.

PRESSURE GROUPS, ELITES, AND DOMESTIC POLITICS
Setting the Terms of Policy

As a condition affecting the timing of de-escalation initiatives, pressure groups and elites function much like more general public opinion; that is, they operate to define and, in some cases, limit the range of policy options that can be considered. For example, Middle East policy in the United States is always created with an awareness of the interests of Israel's American supporters (Quandt 1986, 12–13). American policy toward Cyprus, Greece, and Turkey has likewise felt the effects of well-organized Greek-American groups (Deering 1980). Supporters of Taiwan were able to block any attempts to normalize relations between the United States and the People's Republic for over twenty years. With the advent of major grain sales to the Soviet Union, American farmers could be counted on to oppose attempts to use economic leverage in U.S.-Soviet relations, just as business groups have generally supported increased trade (Goldman and Vernon 1984; Morgan 1979).

Over time, the relative power and influence of such organizations may change, but they still should be considered part of the fundamental political landscape. Any leader contemplating an initiative must take into account the likelihood of support or opposition from key groups within society. Such groups may provide vital sources of support to mobilize the broader public in support of an initiative or to mount a concerted opposition that can doom de-escalation attempts from the beginning. The groups and coalitions will vary with the issues, and few generalizations can be made beyond specific cases except to note the importance of this defining function. An understanding of the relative power of various groups in a society would provide a useful measure of the likelihood and prospects for any de-escalation initiative.

Elites and the "attentive public" also help to set the terms of the policy debate, sometimes in opposition to the basic tendencies of the general public.

> During the immediate postwar years, leaders were more hawkish in private than in public, being fearful that the public was not yet prepared for a major new internationalist commitment. In the 1950s and early 1960s, this relationship reversed, as officials whose private views were moderate and flexible found it necessary to over simplify the antagonism with the Soviet Union and to exaggerate the nature and immediacy of the peril it entailed. The point was to keep the public, and therefore Congress, from questioning or challenging the internationalist thrust of cold war policy. . . . Support for such policies is not natural; it must be mobilized and maintained against the constant threat of unraveling (Schneider 1984, 31).

A major topic in discussions about the role of American elites is the impact of the Vietnam War in shattering the bipartisan consensus that supposedly governed foreign policy in the postwar period (Holsti and Rosenau 1984). It is worth noting that, at least for some on the left, the elite consensus was not a welcome stabilizer but a stultifying force that prevented the initiatives necessary to achieve genuine progress in reducing the U.S.-Soviet conflict (Barnett 1972). (Staunch conservatives would probably agree about the perils of moderation, although obviously not about the goals to be sought.) As one might expect for any highly political issue, one's view of the role of elites or organizations is likely to be significantly colored by the impact those groups have on one's own political agenda.

Groups, Movements, Elites, and the Effort to De-escalate Conflicts

The sheer variety of domestic pressure groups that could affect the content and timing of de-escalation initiatives confronts researchers with a daunting task of classification. No comprehensive, centralized list of organizations that focuses on peace or U.S.-Soviet relations exists, although there are a number of guides and handbooks. The Washington-based Forum Institute's 1983 list of "arms control and peace organizations," for example, included more than 130 national groups. A second handbook by the Institute for Soviet-American Relations (1986) of organizations concerned with U.S.-Soviet relations listed 194 groups, although there was considerable overlap with that of the Forum Institute. Databases that attempt to include affiliates of national organizations as well as independent local groups invariably run into thousands of entries. As a first step to assessing the impact of these organizations, some basic classification scheme seems necessary.

The simplest distinction is probably between organizations that exist to promote a general cause, such as peace, and those that are formed to promote focused, particular interests. Jeff Berry defines the former as "public interest group[s]," which "seek[s] a collective good, the achievement of which will not selectively and materially benefit the membership or activists of the organization" (Berry 1977). Ground Zero, Physicians for Social Responsibility, and the Committee on the Present Danger would probably all qualify as public interest groups. Other organizations are classic pressure groups that seek to promote particular economic, ethnic, or policy interests. One interesting phenomenon in the 1980s within the peace and arms control community was the development of "guild groups," organizations that sought to promote a broad public interest goal but whose membership was based on the type of common ties and interests that underlie traditional pressure groups. Scientists have been organized in this way for decades—the

Federation of American Scientists, for example, was founded in 1946—but in the last decade, the approach has been copied by physicians, performing artists, computer experts, and teachers.

The boundaries between the public interests and pressure groups are obviously porous and shifting, but the two basic types nevertheless provide a useful starting point. The interactions between the two types, some argue, have affected the basic political landscape. "Interest groups must also operate in a more ideological context. Ethnic constituencies, business interests, and farmers used to participate in foreign-policymaking as nonideological 'interests' pressuring for their private advantage or special concern. All now find themselves embroiled in politics of values and ideologies. Business groups and farmers are challenged by conservatives, who argue that they are enriching themselves and selling out America's larger interests by supporting detente and pressuring for increased foreign trade. . . . In the new style of pressure-group politics, values are more at stake than interests" (Schneider 1984, 33).

Targets and tactics are not especially helpful to distinguish among interest groups. Over the years, public interest groups have adopted most of the tactics associated with classic lobbying groups—direct mail campaigns, political action committees (PACs), coordinated lobbying strategies—while still retaining the demonstrations and marches traditionally associated with social movements. Public interest groups also maintain Washington offices and organize sophisticated, coordinated lobbying efforts. Their activities are generally directed toward Congress rather than the executive branch, and this may be a difference from traditional interest groups, which usually target both. This may simply be an effect of the administration in office at any given time; the Reagan administration, for example, was generally considered beyond the reach of peace and arms control groups. Organizations with focused, often economic goals may also find it easier to make and use contacts within the functionally organized departments of the executive branch.

Groups are frequently given credit or blame for their impact on de-escalation initiatives. In at least two cases, peace movements had a substantial role in bringing about efforts to de-escalate U.S.-Soviet conflict. The first was the popular movement against nuclear testing in the 1950s led by groups such as the National Committee for a Sane Nuclear Policy (SANE). The test ban movement is widely credited as a key factor in the U.S. decision to pursue test ban negotiations, although credit for the Limited Test Ban Treaty is usually shared with the shock effect of the Cuban Missile Crisis (Divine 1978). The second was the nuclear freeze movement of the early 1980s, which helped push the

Reagan administration back to the negotiating table with the Soviets, even if the freeze movement could not effectively translate general sentiments into a concrete legislative agenda (Talbott 1984).[5] The peace movements in Western Europe also clearly had a role in bringing the Reagan administration into talks with the Soviets, although they could not prevent their own governments from accepting deployments of U.S. Pershing II and ground-launched cruise missiles (GLCMs), and the achievement of an agreement on intermediate-range missiles in the end depended on the emergence of Mikhail Gorbachev as the new Soviet leader.

In fairness, it should be noted that interest groups are sometimes credited with blocking opportunities for de-escalation. Groups may act to block or thwart initiatives, either through specific legislative action, such as the Jackson-Vanik Amendment, or more general activities, such as the Committee on the Present Danger's campaign to alert the American people to an urgent Soviet threat. The committee, a conservative "public interest group," is often cited as an important factor in the defeat of the SALT II treaty and the general decline in U.S.-Soviet relations in the late 1970s (Talbott 1979). Such organizations helped create a political climate in which initiatives to maintain or improve U.S.-Soviet relations became extraordinarily difficult (Sanders 1983). These groups then enjoyed special access in the Reagan administration as many of their members became high-level officials (Gordon 1981).

To assess interest groups, one has to ask, How much do organizations such as the Freeze Campaign or the Committee on the Present Danger actually mobilize public opinion as opposed to capitalizing on existing or emerging opinion to advance particular goals? Kincade (1987), for example, offers a skeptical analysis of the committee's impact on the American public's support for increased military expenditures. A group's timing is obviously an important factor in shaping its effectiveness and impact. Overall, groups may introduce and promote de-escalation initiatives that were not part of the policy-making agenda—the test ban and the nuclear freeze are obvious examples. Groups may help to make initiatives more acceptable by helping to shape and galvanize public support. They may also act to frame issues and hence set the terms of the policy debate. The activities of groups and movements are not sufficient to bring about de-escalation, and de-escalation may well occur without such activity, but they have on important occasions formed necessary parts of a broader strategy.

Political elites may function in a variety of ways to affect opportunities for de-escalation initiatives. In some cases, elite groups, of which the Committee on the Present Danger is a prime example, function in the political process like any other interest groups. To the extent that political elites serve as opinion leaders, they may also be able to shape general opinion to accept or reject given initiatives. A discussion of elites leads to a consideration of the politics of the policy-making process. "Bureaucratic politics" is now enshrined in foreign policy analysis, and has important implications for understanding the effect of domestic factors (Allison 1971). The American political process is remarkably open to outside effects from a wide variety of sources. Numerous institutions vie for a central role in making all aspects of foreign policy, including that toward the Soviet Union (Nye 1984).

The impact on de-escalation may be severe. In any negotiation, as Druckman has pointed out, negotiators must balance their role as bargainers relating to the other side and as representatives of the coalition of interests that make up a national position (Druckman 1977). Druckman views this as a continuing struggle, in which the effort of keeping the various intranational interests involved in a negotiation together may consume far more time than that spent in bargaining with the other side. For *negotiator* one can substitute *policy maker*. Moreover, in the U.S. security policy process, the advantage rests with those who seek to stifle initiatives (Krepon 1984). Strobe Talbott's *Deadly Gambits* (1984), an account of arms control policy making in the early Reagan years, is a classic study of the power of skilled bureaucrats to block policies they oppose. A thorough understanding of the impact of domestic factors must take account of the policy-making process, particularly the points of access for outside influences.

CONCLUSION

This chapter is primarily an attempt at classification, an effort to specify the ways in which domestic factors may affect the timing and opportunities for initiatives to reduce U.S.-Soviet conflict. I examined three broad classes of domestic variables: the political system and its processes; public opinion; and the activities of elites and interest groups. None of the three provides a sufficient condition to explain the timing of de-escalation initiatives, although in several cases initiatives appear to have been necessary for success. A more fundamental problem has been determining when and whether domestic factors play a positive or negative role. As discussed earlier, there are substantial barriers to gaining a balanced understanding of their effects by trying to extract evidence from studies that sought to test different relationships. Most of the studies cited focused on the causes of war, not the conditions of peace, and their results suggest that domestic factors generally impede de-escalation. Evidence from case studies points toward a positive role, although there are cases of negative impact as well. New data sets, such as the one cited by Roger Hurwitz in his chapter for this volume, may enable researchers to test the competing hypotheses about domestic factors' role in international conflict and efforts at conflict resolution. Systematic, comparative case studies that include examples of both de-escalation successes and failures would also help to specify the variables better and to assess their impact. In the meantime, the best and fairest conclusion appears to be the Scottish verdict, "Not proven."

NOTES

1. This section draws heavily on Levy (1989) and Russett (1989).

2. Much of this research derives from a continuing debate about whether or not "the people" are more or less prone to conflict than their leaders. One article of liberal theory about the causes of war has been that citizens are generally peaceful and are led or aroused to war by their leaders. For a discussion of the evidence, see Levy (1989); for a review of the debate see Howard (1978).

3. It should be noted that even when Stein (1991) proposes "reassurance" as an alternative for deterrence, her analysis of domestic influences still includes considerable negative effects.

4. An ability to "keep the country out of war" has proven to be a valuable electoral asset for both leaders and political parties over the years (Galston and Makins 1988).

5. Ironically, SANE and the Freeze Campaign merged in 1987 to form SANE/Freeze.

PART TWO

STRATEGIES FOR DE-ESCALATION

STRATEGIES FOR DE-ESCALATION

SUSAN FRENCH AND LOUIS KRIESBERG

IN THE GENERAL INTRODUCTION TO THIS BOOK, the components and possible combinations of components for de-escalating strategies were discussed. Particular attention was given to choices about parties, issues, and inducements. These may be combined to bring about a reframing of the conflict so that effective de-escalation occurs. Effective strategies vary with the conflict and its stage of development and with the possible implementor of the strategy.

Roger Hurwitz stresses that the adversaries' definition of their relationship with one another is a key element in assessing the potential for and the process of de-escalation. While taking into account Zartman and Aurik's conditions for ripeness and the construct of the international context outlined by Hopmann, Hurwitz offers an interpretation of de-escalation that posits a new path away from conflict, rather than movement "down the up staircase." Hurwitz presents three relational stages that he believes occur between warring nations as they move from armed conflict to a cold peace. These stages are: adversarial, interdependent, and partnership. Understanding the need for or presence of a change in the conception of the relationship or acting with such a transformation in mind is an important strategy for pursuing de-escalation.

In conjunction with such implications, Hurwitz offers new understandings of the process of de-escalation in terms of mutually defined relationships and game theory. His treatment of game theory offers a refreshing view that encompasses a critique of its limited development for the purpose of understanding de-escalation, results of research carried out at the Artificial Intelligence Laboratory at MIT, and application of these results to real world situations. In the final section of the

119

chapter, he assesses changes in the U.S.-Soviet relationship since the Cuban Missile Crisis in an analysis by using the Sherfacs database.

I. William Zartman and Johannes Aurik add to strategies for understanding de-escalation through their presentation of conceptual models, important variables, and case study analyses. They begin by assessing three different ways of viewing the limits of escalation: through power, patterns of behavior and expectation, and each party's decision-making process. They then consider each of these within the traditional analytical perspectives of system, interaction, and purposive actor.

Zartman and Aurik explore the various types of actions in a decision process through a matrix that divides acts into volitional/nonvolitional and gratification/deprivation. Zartman and Aurik view the conflict process as a three-phase entity and place the "decision to come to the table" as the crucial and underrated element in the process of de-escalation. This assertion is then tested through the examination of nine examples of successful and unsuccessful de-escalations.

In the three remaining chapters, various aspects of third party intervention are discussed. Juergen Dedring presents a view of the United Nations that complements that outlined by Rikhye in the previous section. Whereas Rikhye focuses on some of the ways in which the role of the U.N. secretary general allows for a special approach to de-escalation, Dedring explores factors that may inhibit the effective functioning of the U.N. Security Council as a peacemaking factor in international conflicts.

Dedring focuses upon the impact of U.S. and Soviet vetoes of the Security Council peacekeeping proposal during the invasion of Southern Lebanon and subsequent occupation by Israeli troops between 1982 and 1984. Dedring's examination of the relational dynamics existing between the superpowers and between their clients over a two-year period illustrates how conditions changed and thereby called forth a Soviet veto in 1984 to a peacekeeping proposal that had been vetoed by the United States two years earlier. In addition to adding depth to the notion of timing and insight into the malleability of conflict variables, Dedring sheds light on the impact of Cold War politics on the United Nations' attempts to act as an effective intermediary in de-escalation.

A more informal type of third party intervention has come to be known as Track Two diplomacy. Chapters by two former U.S. ambassadors expand upon this concept through both analysis and personal experience.

John McDonald frames his exploration of Track Two diplomacy by noting that, of the thirty-six wars in 1987 with greater than one thousand casualties, only four were cross-border wars. Civil wars tend to destabilize the international system through their potential for escalating or becoming cross-border wars. Given the constraints that national governments, and even international governmental organizations, have in intervening in the internal affairs of countries, McDonald suggests Track Two diplomacy as an effective channel in a strategy to deescalate these and other conflicts. McDonald contrasts Track Two diplomacy with traditional government negotiations, noting the different benefits of each and their inherent complementarity.

One of the problems with the concept of Track Two diplomacy, according to McDonald, is that it is simply too general. At present, Track Two diplomacy can refer to the efforts of a former head of state or a prominent religious figure, or those of an enthusiastic tourist group. McDonald suggests that a more detailed understanding is needed, and elaborates upon a typology of *multitrack* diplomacy. He distinguishes among different types of citizen diplomacy in both their positional influence in the international context and their relationship to official governmental negotiation. This typology is accompanied by a description of each track and the presentation of examples or current efforts occurring at each level.

McDonald ends his contribution with a list of qualifications and considerations useful to any potential citizen diplomat, noting that nonofficial diplomacy, if undertaken, must be conducted in a cautious and thoughtful manner.

This note of caution is expanded upon in Ralph Earle's discussion of Track Two diplomacy. He begins his paper by outlining the history of Track Two diplomacy dating back to the Logan Act of 1798. Earle, who has been involved in both formal and informal international negotiations, offers his view of some of the risks and benefits of these two strategies.

From personal experience, Earle moves to more general and recent examples of Track Two efforts. In reviewing several cases dating from 1968, Earle points out that although some of the efforts at Track Two diplomacy were in the interest of the U.S. government and its people, others clearly were not. These were most often unofficial attempts to influence events on an international level for an individual's personal gain or political agenda.

The chapter ends with the suggestion that three different categories of unofficial negotiators exist. Earle goes on to outline what is, in his opinion, the appropriate realm of each. Earle concludes that Track Two efforts can indeed be an effective strategy for de-escalation of international conflicts. However, it should not be thought of as a standard operating procedure. When it is attempted, it is essential that the State Department be kept informed of such efforts and that unofficial diplomats know when to step back and allow the efforts of formal negotiators to take over. Earle includes a brief list of negotiation "don'ts" at the end of his chapter.

Traditional approaches to de-escalation strategies in international conflicts have often concentrated upon various types of negotiation tactics, policy conjecture, or win/lose game theory. In these chapters, the authors attempt to move beyond established frameworks into new areas of understanding and endeavor. The conceptual frameworks presented in each of the papers provide rich material for the scholar whose objective is to more fully understand the dynamics and prerequisites of de-escalation. Practitioners, regardless of their roles in the international system, are offered further insights from the authors' personal experience in the field.

5

UP THE DOWN STAIRCASE?
A Practical Theory of De-escalation

ROGER HURWITZ

W HAT CONSTITUTES COMMONSENSE BEHAVIOR FOR STATES is relative to how they construct their relationships with one another.
This is a useful point to recall when trying to identify the conditions
and logic for de-escalation or voluntary reduction of conflictual behavior by states. In a world that agrees with Von Clausewitz's commonsense
idea that conflicts and war escalate until victory and defeat, such a
move is an anomaly unless treated as a momentary relaxation, a loss of
will, or panic. De-escalation may, however, comprise efforts by states to
abandon the common sense of adversaries and to redefine their relationships according to different principles. Full de-escalation from hot or
cold war to peaceful cooperation involves several successive redefinitions. Moreover, the structuring or defining principles can by typified;
their appearance in de-escalation follows a particular order; and their
appropriateness is often a matter of public reflection and debate (see
Kriesberg's discussion of "sequence" in the introduction).

De-escalation then is not a retreat down an up-staircase of hostilities but a climb up a war-to-peace staircase with turnings where the
character of the relationship between the parties in conflict changes.
The histories of American-Soviet and Egyptian-Israeli relations support
this claim, as do laboratory gaming experiments that simulate conflict

Research for this chapter was partly supported by the John D. and Catherine T. MacArthur
Foundation. Research was partly conducted at the Artificial Intelligence Laboratory of the
Massachusetts Institute of Technology. Support for the laboratory's artificial intelligence
research was provided in part by the Advanced Research Projects Agency of the Department
of Defense under the Office of Naval Research contract number N00014-85-K-0124.

and cooperation between two players over repeated interactions. This evidence also indicates that dramatic events, including sharp, sudden increases in tensions and unilateral bids for peace, often motivate the turning points of mutual de-escalation. Events like the Cuban Missile Crisis and Sadat's visit to Jerusalem make it difficult for decision makers on both sides to maintain their established assumptions about the relationship and may force them to recognize the extent of their interdependence.

SOME CONDITIONS

De-escalations are easily attributed to the exercise of common sense as formulated in strategic or behavioral logics. De-escalations often occur after sudden rises in either diplomatic tensions or military hostilities, and this suggests such moves are pragmatic responses by one or both sides to the fear of "things getting out-of-hand." For example, during the Cuban Missile Crisis, most U.S. decision makers agreed on the need for a strong, escalatory response to the Soviet placement of missiles in Cuba. However, whereas the hawks proposed an air strike on the missile sites or even an invasion of Cuba, the doves feared that a more general conflict and perhaps even nuclear war could result from inadvertence (Blight and Welch 1989).[1] Once the quarantine on Cuba was implemented, they sought its relaxation as soon as the Soviets indicated a willingness to negotiate the removal of the missiles. In a famous incident, dovish Defense Secretary McNamara warned the admiral overseeing the blockade not to let it lead to a violent naval engagement with Soviet ships. President Kennedy favored the quarantine because it sent a strong signal of U.S. determination to have the missiles removed, but in itself it was an action that could be selectively implemented and quickly rescinded. Kennedy reportedly worried that misperceptions and unreflective displays of force could lead to rapid, irreversible escalation (Abel 1966, 93–94; Kennedy 1969, 127–28).[2] Even in a realist view of international relations, which emphasizes the need for states and leaders to act forcefully, such pragmatism is quite common and appropriate. Hobbes observed in his "state of nature," a commonly invoked realist image, that the fear of death has remarkable powers to curb human passions and instill prudence.

De-escalation seems especially sensible (and perhaps more likely for that reason) if the decision makers believe their antagonist would reciprocate a unilateral de-escalation. Such a belief could be warranted, if the other side communicates that intention or is known to have planned the preceding escalation. In that case, the escalation and de-escalation can be interpreted as moves in strategic bargaining, a combination of threats and offers (or "sticks" and "carrots"), which Schelling (1960) and Shubik (1970) modeled in game theoretic terms and Bennett (1986) reconstructed as speech acts. A's escalation would signal both a threat of more costly conflict and an offer to de-escalate, if B started doing so. This commonsense construction of de-escalation as accepting an inferred offer contradicts the expectation of tit-for-tat reciprocity that Axelrod claims is the basic pattern of human behavior. Strict tit-for-tat reciprocity, however, cannot explain escalation or de-escalation (Axelrod 1984; Goldstein and Freeman 1988).[3]

In contrast to this idea of a well-calculated de-escalation, common sense of a more visceral variety appears behind reductions in conflict that follow sudden, intensely hostile, ostensibly unintended incidents. In these cases, the de-escalation responds to accumulated pain, disgust, or despair. Many commentators thus characterized Iran's acceptance of a cease-fire with Iraq, in July 1988, several days after U.S. missiles had mistakenly shot down an Iranian airbus, killing several hundred people. Despite having demonized the United States, the Iranians probably did not believe the United States was threatening to continue to attack civilian aircraft until Iran accepted the cease-fire. More likely, the shootdown epitomized the enormous losses Iranians had already suffered in their war with Iraq and reduced their tolerance for more losses. To summarize the cases, de-escalation appears as a form of flight from conflict, which is motivated by the experience or anticipation of considerable pain. This motive can be restrained or supported by calculations of the costs for continuing or trying to quite the conflict (Singer and Small 1972).[4]

Unfortunately, for several reasons this insight provides little operational basis for predicting or stimulating de-escalation. First, a belligerent's threshold of pain is indeterminable beforehand. Protracted, bloody conflicts like the Lebanese civil war show the threshold may be surprisingly high. Second, an antagonist's escalations can cause a party to increase its tolerance for pain and its willingness to pay the costs of conflict. That is, the accumulated costs and pain often become reasons for pursuing the conflict as expressed in clichés like "Don't betray our boys" or "We owe our martyrs a victory" (Brockner and Rubin 1985).[5] Third, as the level of conflict increases so does the stress on leaders. This pressure contracts their planning horizons and may keep them from foreseeing the higher costs of continuing the fight that the escalations are intended to demonstrate (see Hopmann's chap.). Fourth, leaders may also have problems deciding what an opponent's motive may be in escalating. Is the enemy seeking to destroy one's will to resist or paradoxically attempting to signal an offer to de-escalate?[6] The decision makers can easily believe the worse and justify an escalation of their own on the grounds of "no choice." Finally, the decision makers may choose to de-escalate for purely tactical reasons, that is, to stabilize temporarily the conflict at a lower, manageable level of pain without seeking more peaceful relations.

A more adequate approach to de-escalation should, therefore, acknowledge that decision makers interpret and evaluate interactions with other states within the context of the relationships that they believe were created in previous interactions with those states. Relativism of meaning abounds in international affairs, for example, in the difference between the Reagan administration's response to Iraq's attack on the *U.S.S. Stark* and its reaction to the Soviet shootdown of KAL 007. So, the meaning of an escalation or a peace feeler will vary for initiator and target according to their respective definitions of their relationship and the anomalies that these actions create for that definition. One side is unlikely to see the other's escalation (or de-escalation) as a bargaining move, if it believes that the other has been committed to its utter destruction.

Belligerents in the heat of battle usually define themselves as enemies or adversaries whose respective overriding goal is to dominate the other or to thwart the other's attempts at domination. This relationship can be modeled as a zero-sum game in which the defeat of the enemy is the end in itself and not just a means to an end, and the players' rankings of preferences over outcomes are necessarily and not just contingently opposed.[7] Within the context of this relationship, escalation must be read as a bid for local advantage or a demand for the opponent's surrender, whereas de-escalation symptomizes exhaustion or a ploy to lull the unwary. Thus whether its opponent escalates or de-escalates, a party should itself escalate, always seeking advantage. A second order effect helps assure compliance with this action rule. Even if a party foresees that continued escalation will generate only higher costs and no advantage, it should not de-escalate to signal a willingness for a lower level of conflict. Instead it must anticipate that the enemy would take this move as a sign of weakness or a ploy and try to exploit it.

In the first redefinition of the relationship that supports de-escalation, each belligerent realizes that it can make the other pay a terrible price for trying to dominate it and that the other knows this. Such knowledge gives the belligerent reason to assume the opponent will set some limits on its aims and, in view of the other's capabilities, reason to set limits on its own aims. To be sure, each side continues to believe that its welfare and security would be enhanced if only it could defeat the other side without gravely weakening itself. So although the basic situation can be modeled as a nonzero-sum game, the agents remain antagonistically disposed as in a zero-sum game. The principles of mutual deterrence and reciprocal self-restraint define the relationship, which means they are forced to "let live in order to live." To stabilize this relationship, each side must be quick to match any escalation by the other side. In this context, an escalation must be read as either a probe of defenses or an effort to gain a local advantage, whereas de-escalation signals a readiness to return the conflict to a less intense, more sustainable level.

A second redefinition occurs when antagonists find that each can benefit by offering some sort of self-restraint in exchange for the other's similar behavior. Such discoveries form the basis of strategic bargaining like arms control talks. They are facilitated by the agents' recognition of involvement in a conflict of interests rather than a competition in the sense that each does not need to dominate the other if it can otherwise satisfactorily realize its security interests. The basic situation can be described as a nonzero-sum game, particularly the Prisoner's Dilemma, where agents have reasons to cooperate but might be restrained by fears of their cooperation being exploited. The exchange relationship that arises in this situation is consequently stabilized by mutual trust or, failing that, by credible retaliation policies. Agents will, therefore, follow tit-for-tat reciprocity and occasionally try to initiate additional de-escalation. In this context, de-escalation signals a willingness to practice self-restraint, whereas escalation ordinarily indicates a lack of trustworthiness and an intention to exploit the opponent.

In the next possible redefinition of their relationship, the former antagonists begin to see themselves as partners in producing a commonly desired state of affairs and even as concerned for one another's welfare. Recent Soviet-U.S. relations display some hints of this, for example, in a general agreement on the need for environmental protection and U.S. hopes for the success of peristroika. Each agent recognizes that its own and the other's actions are limited by agreements, which usually distribute rights and obligations according to some recognized social standard. The agents thus form a normative order, and their actions can consequently be evaluated for compliance with or violation of this order. Because the agents are expected to comply unconditionally with the agreement, any escalation or other attempt to seek unilateral advantage will be seen as a violation and require an explanation. Violations with acceptable explanations, however, have the effect of respecifying rather than destroying the normative order.

The sequence of these relationships that can transform international relations from belligerency to alliance is highly constrained. The rise of a partnership or alliance presupposes that its members have already practiced self-restraint toward one another and acknowledged their interdependence. Thus one rarely finds nations going from hot wars to warm friendships without first having states of nonbelligerency and cold peace. A similar constraint is found in Turner's empirically induced grammar for "social drama" (also known as "constitutive conflict"), a disintegrative/reintegrative social process, in which a crisis is precipitated by a breach of normative order. That order can be restored only after a phase of redress in which the origins of the conflict are reviewed and animosity is channeled into rituals (Turner 1974). In both de-escalation and social drama, the procession through the phases to a final resolution is neither inevitable nor irreversible. Hostilities can recommence or the parties can remain in a cold truce enforced by mutual threats of retaliation. In Turner's grammar a crisis phase can follow redress, and the resolution of the drama can involve the belligerents' acknowledgment of each other's autonomy and separateness rather than the achievement of social reintegration.

The hypothesis of a constrained order or grammar of de-escalation is also supported by analyses of phase sequences in experimental Sequential Prisoner's Dilemma (SPD) games and in post–World War II international disputes (Sherman 1987, 1985).[8] The dyadic SPD games, each about fifty rounds, were played by undergraduate and graduate students at the Massachusetts Institute of Technology in the early 1980s. Games that began in mutual competition, with both players choosing their noncooperative options, frequently ended in mutual cooperation but only after intervening phases in which one player chose cooperation and the other did not. Changes in the players' perceptions of themselves and the other player, as revealed in their explanations and expectations for moves, accompanied this evolution of cooperation. During the intervening phases, the players came to see noncooperation as reflecting a more defensive, less aggressive orientation.

Of the nearly 700 international disputes coded by Sherman, 107 disputes had a phase of either unilateral or bilateral armed violence and a later settlement. But in only three cases did the settlement phase follow directly after the most violent phase. In contrast, in nearly half these cases, the de-escalation from the most violent phase involved at least one relapse from a less violent to a more violent phase. The pattern of U.S.-Soviet bilateral relations since World War II demonstrates similar constraints. The Cold War, a phase of fierce, warlike competition that lasted through the 1950s was followed by rapprochement in the 1960s and détente in the 1970s. This last phase, however, was interrupted by the reassertion of animosity in the late 1970s and early 1980s.

HOW IS DE-ESCALATION POSSIBLE?

Parties to a conflict will often have difficulties in redefining their relationship and the accompanying postures toward one another. If each views the other side as an enemy, each is likely to deny the possibility of common interests and reject any step that could benefit the other, no matter how much each would benefit.[9] But for several reasons, that view can be firmly entrenched. First, it is a cognitively useful means to assess the meanings of events and so reduce ambiguity. As Larson notes, no international event speaks for itself. "Whether an act is even *described* as cooperation or defection is heavily influenced by the goals perceived to underlie it. Was Gorbachev's offer at the Reykjavík summit to eliminate nuclear weapons in ten years a cooperative move or a defection? It depends on whether one believes that the Soviet leader was carried away by the exhilaration of the moment, or was trying to trap an aged, ill-informed President and divide NATO" (Larson 1987).

Here the image of the Soviet leader as an enemy would constitute the offer according to the latter meaning. Second, memories of earlier conflicts with the same country will tend to contextualize the present dispute as part of a historical competition rather than an isolated conflict of interests. For example, U.S. decision makers explained Soviet actions in Eastern Europe in terms of the scary image of world Bolshevik revolution popularized during the Red Scare and the U.S. intervention in the Russian Civil War (1919–1921). Third, cooperative initiatives that could challenge the view of the other as the enemy are discouraged by warnings that the opponent would exploit such initiatives (Goldstein and Freedman 1987).[10] Finally, politicians and organizations will labor to keep the view dominant if their careers and budgets, respectively, depend on it.

Fortunately, ideological hegemony is repeatedly upset by human imagination. For example, during the Cold War and its reprise in the early 1980s, the official U.S. demonic image of the Soviet Union was eroded in two principal ways, despite the U.S. government's efforts to enforce it. First, there was a small-scale exchange of information, ideas, and products between U.S. and Soviet peace activists, scientists, and business people. Within the context of such exchanges, the Soviets were necessarily constituted as human beings with whom one could talk and seek mutual benefit (see the Husbands and MacDonald chaps.).[11] Second, peace researchers and even some defense intellectuals argued that the U.S.-Soviet conflict should not be constituted in win-loss or zero-sum terms because it could terminate in a major loss for both sides (Kull 1988).[12] Frequent threats of massive retaliation, civil defense charades, and escalation to the apparent brink of nuclear war over the Cuban missiles spurred acceptance of this point by Americans. This position implied that the Soviet should not be cast as an enemy which would seek to defeat one's own side at all costs and whose defeat would automatically constitute a victory.

Hegemony is further eroded by the appearance of new leaders whose careers are less dependent upon seeing the other as an enemy to defeat and who are, therefore, less inhibited about seeking arrangements that could benefit both sides.[13] To the extent that such new leaders also interpret the rival state's hostility as a response to their own state's hostility, they can imagine that the rival might reciprocate rather than exploit a cooperative initiative. In the SPD simulations, players who thought in this way, that is, who had more differentiated, context-sensitive understandings of their opponents' motives were more likely to move toward cooperative relations (Hurwitz and Mallery 1989). In international disputes and these games, such thoughts and imagination can inspire bold, persistent signals intended to encourage the other side to participate in moving toward a less adversarial relationship. Egyptian president Sadat, for example, had more space to disengage Egypt from its conflict with Israel than could his predecessor, Nasser, because Sadat did not have a public career investment in vanquishing Israel. He was also able to acknowledge Israel's concern for security as the principal motivation of its conflict with Egypt rather than interpreting the expressions of this concern as masks for an Israeli expansionism. Nevertheless, his 1977 flight to Jerusalem, Gorbachev's *glastnost* policy and similar dramatic moves enable change but do not make it inevitable. Sadat's case shows that a unilateral bid for cooperation risks indifference or rebuff from the other side and consequent criticism at home. The Israeli government was at first cool to Sadat's initiative and only began to negotiate earnestly in 1978 after pressure from both the United States and a large, indigenous peace movement.

These dramatic moves, in which leaders stake reputations and/or domestic support, help ripen the definition of their states' interdependence by unexpectedly highlighting previously inappropriate questions of trust. Can the other be trusted to respond favorably to a peace feeler? Is the sender acting sincerely? These questions do not fit the adversarial definition, according to which the other always acts hostilely and practices deceit. Such questions are also strange in certain interdependent relationships, like mutual deterrence, which use threats of retaliation to minimize the need for trust. Yet, the intrusion of the trust theme opens up an imaginative space in which decision makers can see themselves making and keeping agreements. This imagined future can appeal on pragmatic grounds because a relationship that included trust could reduce a state's expenditures on its defense or retaliatory force. Thus de-escalation can be sustained by the introduction of a mutual confidence-building program following a dramatic event, crisis, or initiative that highlights the two sides' interdependence. President Kennedy initiated one such program, which reciprocated reductions in force structures and included the withdrawal of U.S. missiles from Turkey, in spring 1963 after the Cuban Missile Crisis. The program proved successful and produced the Test Ban Treaty before being cut off by the assassination of Kennedy (Etzioni in White 1986, 204–7; Osgood in White 1986, 194–203).

The de-escalation process can ripen further if decision makers use the dramatic event or crisis as a precedent for solving their subsequent or outstanding dyadic conflicts of interest. Following the Cuban Missile Crisis, relations between the United States and the Soviet Union began to improve and reached an officially declared détente in the early 1970s. The post–World War II international dispute data show that after the missile crisis the superpowers no longer disputed the global military balance as they had earlier, for example, in the various Berlin crises. This change was not for lack of opportunity. The Soviet Union, for example, could have become more directly involved in Vietnam, and both superpowers could have tried to intervene directly in the Yom Kippur/October War (1973). They instead confined their competition to struggles through proxies for influence over nonaligned states. This new pattern suggests that Soviet and U.S. decision makers were repeating and refining the self-restraint and disengagement with which they resolved the missile crisis. As Lévi-Strauss explained in a justly famous passage, the repetition of a preferred instance of a game or interaction is not the coincidental result of a decision or plan freshly made for the occasion. It is the performance of a ritual, and ritual itself implies the development of a normative order. "All games are defined by a set of rules which in practice allow the playing of any number of matches. Ritual, which is also 'played,' is, on the other hand, like a favored instance of a game, remembered from among the possible ones because it is the only one which results in a particular type of equilibrium between the two sides (1962, 30).

THEORY CONSTRAINTS

U.S. international relations theorists and practitioners have seldom seen changes in parties' mentalities and social relations as necessary conditions for long-term de-escalation. One reason for this oversight may be the influence of theories of international relations that assume that states have fixed or transcendent motives and only contingent bonds with one another. Worse yet, the theories cannot acknowledge that their own production is embedded within historical processes and may reflect socially created, temporally bounded practices rather than "natural acts." The various flavors of political *realism* are especially ahistorical in this respect. They depict decision makers as constantly seeking to increase their states' power in an essentially anarchic system. Conflicts and cooperation arise because the decision makers meet the constraints, challenges, and opportunities that states create for one another in pursuing their interests. This view reduces international relations to series of isolated strategic interactions, gutted of pasts, memories, passions, ideals, normative constraints, and learning (Elster 1979, 123).[14]

The lack of reflection on change is unfortunate because international relations theories guide and justify practices, contributing to the common sense of foreign policy elites. Different theories may propose default practices and approaches that are specific and appropriate to only one phase in the movement from conflict to cooperation. Inappropriate input can in turn block the progress of this movement. As implied, a liberal flavor of political realism can support the phase of de-escalation in which strategic calculation and bargaining are the main logic and mode, respectively, of interaction. Such realism assumes that decision makers are rational agents who can cooperate when such action benefits both sides (Macpherson 1964).[15] Political realists can thus advocate practices of tit-for-tat reciprocity with other countries, graded retaliations when these countries blatantly violated such reciprocity, and occasional cooperative initiatives that others might reciprocate. In U.S.-Soviet relations, such advocacy became conventional following the Cuban Missile Crisis in which the Soviet Union demonstrated its capacity for rational and reciprocal conduct to the satisfaction of even the most hawkish in the Kennedy administration.

In contrast, World War II vintage attrition theories support practices in the escalatory phase of disputes. These theories attribute conflict to innate human aggressiveness or to the enemy's culture or ideology, factors that exclude the possibility of conflict resolution through negotiations or bargaining. Peace can be achieved only through pacification of the enemy. Because any cooperation by the enemy must, therefore, be a ploy, tit-for-tat policies and the idea of cooperative initiatives are rejected. Behavior toward the enemy should instead be energetic and aggressive with a readiness to exploit any concessions. Formulated during World War II, initially toward Germany and Japan, these views constituted much of the U.S. conventional wisdom toward relations with the Soviet Union during the onset of the Cold War, the Berlin Crisis, and the Korean War. Their influence, although challenged by containment and deterrence theories, continued through the 1950s with Secretary of State John Foster Dulles a leading exponent. "There was nothing the Soviets could do to change Dulles's mind about the dangers of negotiating with communists." Dulles explained the unilateral, cooperative initiatives by the Soviet leadership following Stalin's death in 1953 as efforts "to relieve the ever-increasing pressure upon their regime." He told the U.S. cabinet that "the big thing is to exploit Soviet weakness . . . to crowd the enemy and maybe finish him once and for all" (Larson 1986, 11).

Containment and deterrence theories that became prominent in the United States during the 1950s can support a phase of limited de-escalation effected through the replacement of military maneuvers by verbal threats and the practice of limited reciprocity. To be sure, the enemy continues to be seen as aggressive and power-seeking but also sufficiently responsive to contain its aggressiveness in the face of force and massive threats. As put by a Truman aide in 1946 and echoed by Reagan and his handlers more than thirty-five years later in regard to the Soviet Union, the target of containment; "The language of military power is the only language which disciples of power politics understand. The United States must use that language in order that Soviet leaders will realize that our government is determined to uphold the interests of its citizens and the rights of small countries. Compromise and concessions are considered, by the Soviets, to be evidences of weakness and they are encouraged by our 'retreats' to make new and greater demands (Clifford, quoted in Freedman 1981, 38). Although this assessment rejects cooperative initiatives, it does not exclude positive responses to the other side's cooperative initiatives.

Containment and deterrence theorists were also more sanguine than attrition theorists regarding the Soviet Union's use of nuclear weapons. The latter believed the Soviets would pursue an aggressive nuclear strategy because nuclear weapons appeared particularly suitable for aggressors who were unconstrained by world opinion and insensitive to the damage caused to their own or other people. In the mid-1950s, some considered the large number of Soviet World War II casualties to be evidence that the Soviet Union would tolerate the losses caused by a nuclear war (Freedman 1981, 56). The deterrence theorists, instead, argued that the Soviet Union or any generic enemy would draw back when it knew the costs for its expansionist efforts would exceed some price it did not want to pay. One only needed to communicate a resolute and credible intention to inflict such a punishment in case of attack. By the Cuban Missile Crisis, this thinking had supplanted attrition theories among U.S. political elite members, and in keeping with it, none of the key decision makers in the Kennedy administration believed either side would deliberately risk a nuclear war.

Although reliance on nuclear deterrence supported restraint in conventional military expenditures and less military violence, it did not provide very much of a social relationship between two superpowers. In effect, the anticipated consequences of using their nuclear options put the superpowers in the nonzero-sum game of chicken, in which both players lose by engaging one another and each wins by not challenging the other. Thus players in the chicken game can produce a mutually tolerable outcome through mutual avoidance without any need for extensive negotiations or acknowledgment of a positive common interest (Brams 1985).[16] Another limit to this de-escalation was that nuclear retaliation policies generated a nuclear arms race as each side strived to guarantee that enough of its weapons for effective retaliation would survive a first strike by the other side. The motives for continuing weapons escalation can be represented by the well-known nonzero sum game of Prisoner's Dilemma, in which players have cooperative and noncooperative options. Although in this game, both players would do better to cooperate than not to cooperate, neither player wants to choose cooperation unilaterally in the absence of an enforceable agreement because one risks large loss if the other player does not cooperate. Similarly, the Soviet Union and the United States may have had a common interest in building fewer bombs but neither trusted the other to do so.

Actually, until the Cuban Missile Crisis, superpower decision makers had little appreciation of the idea that nuclear deterrence policies should be accompanied by arms control talks and agreements. "[Deterrence theory] was propounded at a time when the super-power relations did not seem at all stable in either political or military terms. The Cold War was at its height and America was storming ahead in the quality and quantity of its nuclear arms. The new doctrines could not but be understood in the context of a buildup of military strength that spoke of a drive for superiority . . . which meant inevitably that they were misunderstood" (Freedman 1981, 228).

But following the missile crisis, as part of the trend toward détente, a more appropriate reading of deterrence theory developed and assimilated the theory with political realism. The Soviet Union was increasingly accepted by the U.S. leaders as a great power with its own particular, not absolutely competitive, concerns. The staggering number of Soviet World War II casualties was now considered a reason for the Soviet leaders to want to avoid a nuclear war. At the beginning of the 1970s, it was accepted in the United States that nuclear weapons had become more of a problem than the Soviet Union and that the superpowers should work together to solve the problem of the potential use of such weapons. At the same time, arms races and other security dilemmas were recognized as stemming as much from bureaucratic interests and inertia as from drives for domination or perceptions of threats.

Deterrence theory and political realism can highlight the need for a further phase of de-escalation that involves the development of trust and consensus building, but they do not provide much insight to practices that could support such a phase. Nearly thirty years ago Rapoport recognized this limitation in game theory, which models interactions according to the precepts of political realism. He proposed instead to model the process of coming to agreement as a debate in which speakers start by summarizing their opponents' as well as their own positions—the so-called "double focus" method (Rapoport 1960). Rapoport seemed to be searching for some means to formalize and stimulate empathic understanding, but it is not clear that his notion of a debate, where speakers still compete, serves this purpose.[17] Nevertheless, debates have several basic features not found in experimental gaming, which suggest practices that could contribute to an agreement-seeking phase of de-escalation. These practices include the use of language, a set of procedural rules, and a commitment to changing positions and behavior rather than eliminating participants. Language and speaking implicate principles of (1) reciprocity, evident in the turn taking of conversations and (2) charity toward the other, evident in the recursive clarifications of meaning. The rules of debate, including limits on time and rights to rebut, enforce principles of self-limitation and equity. Finally, the debate presupposes that disputants are members of some political community.

DEFINITIONS AND DE-ESCALATION IN LABORATORY GAMES

Sequential Prisoner's Dilemma (SPD) is a laboratory game whose play simulates patterns of cooperative and competitive interactions in nonregulated environments (Alker and Hurwitz 1980).[18] Players are isolated from each other and choose on successive rounds between a *cooperation* and a noncooperation, or *defection*, option for the same Prisoner's Dilemma game, represented in a payoff matrix, which the players can see. Players are told that their scores for the game are the respective cumulative scores over all the rounds, and they are also told the outcome for each round after it is played. In almost all SPD games, the players vary their choices among the options. Attempts to explain these changes have been based, respectively, on behavior-learning models and the assumption that players follow fixed strategies or policies that specify choice according to the other players' previous or expected choice(s) (Axelrod 1984; Emshoff and Ackoff 1970, 77–89; Rapoport and Chammah 1965). These models do not explain certain interesting patterns, such as a sudden, sustained change in a player's choice after both players have chosen the same option for many trials.

These anomalies argue that players do not have fixed behavioral propensities or permanent motives and strategies when playing the game, and other experiments have found a variability among players' choices according to the verbal instructions they receive regarding goals. Regardless of the other players' choices, players who were instructed to work for mutual benefits cooperated more frequently than players told to maximize individual payoffs, and the latter cooperated more frequently than players who were told to maximize relative advantage (Deutsch 1973). These results suggest that players took these instructions to assign themselves roles in the game, and these roles are acted out by applying rules that specify the choices an agent makes in the game or in specific contexts in the game. In the absence of an experimenter's instructions, players probably assign their own goals or conceptions of the game to themselves with past experience of such games, psychological experiments, or the situations they think the game might represent. But positing the dependency of choices on such instructions does not explain why and how some players change their choices and apparently their conceptions of the game during its course.

Experiments at the Massachusetts Institute of Technology in the early 1980s focused on these puzzles by asking players to report their beliefs about the game and its moves as they played.[19] To analyze the resulting protocols, the records of the game outcomes were divided into phases or regions of moves in which at least 80 percent of any series of trials had the same outcome type, that is, mutual cooperation, mutual defection, first player's unilateral defection, and first player's unilateral cooperation. A player's belief statements in each of the phases were retrieved and compared across phases for the same player and with belief statements of other players in the same phase. The belief statements included rationales for their own and the other player's moves, conceptions of the game, statements of intentions, and expectations of the other player. The semantic content analysis tasks were formalized and executed in a computer environment, the Relatus Natural Language Processing System, which has the capability of parsing, building textual models, and retrieving textual material according to specified thematic content and function, for example, expectations, rationales, statements of intention, and causal statements.[20]

The analysis found that players' beliefs about the game, its possible development, and the meanings of choices varied over the phases. These changes resulted from situations arising in the game, and they affected subsequent choices. If one assumes that mutual noncooperation in the game simulates real world conflict and mutual cooperation simulates de-escalation, the findings of the experiments provide some insight on cognitive aspects of de-escalation.

> 1. Most players had a general idea or concept of the game conveyed through beliefs about their purposes in the game, expectations of realizing these purposes, and expectations of the other player. With many players, the contents of these beliefs changed as the game unfolded. Players used metaphors, like *game* and *partnership* to understand their interactions and their relationships with the other players. These terms helped constrain the players' choices because they assigned roles like *competitor, helper,* and so forth, which were realized through a particular, sometimes context-

sensitive choice. One-third of the players reported they chose the noncooperative strategy because they thought of the SPD as a game to be won or lost, and the noncooperative strategy was the only possible means to gain more points than the other players.

2. Players tended to attribute their conceptions of the game to the other players and to interpret their own and the other players' moves according to it. Some players who defined the situation as a game were puzzled by the other players' cooperation and speculated that the other players might have a different payoff matrix, in which *cooperation* was less risky or produced a higher payoff. These players tended to see the other's *defection* as a bid to win rather than a defensive move in response to their own defection. In contrast, players who believed that mutual cooperation was in both players' interests often interpreted the other players' choices of noncooperation as signs of distrust.

3. Most players considered their own and the other players' choices a means to signal a preferred course of interaction as well as to acquire points. Consequently, some interactions were interpreted as a conversation or argument about playing the game. One typical pattern occurred when a player who desired mutual cooperation believed that the second player's choice of noncooperation was motivated by distrust. The first player would then choose the cooperation for several trials to indicate his or her own commitment to cooperation. Signals, however, were frequently misunderstood because the sender's and recipient's conceptions of the game differed. As mentioned, players who thought unilateral victory was the purpose of the game (and attributed this belief to the other player) either could not understand the signal or doubted its sincerity and instead believed it to be a ploy.

4. Stable patterns of mutual cooperation or mutual defection developed in the majority of the games, and these patterns were sustained by the players having similar understandings of the game and expectations of one another. Over 75 percent of the games ended in a phase of mutual cooperation or defection longer than twenty-five trials. One explanation for this phenomenon claims that players try to match each other's choices and become more accurate in predicting the other's choices as the game progresses (Emshoff and Ackoff 1970). However, the belief statements show that players in

mutual defection saw the game as strict competition whereas the players in mutual cooperation did not.

5. Such conceptions were frequently altered by outcomes, particularly when the other player did not make the expected choices over several consecutive rounds. Yet, generally unilateral cooperative initiatives which were intended to change a competitor's concept of the game were short-lived. Either the competitor soon reciprocated with cooperation or the initiator abandoned the effort. Such an initiative extended beyond four trials in only one game. It was sustained because the initiator changed his concept of a role from a co-equal seeking mutual cooperation to a helper of the other player.

6. The way players characterized the moves ultimately depended on their beliefs about the appropriate norms or principles for structuring their relationships, such as competition, reciprocity, social responsibility, or equity. This response is illustrated by different attitudes among players toward occasional defections by a player during a mutual cooperation phase. Two mutual cooperation patterns appeared in the experiments as a result of an asymmetrical PD payoff matrix that benefited one player more than the other in mutual cooperation and cost the first player more in mutual defection. In the first pattern, both players cooperated on every trial. They considered any unilateral defection a violation of cooperation because it violated reciprocity. The aggrieved party often tried to prevent the repetition of such defection by playing tit-for-tat, forcing the other player to a redress of unilateral cooperation before the resumption of mutual cooperation. In the second pattern, the player receiving more points in mutual cooperation consistently cooperated, whereas the other defected periodically. The frequency of defection was chosen so the points gained over the other player in this unilateral defection equaled the total extra points the other accumulated in the preceding rounds of mutual cooperation.[21] Players in the second pattern interpreted the unilateral defection as part of a larger pattern of cooperation that also assured equitable results. One player even dubbed the pattern "affirmative action."

The players' concern to satisfy a principle of equity rather than exercise their respective bargaining powers generated this pattern. Because the *advantaged* player had a greater incentive to avoid prolonged mutual defection, the *disadvantaged* player could have used this source of bargaining power to force the advantaged player to accept far more frequent defections.[22] However, only one player actually adopted this strategy. Moreover, most players who followed the compensatory pattern reported early in the game that they were troubled by the imbalance in payoffs for mutual cooperation. Once the pattern was established, they regarded their adherence to it as an obligation toward the other, whom they described as a "partner" or "friend." Several players counted out the trials between the defections, thus completing the transformation of the game from a competition to a coordinated, norm-controlled performance and removing the exercise of choice on each trial. One player later wrote about the game; "Once my partner and I fell into the pattern, however, my mood changed, from one of apprehension to one of deep satisfaction of having 'won.' I also experienced a joyful anticipation of each move, knowing exactly what it would be and that it was one of the best. My feelings toward my partner were those of respect for his playing ability and comraderie, for we had unified to beat the system."

7. Sustained change or de-escalation from mutual defection to mutual cooperation normally occurred before a mutual defection phase exceeded ten trials. When a mutual defection phase became longer, players were less cognitively and emotionally able to change their patterns of play. They became more certain that the SPD was a competitive game and that conception invalidated an interpretation of a choice of *cooperation* as a signal of the desire for mutual cooperation. Players also occasionally justified their rejection of cooperation with doubts that the other player would respond favorably to any initiative. They cited as grounds for these doubts earlier trials (precedents) in which their cooperation had been matched by the other players' defections.

For such reasons, players who felt frustrated, stuck, or helpless in a long phase of mutual defection refrained from attempting to breakout, preferring to let the other players make the first move. There were valid grounds for their reluctance. The more rounds of mutual defection that preceded a unilateral cooperation initiative, the less likely the other player was to understand this move as a demonstration of trustworthiness or at least a signal for an alternative, non-competitive relationship between the players. Such intentions were also better understood when there had been an earlier phase of mutual cooperation and particularly when the initiator had been the one who had departed first from the earlier mutual cooperation. In that case, the other player could regard the cooperation signal as redress for that earlier defection, the act of a "reformed sinner."

The laboratory game format supports such a double interpretation more easily than real world interactions in which concrete actions or social forms, like apologies or aid, can reduce the ambiguity of motives. Nevertheless, a de-escalation in real world conflicts that can be interpreted as both a demonstration of good faith and a redress for a past provocation might be particularly effective in stimulating change in a conflictual relationship. In the Cuban Missile Crisis, the U.S. announcement that it would not invade Cuba might have had such appeal, especially for Soviet Premier Khrushchev, who claimed that he installed missiles in Cuba to forestall a U.S. invasion of the island.

THE CUBAN MISSILE CRISIS AND SADAT'S INITIATIVE

Kennedy's quarantine of Cuba and Sadat's flight to Jerusalem have become standard examples of how strong, dramatic signals can communicate resolve, reduce ambiguity about intentions, and thereby defuse a crisis or promote negotiations. These acts and the responses to them also change the respective definitions of the relationship between the principal actors. Kennedy's move, if perceived as an ultimatum, communicated to the Soviet Union that from the U.S. perspective the superpowers were playing chicken (Steinberg 1989).[23] It defined the superpowers as sharing a certain interdependence with a partial conflict of interest rather than a straight adversarial relationship. However, mutual avoidance rather than negotiations or collective problem solving was proposed as the best means for resolving the conflict, that is, "Remove the missiles and we will not invade Cuba and possibly blunder into nuclear war."

In a recent Soviet study, V. Sergeev and associates argue that the missile crisis contributed to a more positive redefinition of the superpower relationship than may be inferred from the usual construction of the crisis as a chicken game resolved through mutual avoidance (Sergeev, Akimov, Lukov, and Parshin 1987).[24] While mapping the dependencies in Kennedy's foreign policy pronouncements during 1962, the researchers found that as the missile crisis deepened Kennedy stopped believing that the United States could achieve its security goals through unilateral action. The attainment of these goals instead depended on Soviet cooperation and restraint. Kennedy became almost totally confident that his control measures to counter the placement of the missiles would attain their goals if the Soviets were sincere in their declared peaceful intentions and practiced self-restraint.

> The recognition of the role of interdependence by the US leaders of that period seemed to lead them to the reconstruction of a crucial role of such a category as sincerity (both one's own and the partner's). While the previous assumption about the interdependence from the environment made the US leaders ignore the category of sincerity ("I don't care whether the partner is sincere or not, since the power is on my side"), the new situation turned sincerity into a major resource promoting one's goals (Sergeev, Akimov, Lukov, and Parshin 1987, 29).

This conclusion is also supported by Kennedy's apparent realization that the Soviets could have regarded the U.S. installation of missiles in Turkey as a provocation. According to then Secretary of State Rusk, Kennedy had prepared a fallback position in case the Soviets refused the first demand to remove the missiles, under which the United States would pledge to remove the missiles in Turkey in exchange for the removal of the missiles in Cuba (Blight and Welch 1989, 113 ff.). His acknowledgment of interdependence, emphasis on sincerity, and readiness to bargain indicate that Kennedy had certainly abandoned attrition and containment theories for dealing with the Soviet Union. This change in mentality is consistent with Sergeev and associates' useful definition of crisis as a "situation where mutual perception[s] of participants change rapidly and this change is linked with threats to mutual security." The change also helps explain the sudden, rapid thaw that occurred in the bilateral relations the following year, which resulted in the Test Ban Treaty. The cooperative Soviet responses to Kennedy's initiative supported the idea that superpower relations could be based on reciprocity and mutual benefit.

This crisis, rather than earlier crises, had such transformative power primarily because the risks and costs of nuclear war seemed more salient. Most of the decision makers did not regard the Soviet move as threatening the global balance of power, and they believed that the United States would triumph in the event of nuclear war. However, they were informed by U.S. intelligence that if the Soviet missiles were operational and launched, at least 4 million people on the U.S. East Coast would be killed. The prospect of such a loss diminished the possibility of a military solution and made a negotiated solution imperative. But in addition, by the early 1960s, the theories of attrition and containment were clearly not working. Despite their associated practices, Soviet influence had spread to the emerging Third World, and the U.S. alliance systems in the Middle East and Southeast Asia had crumbled. The full achievement of U.S. interests had, therefore, become factually dependent on Soviet cooperation or restraint.

Sadat's peace initiative in 1977 was intended to tell the Israelis that Egypt and Israel were effectively in a Prisoner's Dilemma, which could be successfully resolved through negotiations and some mutual trust. The two countries were currently nonbelligerent, and the Kissinger-brokered disengagements between Israel and Egypt had created a small tradition of limited trust and reciprocity. However, the relationship was shaky and depended on self-restraint at a time when national interests had still not been satisfied. The Egyptians had not achieved their goal of recovering sovereignty over the entire Sinai, whereas the Israelis felt they had not reasserted their deterrent power vis-à-vis Egypt and other Arab states. Thus there were reasons to fear that without moves that expanded the basis of the relationship, Egypt and Israel could slip back to war.

Sadat's initiative proposed to move well beyond those precedents and to dismantle the grievance structure between Israel and Egypt by exchanging peace for land and thus satisfy each side's main stated concern. As mentioned earlier, he could propose this because he had no career investment in vanquishing Israel. His main national interest was to restore Egyptian sovereignty to the Sinai and reestablish beneficial relations with the West. He felt few constraints about meeting Israeli security interest to facilitate those goals. Israeli leaders were, however, initially reluctant to concede anything vital to Egypt. Some believed Egyptians still harbored the desire to destroy Israel, and others had no inclination to let any of Israel's security depend on Egyptian restraint. Sadat's dramatic initiative did much to dispel the Israeli distrust about his intentions. On one hand, Israelis were aware of the great personal risks he was taking vis-à-vis the Arab world, which excoriated the initiative. On the other hand, Sadat in coming to Jerusalem undercut the standard Israeli excuse for not negotiating because "there is no one to talk to."[25]

By raising and answering the question of trust, Sadat forced Egyptian and Israeli elites to imagine a new basis for the relationship between their countries. Certainly, he was the first and only credible Arab leader to make such a direct appeal to Israel for peace. But several other factors besides the drama and intensity of the initiative accounted for its eventual success. As is well known, Israel's Begin government nearly discarded the opportunity that Sadat gave it, first in the winter, 1977–78, and then at Camp David, September 1978. However, a large, spontaneous Israeli peace movement inspired by Sadat's initiative and U.S. diplomatic pressure, political support, and economic aid brought Israel to accept terms that were as basically beneficial to it as to Egypt. In addition, the substance of the exchange with Egypt was probably easier for Israel than any other imaginable exchange of land for peace with an Arab state or group. In light of the Yom Kippur/October War, the Sinai had proved of questionable strategic value for Israel and it had no ideological or religious significance for Jews. On the other hand, by relinquishing the Sinai, Israel split the most populous Arab state from the Arab coalition. The possible exchange of the West Bank for peace with the Palestinians or the Golan Heights for peace with Syria would have Israel relinquish lands of greater religious or security value for peace with less formidable enemies.

An irony of framing the situation that Sadat's initiative addressed as a Prisoner's Dilemma game is that Sadat himself had firsthand experience in resolving the problem from which the game derives its name. Arrested in 1946 with some twenty others as a conspirator in the assassination of a pro-British Egyptian politician, he was held incommunicado and repeatedly urged to confess and implicate his coconspirators. He refused and inferred by the continual demand for his confession that others had also remained silent. "Having thought it out thoroughly, I had come to the conclusion that Muhammad Kamil [later Sadat's foreign minister] couldn't have made a confession. Young as he was, he should hold out, if anyone could. I tried to contact him through the warden and eventually succeeded. His response encouraged me. He was dependable and, working together, I hoped we could pull the case apart" (Sadat 1978). Eventually, Sadat, Kamil, and two others were acquitted for lack of evidence. Sadat credited his ability to trust others, learned in a traditional Egyptian village where he spent some of his youth, for his conduct in this episode. In his autobiography, he intimates that its lesson was in his thoughts at the time of the Jerusalem initiative.

LEARNING FROM THE CUBAN MISSILE CRISIS

The successful resolution of the Cuban Missile Crisis[26] involved a major redefinition in the U.S.-Soviet Union relationship, as indicated by the ensuing de-escalation in conflict and increased cooperation between the two superpowers. Soon after October 1962, their relations improved dramatically, highlighted by the signing of the Test Ban Treaty less than one year later. The change is more systematically indicated by a rising curve into 1967 for the monthly average level of net cooperation in each superpower's actions directed at the other superpower, as indicated by event data series (Goldstein and Freeman 1988, 1987). Interestingly, the Vietnam War did not block this trend although the United States was a primary actor on one side of that war while the Soviet Union was a secondary actor on the other side. Middle East disputes, however, had a negative effect: the average level of cooperation dropped around the Six Day War and later during the Canal War (1968–70). The level of cooperation rose to a peak with the quasi-formal U.S.-Soviet détente at the end of the first Nixon administration but deteriorated somewhat after the Yom Kippur/October War in 1973 and more so after the passage of the Jackson-Vanik Amendment, the following year. Nevertheless, until the conscious revival of the Cold War by the first Reagan administration, the level of net cooperation between the superpowers remained consistently higher than before the missile crisis.

One reason for this trend is that the superpowers apparently learned from the missile crisis to avoid entering disputes that could lead to military confrontation with each other and to avoid participating in disputes that directly threatened the other's vital interests. This claim derives from an analysis of the nearly seven hundred post-World War II international disputes, which Sherman coded for actors in the dispute, types of phases, sequence of phases, issues, actions by actors in phases, threats to superpowers, threat level, casualties, presence of management agent, and type of dispute settlement (Mallery 1988; Duffy 1991).[27] The analysis developed a chronology of disputes involving both the United States and the Soviet Union with partitioning for presence of one or both superpowers, level of superpower involvement (as primary or secondary actor), violence of the dispute measured by phase types and casualties, and threat to the superpower. Disputes involving the United States and the Soviet Union were significantly fewer and less severe in the decade following the missile crisis than in either of the two postwar decades preceding it.

Only seventeen such disputes were initiated between the missile crisis and the Yom Kippur war, compared to forty-seven in 1940–1950 (Korean War), forty-nine in 1950–1962, and twenty-nine in 1974–1985. New disputes in which the Soviet Union and the United States were primary actors dropped sharply from twenty-seven in the 1940–1950, and twenty-five in 1950–1962, to seven in 1962–1973 and four in

1973–1985. Because several unresolved disputes from earlier periods were settled or became dormant in the decade after the Cuban Missile Crisis, total dispute participation also dropped in the later period. Moreover, no disputes occurred after the Cuban Missile Crisis in which both superpowers used military force to achieve objectives.

The post–missile crisis disputes that included the United States and the Soviet Union were qualitatively different from earlier ones. The later crises did not involve attempts to change the global military balance or to reduce either side's sphere of influence. For the entire post–World War II period, fifty-six disputes involving the United States and the Soviet Union concerned the global military balance, but of these only the Yom Kippur War and the Angolan Civil War started after 1962. However, after the missile crisis, ten-year totals increased for new disputes that threatened the influence of the United States or the Soviet Union over members of the adversary bloc. This increase may indicate the superpowers' declining prestige with each becoming less able to intimidate the other one's allies and less able to discourage its own allies from challenging the other superpower.

The superpowers' apparent rule of avoiding confrontations with one another is also supported by the restraint of each from exploiting the other's difficulties within its own bloc. The number of intrablock disputes increased in the 1970s and 1980s, but since 1973, the United States was a primary actor in only two such disputes threatening Soviet influence, namely, relations with Cuba in the late 1970s and Polish Solidarity. The Soviet Union was not actively involved in any dispute involving a threat to U.S. influence in the Western bloc. Notwithstanding U.S. verbal attacks on the Brezhnev Doctrine, this restraint acknowledges spheres of influence, and it appears to trace to the missile crisis resolution. In a sense, the U.S. involvement in the Polish Solidarity dispute is the exception that proves the rule. The large Polish population in the United States forces any president to respond to Soviet actions in Poland, but the U.S. reaction to the Soviet-backed suppression of Solidarity was relatively mild compared to the Truman administration's vigorous, Cold War–precipitating reaction to the Soviet actions in Poland in 1945–46.

In the 1970s and 1980s, competition between the United States and the Soviet Union was mainly confined to that for influence over Third World states. The number of new disputes that cast both superpowers in secondary support roles in regional conflicts climbed from seven in 1962–73, to eighteen after 1973, and the intensity of these disputes, as measured by their casualties, also increased. Such confrontation through proxies, however, does not evidence serious rivalry. With the exception of the Soviet action in Afghanistan and the U.S. involvement in Grenada and Panama, the superpowers were not directly active militarily. Again, with the possible exception of the Soviet action in Afghanistan, their respective interests were not seriously affected by the results of the fighting. In any case, the increase has just barely kept pace with the dramatic increase of disputes among nonaligned states. As recent negotiations on Nicaragua, Afghanistan, and Angola demonstrate, the superpowers can reduce their involvements by urging accommodation on their proxies when these become expensive or threaten to escalate rapidly.

A SMALL CONCLUSION

De-escalation is sustained by changes in how parties in a conflict define their relationship. Dramatic events and initiatives are often responsible for these changes. Sadat's peace initiative in 1977 convinced most Israelis that he could bargain in good faith. Following the initiative, the respective decision makers and public opinion recognized that an Egyptian-Israeli relationship could be grounded on an exchange that satisfied respective interests rather than on enmity and fights for survival.

The Cuban Missile Crisis taught Washington and Moscow decision makers the dangerous consequences of remaining strict adversaries. The decision makers recognized that in the nuclear age the defeat of one superpower must entail defeat of the other, and they learned that the satisfaction of each side's security interests depended on the satisfaction of the other's. An American academic, keenly aware of the ironies of strategic calculation, observed, "the Cuban missile crisis was the best thing to happen to [the United States] since the Second World War. It helped [the United States] avoid further confrontation with the Soviets, it resolved the Berlin issue and it established new basic understandings about American-Soviet interaction" (Schelling in Blight and Welch 1987, 104). Since the crisis, the superpowers have practiced and refined the lessons they learned. They have followed principles that avoided direct confrontation and deferred to interests that the other state considers vital. Their present willingness to resolve outstanding disputes and their respect for one another's sphere of influence suggest that the superpowers may now be taking turns in letting the other or its allies gain limited advantages. Such coordination or reciprocity over successive chicken situations would be reasonable. By taking turns in bolstering allies and proxies, the superpowers can gain more influence than if they both avoid all dispute involvements for fear of direct confrontations. Such a "regime" indicates a relationship based on both individual self-interest and a desire to keep the partner in the game.

NOTES

1. Secretary of Defense Robert McNamara recalled: "In my mind I attached a very low probability to the ultimate escalation to nuclear war, but a higher probability to the escalation to a conventional confrontation somewhere. And that would be very dangerous, both in and of itself and also because it might escalate further, leading possibly to nuclear war" (Blight and Welch 1989, 187).

2. Kennedy was influenced by the recently published book by Barbara Tuchman (1962), which attributed the outbreak of World War I to decision makers' misjudgments and their inability to halt war preparations once the diplomatic crisis following the assassination in Sarjevo had passed its peak (see also Kennedy [1969, 127–28]; Abel [1966, 93–94]).

3. J. Goldstein and J. Freeman (1988) argue that the United States, the Soviet Union, and China followed tit-for-tat reciprocity in their behavior toward one another during 1953–80. They acknowledge a puzzle in the various changes in these relations from increasing mutual hostility to increasing mutual cooperation and vice versa.

4. The conjecture is supported by studies that find that nineteenth- and twentieth-century conventional wars usually wound down only after 0.1 percent to 1 percent of the parties' populations was killed (Singer and Small 1972).

5. A similar phenomenon is found in a corporation using its sunk costs as reason to continue a doomed project, vide the building of most nuclear power plants today. In folk economics this practice is called "throwing good money after bad" and in neopopulist economics is called the "overcapitalization ripoff." Its logic is partially captured in the dollar auction game discussed in J. Brockner and J. Rubin (1985).

6. The use of a "stick-and-carrot" strategy can reduce the ambiguity. The "carrot," or de-escalation, signals that an earlier escalation was intended to warn rather than to defeat the other party, whereas the "stick," or escalation, signals that any de-escalation was a matter of choice—not the result of exhaustion.

7. As presented here, the enemy relationship is bilateral but not necessarily symmetrical. That is, if A is B's enemy, B is A's enemy; but it is not necessarily the case that if A wants to dominate B, B wants to dominate A. B might only want to resist A. Arguably, the enemy relationship is only bilateral if both want to dominate the other. Of course, A and B might have divergent readings on respective motives. During the Vietnam War, U.S. administrations claimed that they did not want to dominate Vietnam but that the North Vietnamese as part of an international Communist movement wanted to dominate the United States—therefore, North Vietnam was an enemy of the United States but not vice versa.

8. A phase is one of six levels of disagreement and conflict through which a dispute may pass one or more times. The dispute phase is essentially a verbal, diplomatic quarrel or disagreement claimed by at least one party to be an issue of substantive international political significance. The conflict phase is characterized by the threat of one or more of the parties to use military force to resolve the dispute. In the hostilities phase, military force is used systematically for specific objectives, whereas in the posthostilities-conflict phase, fighting does not occur but at least one party continues to view the quarrel in military terms. In the posthostility dispute, the quarrel remains but is no longer viewed in military terms. Finally, in the settlement phase, the dispute is resolved or the parties no longer cared about it (Sherman 1985, 1987).

9. This rigidity helps explain the failure of proposals like the 1950s Johnson Plan for Jordan River waters that intend to end conflict by offering enemies economic development programs whose realization depends on their cooperation.

10. Containment theory's notion that the Soviet Union would exploit any cooperative move by the United States is disproved by an analysis of event data for the 1953 to 1978 period (see Goldstein and Freeman [1987]). The Soviet Union was more positively responsive to U.S. cooperative innovations than the United States was responsive to Soviet turns to cooperation. (Under the definition of the relationship specified in containment, American decision makers may have coded Soviet moves as less cooperative than did the COPDAB coders upon whom Goldstein and Freeman rely.)

11. In the 1950s, the U.S. government worked to prevent such contacts. Similarly, Israel has tried to preserve the image of the Palestinians as implacable enemies by outlawing any contacts between Israeli citizens and members of the Palestine Liberation Organization (PLO).

12. Traditional ideas nevertheless die hard. Thirty years later, a social psychologist found that many defense planners in both the United States and the Soviet Union still thought of nuclear war as winnable (see Kull [1988]).

13. Conventional wisdom claims only hardliners can initiate such moves. Examples include Menahem Begin's peace agreement with Anwar el-Sadat, Richard Nixon's China initiative, Ronald Reagan's positive response on Russian arms control bids, and Charles DeGaulle's decision to end France's colonial rule in Algeria. However, I know of no systematic study of this claim, and counterexamples are easily found, for example, Franklin Roosevelt's recognition of the Soviet Union and Neville Chamberlain's ill-fated attempt to appease Hitler.

14. This representation is consistent with Leibniz's notion of individuals as "windowless monads" and with doctrines of national sovereignty (Elster 1979, 123).

15. In the Leo Strauss *Political Philosophy of Hobbes: Its Basis and Genesis* reading of Hobbes's state of nature, agents incessantly seek relative advantage and preeminence as much as their own welfare. These substantive irrational drives give rise to the war of all against all. C. Macpherson (1964) argues, however, that Hobbes does not attribute such drives to all agents at all times.

16. See S. Brams (1985) for a formal model of nuclear deterrence as a two trial chicken supergame that specifies the conditions under which nuclear retaliation is a credible threat. The chicken game derives its name from a game with automobiles popular among American teenagers in the 1950s, in which two drivers drive their cars toward each other on a collision course. The driver who swerves first or "chickens out" is the loser.

17. Debates frequently leave positions more hardened, and experimental evidence indicated that the "double focus" method produces no more agreement than does each side's single focus on its own position.

18. The earliest known experiments were conducted by M. Flood at RAND Corporation (see Alker and Hurwitz [1980]).

19. Students in upper division courses on war and conflict were paired and played an SPD of approximately fifty trials. The subjects were given no prior indication of this length in order to discourage strategies of shifting to competitive choices as the anticipated end of the game approached. On every move, the players listed their choices, the choices expected from the other players, and the choices those players actually made. On every fourth move, they gave reasons for their own and the others' choices on the previous trial, for the choices they intended on the current trial, and for the others' expected choices. They also reported how well they thought they were doing in relation to their original expectations.

20. Computerization of textual analysis reduces the amount of random variation in interpretation by the analyst. Grouping sentences with similar contents but different wording was handled by retrieving on lexical classifiers. Lexical classifiers are essentially sets of synonyms with specified syntactical and semantic relations that restrict individual words to the sense that warrants their inclusion in the set. The restriction of sense overcomes a typical difficulty in automatic content analysis and information retrieval, for example, retrieving articles on cookies rather than semi-conductors when searching on the word *chips*.

21. Or every $X + 1$ round, where $(T_b - S_a) = [X^*(R_a - R_b)]$, where T_b and R_b are B's payoffs under B's unilateral defection and under mutual cooperation, respectively, and S_a and R_a are A's payoffs under B's unilateral defection and under mutual cooperation, respectively. For the matrix actually used, the solution was a defection every sixth round.

22. It is in A's interest to acquiesce as long as $Z^*R_a + Y^*S_a > (Z + Y)^*P_a$, where Z is the number of times A cooperates while B defects, and Y is the number of times both A and B cooperate. For the matrix used, $Z = Y = 3$. Hence the player hurt more by mutual defection could have been forced to accept twice as many unilateral defections by an opponent than the number dictated by equity considerations.

23. B. Steinberg (1989), using recently available data, skillfully argues that Khrushchev, in placing missiles in Cuba, and Kennedy, in demanding their removal, were motivated by fierce competitive drives and rage over perceived humiliation at the hands of the other. Steinberg explains that the crisis was resolved because the leaders were flexible enough to rein in their emotions when facing the threat of nuclear war.

24. This paper's title "Interdependence in a Crisis Situation: Simulating the Caribbean Crisis," (Sergeev, Akimov, Lukov, and Parshin 1987) embeds the missile crisis in a series of moves and countermoves affecting each superpower's interests regarding Cuba and environs.

25. Nevertheless, some Israelis had difficulty in shaking the earlier definition of the relationship. The Israel Defense Forces' chief of staff at the time believed until the very moment that the plan landed at Lod airport that Sadat had planned some trick.

26. The research for this section was completed with the help of John Mallery, Gavan Duffy of MIT, and Frank Sherman of Miami Univ. (Ohio).

27. A feature vector that overviewed the dispute was constructed from these vectors. The feature vector editor has procedures for filtering through the composites and

phase vectors for particular feature values. Sequences of disputes that have arbitrary intersections or disjoints of features are obtained through successive filtering. A timebase or database manager for time intervals, implemented by Gavan Duffy, can display the beginning and end points of an arbitrary set of events and construct a chronology for any specified region in the temporal space. A chronology represents by discreet lines parallel to an axis all the durations of events within the region (Duffy 1991). Hence the number of co-occurring events or episodes at any particular time can be seen at a glance.

6

POWER STRATEGIES IN DE-ESCALATION

I. WILLIAM ZARTMAN AND JOHANNES AURIK

WHY DE-ESCALATE? One answer in the intuitive world would be that the last escalation was successful, carrying our side over the top and making further effort unnecessary. The other answer would be that something had occurred that made further escalation undesirable, no matter how necessary it might appear to the pursuit of conflict. We will pursue that limitation in this chapter in regard to regional conflict in Third World areas that involves the great powers.

Three different ways of identifying that limitation can be proposed, depending on the analytical perspective chosen. One would associate limits of escalation with power—counterefforts and counterinducements applied by the other side that limit the first party's ability or willingness to escalate. Power as a concept points to an important supplementary question for analysis: Are positive or negative inducements more effective exercises of power to produce de-escalation? This was a salient question in the mind of President Reagan during a press conference on March 19, 1988, but, as posed, it was probably the wrong question. Doubtless both positive and negative inducements are effective in some way. The questions are rather Which is most effective under what conditions? and If both are effective, which is more efficient?

One could also identify the limits on escalation through patterns of behavior and expectation that govern relations between the conflict-

This chapter was written under a grant from the United States Institute of Peace, which is gratefully acknowledged. Naturally, the opinions, findings, and conclusions or recommendations expressed in this chapter are those of the author not of the United States Institute of Peace.

ing parties. Termed *norms* or *regimes,* these tacit understandings act as ceilings on *normal* behavior as rules of any competition (Krasner 1983). This explanation of de-escalation is not as powerful as the first because it does not apply to all cases, notably those short of the ceiling (or at some more distant relation to it). But that does not mean that the explanation is not absolutely powerful—and, therefore, better than the first—in certain cases.

A third sense of the limits of escalation comes from within the decision-making process of the escalating side in its cost/benefit calculations. A party de-escalates not because of any limitations imposed by the opponent or because of any jointly decided limitations but because of its own internal calculations about the value of the conflict efforts (see the discussion of Gorbachev by Jo Husbands and that of R. Haass and P. T. Hopmann). Such calculations obviously take into account the opposing (cost-imposing) efforts or power of the opponent, but their focus is more on the verbal assessment and disposition of the decision-making group than on the implemented reactions to the opponents. This type of explanation highlights the fact that the same or similar events are perceived and acted upon differently by different people with their different image sets.

These three explanations of conflict behavior relate to basic notions of international relations analysis. One claims that behaviors are best understood in interaction and that the best predictor of a state's action is the opponent's previous action. The other claims that entities are coherent and purposive actors and that the best predictor of a state's action is the same state's previous action (in similar or related circumstances). In between is the fully systemic view that claims that states' actions are part of patterns of behavior either externally or consensually imposed. Coherent as these different analytical approaches are, they are more rigorous than real, and reality is most likely to be found by combining them according to the circumstances. States attempt to act as purposive actors in the process. The result is an interactional system that acts at the same time as a pattern context and constraint for the state actors.

Yet trying to make some, probably overly rigorous, order of behaviors is not a vain exercise. It is necessary in order to establish the effectiveness and efficiency of measures that decision makers must take as well as to understand the areas of interaction that fall outside their decision-making possibilities. But it also means that one must ask further questions about intervening variables, identifying the conditions or situations under which certain effects occur. Thus, relevant questions

are Under what conditions is de-escalation attributable to specific negative and positive measures by the proponent? What distinguishes the
effects of negative from positive measures? Under what conditions is de-
escalation attributable either to the effect of contest rules or to an
independent cost/benefit sense of ceiling? Before answers can be sought
for these questions, three concepts need further discussion: power, ripeness, and escalation/de-escalation.

Power, or leverage, is the basic concept of political science but one
that is still short of agreed identification; a particularly elusive concept,
it seems to occupy the same position to social science that *humours* did
to premedicine or *elements* did to prephysics. Deeper investigation of
the power question leads to the realization—as noted by Simon (1957,
8) and Dahl (1976, 29)—that power is merely the causal question. To
say that one has the power to accomplish a goal means that one has the
ability to cause a goal to be accomplished, and this leads back to the
question of what gives that power or ability or cause? Categories of
answers come from all over, but the most useful for these purposes is
the fourfold typology of contingent gratifications and deprivations
(Schelling 1960, Zartman 1987). After the distinction between positive
and negative inducements (gratifications and deprivations, respectively)
has been made, it can be further divided into other subcategories to test
other effects. The most useful here is between volitional and nonvolitional
contingencies, that is, things one will do and things that one perceives
will take place without any specific intent. The resulting matrix is as
follows:

	Gratifications	Deprivations
Volitional	Promises	Threats
Non-volitional	Predictions	Warnings

Although distinctions other than volition could be used, this one permits the testing of subcategories of propositions that could be useful to
practitioners.

Another overarching dichotomy relates to power, one that sepa-
rates the previously discussed contingencies from applied gratifications
and deprivations. Curiously, conceptualization of this order of effects is
less developed. But the role of faits accomplis, the concept of power as
the ability to do without the use of coercion as a diplomatic means, the

expansion of alternatives, and the obtention of resources, all refer to the effect of applied increments to cost/benefit calculations in escalation and de-escalation decisions (George et al. 1971). Because of this, both applied and contingent effects can be called power as an added value because the value of the action is added negatively or positively to the evaluation an actor makes of the outcome (Zartman 1974). Because value and evaluation are subjective calculations, this analysis bridges the power and the cost/benefit approaches.

Ripeness has already been identified with a number of characteristics: a mutually hurting stalemate with a recent or impending catastrophe, a way out, and valid spokesmen (Zartman 1989). It is an important contextual feature, for efforts at de-escalation are almost certain to be unrewarding or at least much more difficult if the situation is not propitious for their effects. However, it is also clear that even when the moment is not ripe, third parties can work to make it so in preparation for their mediatory effects. Such efforts are also possible for parties to the conflict, as will be discussed in the next section on escalation. Ripeness stands in a different relation to each of the three analytical perspectives. It is external to the power approach and thus easier to analyze as an independent variable. It is related to the notion of regimes because as conflicts approach agreed ceilings, they help establish their own stalemates. And it can be inherent in cost/benefit calculations. It is important to isolate the concepts of analysis to test them and identify their characteristics.

Escalation and de-escalation also need some refinements as concepts.[1] The two are not opposites; a decision not to escalate is not necessarily a decision to de-escalate nor is a decision to de-escalate necessarily a decision to wind down conflict. To begin with, a distinction is needed between escalation, a steplike increase in the nature of the conflict, and intensification, a gradual increase without a change in nature. Because it marks "a change in saliency" (Smoke 1979), escalation and de-escalation are clearer signals to the adversary than mere intensification, although in reality there is still a good deal of interpretive uncertainty in all of them. Both sets of concepts can refer either to means or to ends. The addition of new ways of carrying out the conflict such as the introduction of foreign troops or a move from guerrilla to conventional war is the usual sense of escalation of means but the expansion of goals, such as a call for the overthrow of the opposing government rather than just a territorial settlement, is an escalation of ends. (Corresponding intensifications would be the introduction of more and more troops or the demand for more and more territory.)

But a check on escalation (or intensification) does not necessarily mean that the de-escalation process has begun. A decision not to escalate often means a decision to carry on the conflict at its present level, and a decision to de-escalate (especially in means) may mean the continuation of the conflict more cheaply. Both decisions refer to a choice of continuing stalemate as a condition of conflict not to the beginnings of its end. The three stages of the conflict cycle should, therefore, be seen as escalation, stalemate, and de-escalation; it is not the introduction of phase two but its transformation from a continuing bearable stalemate into a mutually disadvantageous stalemate that make for a ripe moment for resolution. In this light, the components of the de-escalation decision—the ripe moment for de-escalation—may be reiterated and refined. In addition to valid representatives, a component that is not in question here, they are a perception of futility (disadvantageous stalemate), requitement (a belief that the other party will respond in kind to any concession or de-escalation), and a way out (so that the issues of the conflict will be reduced as well as the means). It is requitement that activates a stalemate and readies it for conflict management and resolution.

Therefore, a number of decisions at the height of the conflict are crucial to winding it down. One is the decision not to escalate, not to go any higher, which produces a stalemate. Because *nonescalations* are the residual situations, a decision not to escalate may be difficult to detect from the outside unless it is trumpeted as a signal. Furthermore, that decision may even take the form of an intensification, a decision to "meet and call" but not to raise. Producing an escalation to meet and call an opponent's escalation is difficult because the act of crossing a saliency is so strong that it may override any attempt to meet and call rather than raise. Once the stalemate is produced, the perception of mutual pain must also be produced; the world is littered with conflicts that sputter on at an acceptable level of stalemate, ready to intensify or escalate at the merest incident but neither managed nor resolved. Only when the components of the de-escalation decision—futility, requitement, and a way out—are on hand and perceived by both sides is the down staircase open for service. It should be clear from this discussion that there is plenty of ambiguity in these components and that this ambiguity is not just an operational problem for the analyst but also a real problem for the practitioner.

The key decision in this general context of winding down is the decision to get to the table, and it is on this decision that we will focus in this chapter—as in the rest of this book. Practitioners have argued, as distinct from "green table" negotiation, that negotiations begin when one party decides or perceives that a solution to the conflict may be obtainable from negotiations (Low in Touval & Zartman 1985; Saunders 1985). The party then sets about to convince the other side not of a specific outcome as yet but of a similar possibility for the other party to achieve an acceptable solution (requitement) through negotiations. In the study presented here, we will examine that decision to come to the table as the crucial decision in de-escalation.

Attempts to answer that question about de-escalation can only be subjective and sensitive, relying on rather soft data and always open to question and debate. In this study we will use ten cases from the 1960s to the 1980s: the January 1975 Agreement signed at Alvor among the three factions of the Angolan nationalist movement, which set up a tripartite government and ended the civil war; the January 1984 Accords signed at Lusaka between Angola and South Africa, which provided mutual disengagement; the nonaggression and mutual disengagement pact signed in March 1984 in Nkomati by Mozambique and South Africa; the peace agreement signed in January 1973 in Paris among the United States, North and South Vietnam, and the Viet Minh to end the war in Vietnam; the withdrawal agreement signed by Israel and Lebanon through the mediation and participation of the United States in May 1983; the Geneva agreement signed by the United States, Soviet Union, Pakistan, and Afghanistan, which provided for the withdrawal of Soviet troops from Afghanistan; the August 1988 acceptance of a cease-fire by Iran and Iraq; the London agreement of 1960, which provided for the independence of Cyprus; the 1964 agreement that restored peace to the warring communities in Cyprus; and the 1967 negotiations to do the same. Only the latter was a case of failed negotiations; an agreement never ensued. However, ironically, all the others were variously flawed in their results, and some of them simply collapsed after signature. The inadequacy of the particular outcomes is the subject of a different study; the subject here is the explanation of how and why the parties decided to enter negotiations in the first place rather than continue to try to impose a unilateral solution.

EVIDENCE

Decision to Negotiate the Alvor Agreement, January 15, 1975

The decision to negotiate in the January 1975 Agreement in Alvor, Portugal, had different bases on the Portuguese and the African sides (Marcum 1978, Bender 1978). The Portuguese Revolution provided its own rationale for de-escalation and then gave the National Liberation Front of Angola (FLNA), the People's Movement for the Liberation of Angola (MPLA), and the National Union for the Total Independence of Angola (UNITA) the fulfillment of both their biggest prize and their biggest fear—independence and the removal of the only thing they had in common, the fight against the colonizer.

Radicalized by the fifteen-year struggle to hold onto the Portuguese colonies in Africa, a group of captains and majors led by Gen. Antonia de Spinola and calling themselves the Armed Forces Movement seized power in Portugal in April 1974 from the regime of Marcello Caetano. Although it was unclear in the immediate aftermath of the takeover what exactly the new rulers had in mind for the colonies (Spinola favored some form of federation whereas others supported total independence), in July, Lisbon announced it had conceded independence to the African territories. Essentially, this was Portugal's decision to negotiate any remaining conditions of implementation. It was preceded by a white backlash in Luanda against the Lisbon revolution and against African calls for independence. More importantly, the death toll in the colonial conflicts had risen sharply and the Portuguese economy lay in shambles. Many of the new rulers felt that any postponement or halfway solutions might lead them to repeat the fate of Caetano's self-defeating repression abroad and at home.

With the help of the Organization of African Unity (OAU) and a number of African states, Lisbon took an active role in trying to bring together the three liberation movements in order to prevent a civil war. In July, UNITA, MPLA, and FNLA agreed at a meeting at Bukavu in Zaire to form a joint front to discuss conditions of independence with the Portuguese, which may be regarded as the liberation movements' decision to negotiate. The need to unite to receive the prize of independence from Portugal was the major cause. Then, on November 25, the presidents of UNITA and FNLA agreed to hold joint negotiations on independence with Portugal and to cease conflict against each other; after discussions with the Portuguese high commissioner, UNITA extended the agreement to MPLA on December 18, 1974 and proposed a tripartite meeting on joint negotiation strategy. The meeting was held in Mombassa on January 5, 1975, under Kenyan President Jomo Kenyatta's auspices and led to the Alvor Agreement ten days later.

No direct constraint or applied power was used to bring the Angolan parties to negotiate. That had been done beforehand, and had failed; instead, the Angolans had effectively applied their own constraints on the Portuguese side, causing its internal collapse and bringing it to its negotiatory decision. Thereafter, the inducements offered to the Angolans were all contingent gratifications—promises and predictions of independence (requitement). No contingent deprivations seem to have been applied or implied except for the inherent warnings of continued stalemate if no negotiations were begun and no agreement was reached. Applied power had caused stalemate and one party's decision to negotiate; the others then responded to the promises and predictions of positive outcomes as intensified beforehand.

Yet despite the fact that the parties eventually signed the Alvor Agreement on a date for independence and a transitional coalition government, animosity between them prevailed throughout the subsequent six months. The parties did not so much decide to negotiate on a transitional government as to reach an agreement on independence that gave each the best chance to seize power in Luanda. The divisions and hostility had already been made plain in their independent cease-fires with Portugal: after the Portuguese unilaterally suspended military operations in Angola on May 19 to create conditions for a truce with the three movements, UNITA arranged a ceasefire on June 14; the FNLA signed on October 12 once they felt they had improved their chances of seizing power; and the MPLA, in the midst of a leadership conflict between Neto and Chipenda, signed an accord to suspend hostilities on October 21. Not surprisingly, the transitional government never functioned as a united body, and its role was very minor in the face of the growing civil war.

Decision to Negotiate the Lusaka Accord of February 16, 1984

In the 1984 disengagement and nonaggression agreement between South Africa and Angola along the Angolan-Namibian borer, the American mediator was crucial in bringing about the decision to negotiate (Zartman 1989, chap. 5; Bender et al. 1985). Since the arrival of Cuban troops in Angola in 1975, U.S. goals had centered on (1) the independence of Namibia from South Africa, (2) the withdrawal of Cuban troops from Angola, and (3) the promotion of a settlement between UNITA and MPLA in Angola. To attain these goals, the United States had tried to develop its greater leverage over Pretoria by concentrating on carrots and only later exerted any sources of pressure on Luanda that concentrated on sticks.

Pretoria's regional posture has been properly described as a "Jekyll and Hyde" policy. Since the end of Angola's and Mozambique's position as friendly buffer states in 1974–75, Pretoria attempted to create a friendly regional constellation through a mixture of aggression and cooperation, both military and economic. Pretoria initiated secret talks with Luanda in December 1982 on the Cape Verde islands over mutual withdrawals along the Angolan-Namibian border, after a decade of operations on Angolan territory, with most recent incursions in November 1981 and March and August 1982. U.S. mediation efforts toward the establishment of a truce failed in the face of the continuing Republic of South Africa (RSA) operations and South West African People's Organization (SWAPO) activity. A truce could bring only limited economic gains to Angola, and the Cuban troops that would continue to be a necessity for Luanda's security would be an obstacle to cooperation.

The situation changed during the fall of 1983. The South African Operation Askari was launched, and UNITA penetrated deeply into northern Angola, even threatening the area around Luanda. The MPLA government felt compelled to increase its dependency on Soviet and Cuban assistance and closed an important arms deal with the Soviet Union in January 1984. Meanwhile, in November 1983, South African Premier P. W. Botha won a two-thirds majority for his proposal for constitutional reform, which increased his freedom for maneuver vis-à-vis the obstinate right. Most importantly, now both parties had much more to gain from a truce than in 1981. Both economies were performing poorly; Luanda's security was acutely threatened, and it chafed under growing dependency on Moscow and Havana; Pretoria could afford some leniency after its military constitutional success and was still looking for ways to silence SWAPO.

In December 1983, U.S. Assistant Secretary of State Chester Crocker, alarmed about the rumors of the new Angolan-Soviet arms deal, persuaded Foreign Minister Rolf Botha in Rome to offer a cease-fire and a unilateral RSA withdrawal from Angola as a confidence-building measure and to demand mutual withdrawal and nonaggression (including SWAPO and UNITA operations) together with the withdrawal of the Cubans. Nevertheless, the real South African decision to negotiate for both can be found in January 1984. Only then were U.S. mediators able to convince Luanda not to exploit the cease-fire and to offer talks based on mutual withdrawal, nonaggression, and the independence of Namibia. Not surprisingly, Pretoria rejected the last clause, but its troop withdrawals continued, and conciliatory words about the future of Namibia were announced. One month later, both sides met and signed the agreement in Lusaka, Zambia.

The decision to negotiate was the result of power applied by both sides in the ever-intensifying conflict and a perception by both sides that they could continue the conflict at a lower, less costly level. This general perception made South Africa amenable to a suggestion that it promise to withdraw from Angola in exchange for an Angolan and SWAPO withdrawal from a no-man's-land in the southern part of the country. As in the Alvor Agreement a decade before, there were warnings inherent in the stalemate, indicating deprivations if a de-escalation were not negotiated but no explicit negative inducements—nor positive ones for that matter—outside of the terms of the agreement itself (requitement). Indeed, any additional sweeteners, such as Namibian independence or Cuban withdrawal, were specifically rejected by the two sides.

As in the case of Alvor, the Lusaka Agreement fell apart. The South African withdrawal was never completed, although much of the SWAPO force moved north. Instead, the agreement provided the springboard for wider negotiations on a full agreement over Cuban withdrawal from Angola paired with South African withdrawal from Namibia, which would become independent under U.N. Resolution 435. Although the terms of the agreement began to come into focus, the decision to agree never seems to have been taken by the two parties, and the talks collapsed when South Africa raided the northern-most enclave of Angola, Cabinda, in early 1985, even after Angola had come through with a negotiable offer. Only after four years, in 1988, was the Lusaka Agreement renewed and fully executed.

Decision to Negotiate Nkomati Agreement of March 16, 1984

Clearly the 1984 Nkomati Accords, a nonaggression treaty signed by South Africa and Mozambique, is a case of conflict management as opposed to conflict resolution (Zartman 1989, chap. 5; Bender et al. 1986). The conflict and acts of aggression continued afterward. Indeed, the basis of the conflict, the struggle against apartheid versus the maintenance of the apartheid state in South Africa and the struggle for and against an MPLA government in Mozambique, remain as unsolved as before Nkomati, and the economic and military warfare go on.

On the way to Nkomati, two periods and events stood out. First, since Mozambique's 1975 independence, Front for the Liberation of Mozambique (FRELIMO) had been in conflict with the RSA and Rhodesia in three ways—through guerilla attacks on Mozambique by the

National Resistance Movement (MNR), FRELIMO support for Zimbabwe African Union/Zimbabwe African People's Union (ZANU/ZAPU) and the African National Congress (ANC), and economic warfare. After the 1979 Lancaster House agreements that turned Rhodesia into independent Zimbabwe, the RSA took over and increased support for the MNR; FRELIMO started to concentrate on rebuilding Mozambique and on reducing its economic dependency on South Africa.

By 1982, it had become clear to the Mozambican government that this would never work without an accommodation with South Africa. It is here that one must look for the FRELIMO decision to negotiate. Crucial to this decision was the realization that the Socialist countries could not and would never provide the needed military and economic assistance, and that MNR and RSA military and economic warfare had destabilized the country politically and had forced it to move the needed economical reforms into a lower priority. Since 1982, Maputo successfully has turned to the West for economic aid and for pressure against the RSA.

In the fall of 1982, the RSA initiated talks proposing a nonaggression pact and promising new markets and investments. Yet despite Pretoria's rising trade deficit, economic crisis, and foreign debt, it did not seem to have made a serious decision to negotiate. It demanded the one-sided expulsion of the ANC, which it knew was unacceptable, and the effort collapsed. However, one year later, in December 1983, Pretoria again agreed to sit down with Maputo for talks on a wider range of problems and relations that would lead through a series of biweekly meetings to the Nkomati Accords. What had happened during 1983 for the RSA to make the decision to negotiate, was the additional Western pressure on Pretoria as a result of a Maputo campaign to convince the West that it was not a Soviet pawn and that its interest was not aided by letting South Africa turn a regional dispute into an East-West conflict.

Once again, the decision to negotiate, taken at roughly the same time by both sides, was the result of the pressure of reciprocally applied power in the mutually hurting stalemate, which led to a perception that it was possible to de-escalate the conflict and conduct it at lower cost to both parties. In the process, some elements of the conflict—reciprocal support to the National Resistance Movement (Renamo) and the ANC—were eliminated, leaving intact the underlying opposition between the two political systems. Based on this willingness to negotiate, the actual decision to do so was provided by contingent gratifications offered by both sides—the promise of economic benefits to South Africa by Mozambique and the promise of mutual support withdrawal for guerrillas and economic benefits by South Africa. There were no warnings except for the contingent deprivations inherent in a breakdown of the agreement and a return to a hurting stalemate and no explicit threats or sticks beyond the ongoing conflict.

Once signed in March 1984, the Nkomati Agreement was reaffirmed in new terms half a year later. Mozambique reined in the ANC but Renamo continued its operations with private South African support. Under this applied power, Mozambique met again with South Africa and Renamo thus formalizing the latter's position as a recognized party, a status not accorded to the ANC. Still the conflict continued with increasing intensity as Renamo found sources for supporting its guerrilla operations. In 1988, the two states met again to reaffirm the agreement; Renamo's applied power was no longer as interesting to South Africa as the predictably better returns from a more cooperative policy; carrots were available from the removal of sticks.

Decision to Negotiate the Vietnam Accords of January 27, 1973

Although the decisive progress to the 1973 Paris Agreement between Hanoi and Washington happened in September–October 1972 and after the December 1972 bombings and although the parties had been talking secretly for years, the crucial North Vietnamese decision to negotiate has to be found in the months of May and June 1972 (Zartman 1983, 5; Kissinger 1982; George et al. 1971; Szulc 1978). Only then had both parties made the decision to proceed seriously toward a negotiated settlement. This was preceded by a change in the U.S. view of an acceptable outcome from victory to a draw that was communicated by the Nixon administration at various times through 1970 and 1971.

The massive Communist spring offensive beginning at the end of March 1972 was essential in fortifying the perception of a stalemate. Effectively stalling the previous exploratory talks, the offensive resulted in the fall of Quang Tri and, more importantly, revealed the vulnerability of Vietnamization and weakening U.S. bargaining power. Nixon and Kissinger responded with a mix of methods to regain bargaining power and to coerce Hanoi into a settlement: sudden and massive escalation in the form of the bombing of Hanoi and the mining of Haiphong from May 8 onwards; new proposals that made the release of POWs no longer an a priori condition and the concession that Hanoi's troops could stay in South Vietnam after the truce; continuing withdrawals of U.S. troops; and "linkage diplomacy" with China and the Soviet Union.

The mixture worked. Between the visit of Soviet President Podgorny to Hanoi on June 13 and the first weeks of July, the Hanoi Politburo set a new policy that led from July 19 onward to renewed negotiations on the basis of the U.S. proposals. Clearly, Hanoi too had concluded in those three or four weeks that a military stalemate had developed. The November elections were perceived by Hanoi as a deadline on the assumption that after the elections it would no longer be possible to deal with Nixon. Furthermore, the costs of the war for Hanoi had increased after the U.S. escalations and after the weakening of the ties with its allies in the face of détente. Hanoi felt secure with its renewed military deployment in the South and saw an increase in the benefits of peace after the new U.S. proposals. Finally, the timing of the U.S. policy (after the spring offensive and Nixon's trip to China, during the Moscow summit, and before the November elections) was crucial as this maximized the pressure on Hanoi before its decision to negotiate.

The two decisions to negotiate must be analyzed separately. The U.S. decision was the result of power applied by Hanoi to make the continuing conflict costly. The United States then tried an assortment of threats and promises coupled with additional applications of military power "to call" but not "to raise." No longer trying to defeat Hanoi outright, the United States sought to induce it to accept the offers to negotiate on the basis of the contingent gratifications. The combination was effective in allowing Hanoi to bargain for outcomes that brought its goals within grasp at a lower cost than that provided by continuing conflict. Threats, and indeed coercion, made the alternatives to negotiation painful and reinforced the nature of the stalemate. Whereas normally the sticks are in the stalemate and the positive inducements are held out as part of the outcome to be negotiated, in Vietnam, additional sticks were piled on in the Hanoi bombings and Haiphong minings plus the undermining of Soviet and Chinese support to bring North Vietnam to negotiations.

The outcome was an agreement, but it was taken within the context of the U.S. decision to withdraw, and it left North Vietnam and the Vietcong in a position to undo it totally within the year and to complete the conquest of South Vietnam.

Decision to Negotiate the Lebanon Agreement of May 17, 1983

Israel's move into Lebanon in June 1982 was dictated by two essentially conflicting goals (Rubin and Blum 1987; Yaniv 1987). The first directly concerned the security of its northern border: its goal was the removal of the PLO and the partial retreat of the Syrian forces from Lebanon and the creation of a security zone south of the Litani River to be controlled by Israel and its proxy militia headed by Sa'ad Haddad. The second goal was to ensure the stability of southern Lebanon indirectly by working toward a stable, friendly government in Beirut that would sign and maintain a peace treaty with Israel. Both goals were complementary in that a strong Israeli position in the south was necessary in the absence of a stable Beirut government or peace treaty and provided leverage in the peace talks but conflicting in that the Israeli presence ultimately weakened the Beirut government. After the assassination of Lebanese President Bashir Gemayel in September this conflict became more pressing. The withdrawal of the Israeli forces and the need for a treaty gained importance in September 1982 after the discovery of the Sabra and Shatila massacre and after the first goal was essentially reached when the PLO was removed from Beirut in August and the Syrians were pushed back to the Bekaa valley.

The strategy of Bashir Gemayel was to drive back the Syrians with Israeli help and then secure a negotiated Israeli withdrawal. Bashir's brother and successor, Amin Gemayel, continued the policy of striving toward the removal of foreign troops from Lebanon but shifted the pro-Israeli orientation of his brother toward a more balanced policy, as became clear when he refused to normalize relations with Israel and communicated with Israel through clandestine channels during the last three months of 1982. Amin hoped to remedy his weak position by accepting U.S. support for his government and army and U.S. arbitration in the negotiations.

The decision of both parties to negotiate was taken around mid-September before the exploratory talks that followed Amin's visit to Washington in mid-October 1982. At this stage Israel was victorious, had reached its direct goals, and could thus hope for a strong bargaining position and the second Israeli-Arab peace treaty. Perhaps more importantly, the negative effects of the occupation were revealed with the publication of the Israeli government's Sabra and Shatila report and with domestic and international pressure (reaching its zenith in the verdict of the Kahan Commission in February 1983) growing more toward withdrawal.

Mid-September also saw the succession in Beirut of Amin Gemayel, whose lack of authority in the balkanized country necessitated negotiations and the acceptance of U.S. mediation. Thus Amin Gemayel essentially took a new decision to negotiate different from his brother's; his first goal was not the removal of Syria, normalization with Israel, or the surpremacy of Maronites but Lebanon's unity, national sovereignty, and the withdrawal of all foreign forces.

Finally, on September 1, 1982, President Reagan announced his Middle East initiative—linking progress on the West Bank with an agreement in Lebanon following the "successful" negotiation for the retreat of the PLO—and put pressure on both parties through diplomacy, the marines in Beirut, and withholding arms to Israel to reach an agreement.

Lebanon's decision to negotiate came from the power applied by the Israeli occupation and the continuing conflict involving Syrians and Palestinians on Lebanese territory; it was precipitated out of this context by U.S. promises to provide support for the Gemayel government and a favorable outcome through U.S. mediation. Israel's decision was necessitated by the favorable victory and the subsequent painful stalemate in which it found itself. Maintaining the occupation without a political agreement would turn victory into defeat, whereas converting the victory into an agreement would exploit its promise. Unfortunately, the assorted threats contained in Reagan's peace plan was directed *against* the very negotiation it sought to promote, making the Israeli decision most reluctant. In a word, the qualified decisions to negotiate on both sides were limited by the fact that power applied in the stalemate was not accompanied by sufficiently attractive promises of a satisfactory agreement. The outcome removed the burden of occupation from the occupier and the occupied, but the other benefits of agreement were illusory. The agreement was rejected by Syria and repudiated by Lebanon soon after it was signed.

Decision to Negotiate Cypriot Independence
Agreement of February 19, 1959

After failure of the 1955 Eden Plan and the 1956 Harding and Radcliffe proposals, Britain was under diplomatic pressure from the United States and its NATO allies to formulate a proposal for an independent Cyprus as finally put forward in the MacMillan Plan, and then to put pressure on Athens and Ankara to give in to the compromise (Attalides 1979).

Britain was one of America's most important allies. However, the growing military cost to secure Cyprus as a base (30,000 troops in 1958) combined with more general motives such as containment of communism (heightened by the Greek experience of 1947 and the Truman

Doctrine), U.S. anticolonialism (heightened after the fiasco of the Suez crisis of 1956), and U.S. pressure for *enosis* (or union with Greece, which would mean control over Cyprus by a country that was economically and militarily dependent on the United States) all pointed to independence. Thus London was pressured by the United States and its NATO allies to resolve the situation and ease the disputes between Athens and Ankara over Cyprus. Britain resisted self-determination and majority-rule (in effect enosis), and as a way to postpone its withdrawal and the transfer of its bases to joint NATO control, recalled the large Turkish minority (thus complicating the self-determination question). Ankara had already as early as May 1956 threatened to go to war over enosis; Greece, on the other hand, had promised NATO that enosis would be rewarded by additional bases in both Greece and Cyprus.

In the end, around 1958, the decision was made in London to change the colonial dispute into a more permanent and complex outcome of independence, by settling for two bases on Cyprus (accessible to any NATO country) instead of Cyprus as a base and by giving both Athens and Ankara influence on the island. For the Greeks and the Turkish it was a take-it-or-leave-it offer. Enosis was excluded, but the Greeks for the first time gained influence on the island; they feared that if they rejected the plan, London would withdraw to its bases and allow the Turks to invade and partition Cyprus. for the Turkish *taksim* (partition) was excluded but they were given an absolute veto over the future of the Cypriot government, and they agreed for fear that British (Labour especially) and American proenosis sentiments would be carried out. The U.S. pressure on Athens and Ankara probably worked because in those Cold War times both Greece and Turkey had been NATO members for only seven years (after much begging) and were highly dependent on U.S. economic and military aid. Thus the pressure was effective because the relationship was a very dependent one. In the negotiation process that led to the July 1960 Zurich-London Accords, the Cypriots did not take part effectively; essentially, the accord was a solution to a NATO problem.

As in many cases of successful negotiations, the decision to negotiate by all parties was the decision to opt for a second-best solution. And that decision, in turn, was prompted by the fact that the preferred outcome for all parties—a different one in each case—was blocked. Applied power brought the parties to a readiness to negotiate; contingent gratifications, in the form of a mutually acceptable—even if not absolutely preferred—outcome, plus some threats and warnings from the mediator brought forth the decision to negotiate. It is noteworthy that in this presentation of the situation the parties themselves had only enough power to block each other but not enough to elicit the positive decision to negotiate. To get that response plus a reinforcement of the stalemate constraints, they needed the mediator. The result was successful in the sense that a viable agreement was reached for Cypriot independence. That it fell apart before half a decade had passed was probably not the fault of the power applied to bring about negotiations or to find an agreeable solution but of lack of available power to make it stick.

Decision to Negotiate in 1963–64 Cyprus Crisis

Following the December 1963 unilateral declaration by Cypriot President Makarios to amend the Constitution in favor of Greek Cypriot majority rule (thus holding out the potential for enosis), intercommunal fighting broke out and Ankara threatened to invade. Britain and the United States proposed a ten-thousand troop force, but Makarios rejected any NATO mediation and peace keeping and instead appealed for Greek, Soviet, Egyptian, and U.N. assistance. He thus transposed the Cyprus dispute to the international level, introducing the foreign policy paradox of seeking non-NATO assistance to bring in enosis and, in the end, Greek and NATO control over the island (Koumoulides 1986; Bendahmane and McDonald 1986; Camp 1980).

President Lyndon Johnson sent a letter in June 1964 to Turkish Prime Minister Ismet Inonu to persuade him to hold off a Turkish invasion, informing him that NATO weapons, paid for by U.S. aid, were not for use in *private* wars and threatening not to help Turkey if the Soviets attacked in support of Greece. As a result, Turkey de-escalated the threat, but the U.S.-Turkey relationship was in ruins for years. Ankara sought a détente with Moscow to reduce its dependency on NATO and to win Soviet support in the Cyprus dispute.

By June 1964, Athens had covertly transported five thousand troops to Cyprus. Greece insisted with Makarios that the dispute should be handled at the U.N. level and refused to enter direct talks with Ankara—a clear signal of escalation to Turkey, which so-far had merely threatened to intervene. Washington responded with threats to Athens that the United States would stop assistance and not support Greece against a Turkish or Soviet attack.

The Soviet Union warned Ankara that it would assist Cyprus if Turkey invaded and would supply the Greek Cypriots with large supplies of arms. But after the Turkish foreign minister traveled to Moscow in a volte-face on the Cyprus issue and argued for Cypriot independence; the Soviet Union left its previous position in the dispute, shifted to the importance of better relations with Turkey, and the next year argued for a just solution for the Turkish minority.

Under great NATO pressure, Athens and Ankara agreed to talks in Geneva and, initially, did not reject the Solomon-like solution of the Acheson Plan: de facto enosis, a Turkish base on Cyprus, cantons for the Turkish Cypriots, and the transfer of the island of Kastellorizon from Greece to Turkey. According to Acheson, Makarios was the one who "threw monkey wrenches into the machinery," rejecting any such solution and arguing for an *unconditional* union with Greece. Makarios strengthened his case by negotiating with the Soviets over arms deliveries, gathering nonaligned support, and presenting plans for guaranteeing minority rights of the Turkish Cypriots before the United Nations. Cyprus was again recognized by the United Nations as an independent state in December 1965.

The decision to negotiate in the second Cyprus case was the exclusive result of a round of threats wielded by all the parties to block the original act of applied power that produced the crisis and also to neutralize everyone else's threats. The result was a total deadlock of all plans to change the status of Cyprus and, therefore, a negotiated return to the status quo, until Makarios found another way to upset it.

Decision to Negotiate in the 1967 Cyprus Crisis

As opposed to the 1959 and 1964 crises, the Greek, Turkish, and especially, Cypriot foreign policies had run a more independent course and Western leverage had decreased in 1967, when a new crisis and new Turkish invasion possibilities erupted over intercommunal fighting. This time, President Johnson did not threaten, as he had in 1964, to abandon Greece or Turkey if the Soviets attacked. Instead, he sent Cyrus Vance on a peace mission. Vance was successful in persuading the new junta in Athens to withdraw Col. George Grivas and the ten thousand Greek troops from Cyprus, resulting in less NATO influence over the island. The considerable U.S. leverage over the weak and newly established pro-Western junta in Greece was crucial to the decision.

During the four years following the 1964 crisis, both countries had expanded their military presence on Cyprus and President Makarios had followed a policy of controlling the island and consolidating its independence while never excluding enosis. The critical event preceding the crisis was the April 1967 coup in Athens. At first, the hard-line military junta continued the Evros talks with Ankara, but these talks failed in September in the face of the junta's preference for enosis. The junta was the main instigator of the November 15, 1967 attack by Grivas and the Greek and National Guard troops on the Turkish enclave in Kophinou, triggering renewed fighting and bringing Greece and Turkey again to the brink of war.

The success of the U.S. mediation and the Greek and Turkish decisions to negotiate and to agree to the proposals also depended critically on the emergence of a new junta in Athens, which overthrew the right-wing military after the failure of its Cyprus meetings. During a ten-day shuttle between Athens and Ankara in November 1967, Cyrus Vance managed for the third time on behalf of the United States to convince the Turks that intervening on the island was not in their or in NATO's best interest. Yet, the reason that Ankara agreed was not so much its willingness to listen to the U.S. warnings as the fact that nearly all its demands were met by the new junta: the withdrawal of Grivas and of all the troops in excess of the legal contingents. The new junta had barely any domestic support and was thus highly dependent on the United States, which could successfully press the colonels to agree to the Turkish demands.

Although they were consulted, the Cypriots did not play a major role in the negotiations. In fact, Makarios strongly opposed the dissolution of the National Guard. The Cypriots did enter intercommunal talks on a new Constitution between June 1968 and September 1971 as a direct result of the Turkish Cypriot declaration of a separate Turkish Cypriot administration. In the latter half of 1968, the parties were near a possible settlement, but Greek President Papadopoulos upstaged the Cypriots in secret talks with Turkey by demanding enosis and other tough concessions, thus forcing Turkish Prime Minister Demirel to reject the proposals and destroying the negotiation.

In the third Cyprus round, the Turkish threat countered the Greek act and created a stalemate, forcing a decision to negotiate. The Turks still felt—or were led to feel—that their threatened invasion would provide a more costly and ultimately less satisfactory solution than the return to a status quo ante that worked, and the Greeks were forced to recognize that an implemented Turkish threat could create a worse situation than the status quo ante that Athens had just destroyed. Thus the threats made the stalemate and made another previous outcome look attractive by comparison. However, the promise of that outcome was blemished by the fact that it had been destroyed twice since independence less than one decade before; although it looked relatively good to two or more sides, it did not look absolutely good, and indeed, the status quo ante was the very outcome that the various unilateral crises set out to upset. Cyprus had sticks but no carrots.

Decision to Negotiate the End of the Gulf War on August 20, 1988

The Iran-Iraq War was such a complete conflict that there is not even agreement on when it began (Bill 1988; de Young 1988; Fuller 1988; Preece 1988; Soudan et al. 1988). Iraq claims that the conflict broke into war on September 4, 1980, when the Iranian artillery bombarded Iraqi border villages after a background of Iranian subversion and propaganda against the regime of Saddam Hussein in Baghdad. For Iran, the war began two weeks later, on September 20, when Iraqi forces crossed the border and invaded Iran, bent on annexing territory and overthrowing the Islamic revolutionary regime of the Ayatollah Khomeiny. Fortunes swung back and forth across the once-settled border until 1988, when Iraq began to gain an upper hand, regain its territory, and press the Iranians beyond their ability to respond. By this time, both sides were exhausted but unable to make any of the concessions required even to start negotiations.

The world community led by the United States, feeling that victory by either side would be both impossible and undesirable, sought to use the United Nations when all other attempts at mediation failed. The Security Council passed resolution 598 on July 20, 1987, demanding a truce and threatening sanctions for noncompliance; Iraq accepted the resolution providing that Iran accepted. The decision was a safe one because Iran was uninterested in a truce. It was coming to the end of an Iranian six-year offensive that had built up a string of Pyrrhic victories that had not been decisive, and Khomeiny maintained his demand that Sadam Hussein be eliminated from power before any de-escalation. Iraq's acceptance of the cease-fire was thus further defiance of Iran, but it was also a willingness to call off an attack that had failed to hold any Iranian territory after seven years of war.

The Iranian decision to meet the Iraqi de-escalation offer was more complicated, although more detailed focus on Iran should not hide the basic fact that Iraq tired of the war and made the first move (much like the U.S. position in Vietnam). In 1987, Iran launched the last of its great "human wave" offensives, Kerbala 5; with fifty thousand Iranian dead and twenty thousand Iraqis, it may turn out "to have been the costliest ever fought, surpassing even Verdun, the Somme or Stalingrad" (Preece 1988, 7). Not only the loss made the battle for Basra the military turning point but also the fact that so much effort failed to achieve its—or any—goal. The other jaw of the deadlock was on the diplomatic front, where refusal of the U.N. resolution led to increasing diplomatic isolation, compounded by the failure of the devious U.S. ploy revealed as Irangate. Although Iraq was able to gain further armaments and renew its military arm, Iran was unable to replenish its old U.S. stocks, and because Iran's military arms was its young population, no replenishment was possible. Economically, too, Iran was on its knees because its military fortunes were tied to the falling oil prices of the mid-1980s. Thus there was no major offensive after Kerbala 5, and by March 1988, it became evident that there would be none and that the morale, manpower, and matériel of the Iranian army were all failing.

Instead, Iran turned to weapons of desperation, and Iraq turned on the offensive. The Iraqi attacks began in mid-April, and they gradually retook Iraqi territory from the Iranians. It was clear that the move was an "escalation to call" rather than an "escalation to raise" because the Iraqis did not try to move far into or stay in Iranian territory. Thus the Iraqi offensive only tightened the jaws of the stalemate. On the other hand, the Iranian move of desperation was turned against itself as a threat that proved the final clincher in the decision to de-escalate. At the end of February 1988, Iran revived the "war of the cities" by launching two SSMs into Baghdad after an Iraqi raid on a Tehran oil refinery. In the next six weeks up to the Iraqi offensive, Iraq responded with 174 surface-to-surface missiles (SSMs) to Iran's 67. Then when Iraq resumed its offensive in mid-1988, reports again arose about its use of chemical weapons, repeating verified uses in 1984, 1986, and 1987; on July 1, Iraq admitted their use. The combination of missiles on civilian targets and the use of poison gas gave Iraq a terrifying threat over Iran, without ever having to mention it explicitly. Tehran, which had already lost several thousand people who fled homes that they felt Iran could not defend, now faced the threat of chemical missiles. On July 17, Saddam Hussein called for negotiations and "an honorable peace"; on the following day, Iran accepted resolution 598.

The dual decision to de-escalate and negotiate was not immediately implemented. Iraq was skeptical, but it increased its offensive in order to take as many prisoners as possible to equalize the numbers of captives and to strengthen its bargaining position. To reinforce its message of an "escalation to call," Iraq drove up to 40 kms into Iran and then withdrew, affirming that Iraq has no ambitions on the territory of Iran. Both Iran and Iraq accepted the cease-fire on August 8 to take effect on August 20 and to withdraw to their own territories under the verification of a 350-man U.N. Iran-Iraq Military Observer Group (UNIIMOG), with direct negotiations to begin in Geneva five days later.

Applied power led to the Iraqi decision and requitement followed by more applied power to close the stalemate. Beyond the military, diplomatic, and economic aspects of the stalemate, however, lay an Iraqi escalation to call and an Iraqi threat, both of which were effective in bringing about Iran's decision to negotiate. Crucial too was the U.N.-backed pressure for a return to a redefined status quo ante, the promise that made the threats work.

Decision to Negotiate in Afghanistan

The crisis over Afghanistan started in April 1978 when the Soviets virtually seized control after a pro-Soviet junta overthrew the Daud regime (Klass 1988). After a year and a half of bitter rivalry in the Afghan Communist party (PDPA) and increasing guerilla attacks by the opposing conservative groups, the Soviets, faced with a possible overthrow of a new regime in Kabul, sent in troops on December 26, 1979. This thrust brought the United States, which previously had followed a low-key approach and had recognized the pro-Soviet junta, into the conflict, resulting in the January 1980 Carter Doctrine and support for the resistance.

Formally, the decision to negotiate was taken by Afghanistan and Pakistan around June 1982, when the two, supported by Moscow and Washington, respectively, responded to the November 18, 1981, General Assembly resolution to start the "proximity talks" in Geneva mediated by Under secretary General Diego Cordovez. Kabul's main reasons to come to Geneva were its hope for recognition by Islamabad, its desire to retain control of the country, and its aim to split the cooperation between Pakistan and the Afghan resistance. For precisely that reason, Islamabad had hesitated to enter the talks, having seen the resistance regarding talks with Kabul as an anathema. Only on May 4, 1985, did Kabul and Islamabad finally meet in Geneva.

The actual decision to negotiate may be found shortly before and during the year 1987. Only after September 1986 did Kabul and Moscow begin to admit that the war was a "bleeding wound" and seriously start to look for initiatives to end the increasingly costly and futile conflict. On January 1, 1987, Kabul offered a cease-fire, which was immediately rejected by the resistance. In July, Moscow admitted for the first time that U.S.-supplied Stinger missiles were effective in the war, and Soviet TV showed for the first time pictures of the war around the city of Khost. Throughout 1987, Kabul and Moscow made extensive preparations to consolidate Communist control and to upgrade the legitimacy of Kabul. Lastly, during the summer of 1987, the resistance launched an extensive offensive, driving the Kabul and Soviet forces away from parts of the Northeast.

In October 1987, Moscow hinted to Cordovez for the first time about the self-determination formula, thus moving away from its previous position that it would withdraw only if an acceptable government in Kabul would be agreed upon. During the Washington summit this change was expressed by Gorbachev's offer of a twelve-month withdrawal timetable, essentially picking up on the 1985 U.S. pledge to stop all aid to the resistance when the Soviet withdrawal began. These openings led the next year to the February 8, 1988, announcement of a proposal by Kabul and Moscow for unilateral withdrawal of the Soviet troops and an independent Afghanistan and to the April 14 agreement in Geneva. Thus the decision to negotiate was essentially taken by Moscow somewhere between the resistance offensive of the summer of 1987 and the October proposals in Geneva.

In this evolution of events, the reason for the decision clearly has to be found in the stalemated war. Only in the fall of 1986 and in 1987 had the war truly become fruitless (the Communist forces only controlled Kabul and a few other major cities) and ever more costly for Kabul and Moscow. On the other side, the resistance continued to boycott the peace talks, but Washington and Islamabad agreed because their goals included bringing stability to the region in addition to removing the Soviet forces and the Kabul regime.

Afghanistan is another case of mutually hurting stalemate in which applied power blocked each party's grasp of its preferred solution. What turned this deadlock to negotiation was the ever-looming threat of a catastrophe, which like the stalemate weighed more heavily on the Soviets than on the Afghan rebels or their sanctuary. Interestingly, there does not appear to have been any specific threat, any explicit deprivation, or any sharp deadline or catastrophe. Linkage with INF and the Pushtu question were minor threats in forcing a decision. Moscow decided to de-escalate as part of the new awareness of Gorbachev's team and era; they came to power with the decision rather than coming to the decision in power. Requitedness, or the promise of an agreeable outcome provided by the United States and the mujahidin, was the complementary element in the actual decision. Yet even in the promised future, it was more and more apparent that the only agreeable part of the outcome to the Soviet Union was its own withdrawal not the situation it would be leaving behind.

DISCUSSION

The first task of analysis will be to separate the role of applied power from contingent power; the second will be to compare the role of gratifications and deprivations among the contingencies. The first will help establish whether and how parties are forced to decide to de-escalate, whereas the second will evaluate the comparative usefulness of carrots and sticks.

Applied Power

Like threats, measures of applied power are not very effective in establishing a long-term relation of trust, but as opposed to threats, do seem more effective in inducing the first decision for a negotiated solution to the conflict. On the one hand, applied power has been effective in inducing the narrowly defined decision to negotiate. The March 25, 1974, decision of the Soviet Union to stop all aid to the MPLA was one of the factors in the latter's agreement to negotiate with the other liberation movements and Portugal that led to the 1973 Alvor Agreement. The U.S. actions to withhold arms deliveries to Israel in 1982 and 1983 and to station marines in Beirut seem to have been a minor inducement to negotiate as compared to the strong Israeli position in Lebanon and the extremely weak position of the Gemayel government, but the moves nonetheless had some effect on the position of the United States as the accepted mediator. The 1972 North Vietnamese spring offensive and the May 1972 bombing and mining of Hanoi and Haiphong by the United States clearly helped to strengthen the U.S. negotiation position and tilt the cost-benefit balance against Hanoi.

However, applied power inducements have also had broader conflict resolution effects in various cases. The riots of Europeans in Luanda in the spring of 1974 helped tip the balance within the newly established Lisbon government to go ahead with full independence instead of solutions toward a federation. The 1981–82 operations of South Africa on Angolan territory, notably Operation Askari in the fall of 1982, made the MPLA government in Luanda realize that some form of condominium with the RSA was a precondition of its survival. Furthermore, the January 1984 arms deals between Luanda and Moscow effectively goaded the U.S. into trying to build a relation of trust with the MPLA.

The increases in both Washington's and Moscow's assistance to their respective allies in the Afghanistan conflict were of a different category. These measures of applied power did not induce the decision to negotiate by the United States or the Soviet Union but merely reflected prenegotiation period escalation and previously determined decisions to negotiate. Nonetheless, these increases in economic and military aid did play an important role in convincing the two states' clients (notably the Kabul government) to decide to negotiate, and they determined the nature of the conflict and the formula for resolution: that is, withdrawal of the great powers but not a solution to the internal Afghan conflicts.

In sum, in all the conflicts, applied power was required to create the hurting stalemate, the necessary precondition for de-escalation and negotiation to take place. Escalation was required before the decision could be made to de-escalate. But the question still remains, why not escalate further? What limited the last round of escalation, leading to a decision to stop, to de-escalate, or at least to "escalate to call" rather than "to raise?" Was it fear of the other party's predictable response, an internal decision about the costs of the escalation itself, or a sense of limits imposed by the system? A review of the cases indicates that it was above all the *cost of the current escalation* that led to an internal evaluation to halt the conflict spiral not the feared response from the other side and not the self-imposed norms of international relations. South Africa and Angola before Lusaka, the United States in Vietnam, the Soviet Union in Afghanistan, Great Britain in Cyprus, and Iraq in the Gulf were all overburdened in their current efforts and suffering under the difficulty of sustaining their latest escalation as a prelude to their decisions to open the way for negotiations. The Alvor and the Lebanese negotiations were even more extreme cases of the same effect. In Portugal, the effort of the war led to a collapse of the government, and in Lebanon the cost of victory was so high, and rising if Israel stayed on, that Israel decided to begin negotiations. Only in the cases of the Lusaka and Nkomati agreements could one say that international norms prevented the next round of escalations; South Africa could have thrown additional resources into the fight behind its local allies, and overthrown the governments in Luanda and Maputo, but the result would have been untenable, even for the pariah state of Pretoria. To these two exceptions can also be added the case of colonial Cyprus, where the norms of international relations made continuing colonial rule unacceptable. On the other side, only in the case of the Gulf war and the later Cyprus cases was the decision to negotiate induced by a fear of the other sides's ability to out-escalate or at least to raise another costly notch. It is, of course, true that in the main body of cases, the decision of the escalating side to de-escalate was induced by the ability of the other side to hold firm and to make that last, flawed escalation costly. But that is to say that it was the present response of the other side not its projected future response that caused the decision to open the way to negotiations. That decision, in sum, was caused by the cost of the current escalation, which turned it from an attempted "escalation to raise" to an actual "escalation to call."

Threats (and Warnings)

When evaluating the effectiveness and manner in which threats (volitional deprivations) influenced the ten cases, a clear distinction must be made between the effect and role of threats in the solution of the conflict and their importance for the decision to negotiate. If the cases are examined from the broad conflict resolution objective, the 1964 threat in President Johnson's letter—that the United States could be forced to not support Turkey against a Soviet attack if Ankara executed its threat to invade Cyprus—had a negative effect on the Cyprus conflict. The relationship with Washington was in ruins for a long time; within a year, Turkey established détente with the Soviet Union, thereby reducing both its dependence on NATO and future chances for influence through deprivative actions. There is a clear link between this threat and the 1974 Cyprus crisis in which Turkey unilaterally invaded despite international and congressional warnings not to do so. This suggests that such a severe threat can only be used once and does not contribute to a solution of any kind. Similarly, the U.S.-Soviet-Chinese linkage threat facing North Vietnam in early 1972 (including Podgorny's June 13 visit); the March 1988 threat to Pakistan by Moscow and Kabul questioning the Afghan-Pakistani border; and the U.S. congressional threat to Moscow linking the Afghan withdrawal to the

INF Treaty did not contribute visibly to any solution or long-term de-escalation.

However, a narrower approach that examines the effectiveness of threats in bringing about a decision to negotiate yields a result that is far more positive. Although its value is difficult to determine, the Podgorny visit and the risk of less Communist support for Hanoi seem to have been one of the major considerations for the North Vietnamese Politburo when it changed the means to establish its goal of a unified Vietnam. The Shevardnadze-Najibullah threat was crucial to Pakistan's decision to drop its demand for the establishment of a coalition government during the Afghanistan Accords of April 1988. The threat to postpone the ratification of the INF Treaty helped convince Moscow to accept the U.S. version of symmetry. The threat of Iraqi chemical missile bombings of Tehran was the final straw that broke the Ayatollah's will. Whatever the long-term negative effects of Johnson's letter to Ankara, the blunt measure was highly effective in stopping serious Turkish preparations for invading Cyprus. The crisis of 1964 is characterized by a myriad of threats. Next to the U.S.-Turkey threat, Johnson also threatened Greece with a decision to stop all U.S. aid and assistance in case of an attack, and the Soviet Union mentioned to Turkey that it would aid Cyprus if Turkey invaded. The result was that the crisis de-escalated rapidly until Athens and Ankara agreed to talks in Geneva in June 1964.

The 1964 crisis in Cyprus was unique in that threats were almost the only means of inducement, in a context in which both Turkey and Greece were highly dependent on the United States. When evaluating the effectiveness of threats, one should also consider the degree of dependency of the threatened on the threatener.

Whenever they were effective, threats tightened the jaws of deadlock, closing off further escalations and checking attempts to break out of the stalemate. At the same time, they also made the possibilities of negotiation appear more attractive, and, more specifically, made the second best look good by comparison.

It is more difficult to sort warnings from threats without turning to a more detailed content analysis of fact-to-face communications (Axelrod 1983; Druckman 1986). Nonetheless, even on the present level of analysis, it can be noted that warnings are generally implied in the breakdown of the negotiations at hand and were often explicitly referred to by the parties. Warnings of a worse situation, independent of specific threats to make it so, were often assorted with their reverse—

predictions of a more favorable situation if the opening opportunities of negotiation were seized.

Promises (and Predictions)

The division of power exercises into contingent gratifications and deprivations permits a very important conclusion about constraints to negotiation. Although stalemate, reinforced by applied and contingent deprivations, is a necessary condition for de-escalation, it is not sufficient. Parties are not bombed and beaten into negotiation. Equally important (and equally insufficient by itself) is the promise of a favorable outcome. Unless a way out is indicated, a promise of requitement, parties will continue to claw at the walls of stalemate no matter how formidable they may be.

The decision of the Portuguese junta to open negotiations before Alvor also opened the prospects of independence explicitly promised by the new regime if the nationalist movements could agree on a way to implement it. They, in turn, promised to cooperate in an independent government; their promise was not kept, but the promised independence took place anyhow. In the negotiations leading to the Lusaka Agreement, South Africa made some vague promises on the independence of Namibia. But the principal agreement was based on an exchange of mutual engagements to withdraw from the no-man's-land of southern Angola, contingent on the other side's agreement to withdraw. SWAPO and the Angolan army withdrew totally; South Africa did not. But the conflict was de-escalated to a less costly level, as predicted, based on a partial implementation of the exchanged promises. The same exchange produced an agreement at Nkomati. South Africa and Mozambique also traded promises (assorted with predictions) of better economic relations. But the major promise was the one that formed the basis of the agreement itself and provided the parties with a less costly alternative to the current conflict and a way out of their increasingly costly stalemate—the mutual withdrawal of support from hosted insurgent movements, contingent on the other party's withdrawal of support. Again, the promises were honored only in part. In Vietnam, promises by the United States to grant certain long-sought conditions of an agreement desired by North Vietnam brought the latter to the table and were much more powerful in producing that decision than were the negative exercises of coercion and threat. Later, coercion was crucial as the

Christmas bombing provided a reverse deadline that kept the parties on the negotiation course, but it reinforced rather than reduced the role of the promises in the agreement. In Afghanistan, the promise of reducing costs or of lifting the coercion and threats induced the Soviet Union to plan withdrawal; and the U.S. promise not to take undue advantage of the withdrawal to bring into power a hostile regime continued the de-escalation. The mujahidin were interested in the agreement for the promise of power that it contained, and in the end the United States (and the Soviet Union) withheld their promises not to aid their allies, turning them into threats to do so that almost undid the agreement. In the Gulf, the promise of peace held out by Iraq was reciprocated by Iran to constitute the agreement; without it, the war continued, facing further escalation. In the first Cyprus crisis, under the British, the promise of an end to the conflict made the second-best solution of independence preferable to all the parties' first-best but unattainable solutions, and the mutual promise was self-reinforcing because it made the outcome attainable. Additional promises—British bases, Greek and Turkish rights of surveillance, NATO guarantees—completed the package and made the agreement more attractive despite its second-best nature.

The cases also provide some tests and limits. In the two crises of independent Cyprus, the apparent opportunities perceived by the Greek Cypriots and the efforts of the Athens Greeks to realize them made both the status quo and the promises of any agreement recede to the earlier position of second best. The imperfect promises that made a new de-escalation and agreement look better again were only a mutual engagement to restore the status quo. That observation brings out the problem of the Cyprus negotiations: the uncertainty of promises and their importance in getting parties to the negotiation table. The remaining case brings the same message. The difficulty in bringing about a successful negotiation in Lebanon was not the weakness of the negative constraints—coercion and threats—but the uncertain attractiveness of the promises within the agreement. The Reagan Plan's "promises" were threats to Israel, and Israeli promises to sign a peace treaty with Lebanon were threats to Amin Gemayel (and, indeed, an implemented threat to his late predecessor brother).

An examination of the forms of power used to bring about de-escalation and to bring parties to the negotiation table has provided some very clear conclusions. Deprivations or negative inducements have their place but only indirectly. The initial decision to negotiate is usually brought about not by a constraint imposed on the other party forcing it to negotiate but by one's own failed escalation, rendered too costly to sustain because of the other party's ability to hold out. Threats are then useful in tightening the jaws of deadlock, making the stalemate more painful and future alternatives more attractive; warnings are implicit in the breakdown of progress toward agreement. But what is crucial to making the deadlock productive is the positive exercise of power to provide incentives to a better alternative, the prospects of requitement, and a formula for a way out of the costly conflict. Some carrots may be found in the lifted sticks of the deadlock, but they alone are not enough because they would only return the conflict to an earlier status quo; some "false de-escalation" agreements do that, maintaining the conflict but simply reducing it to a lower level of cost. For meaningful de-escalation to occur, promises or positive inducements (and predictions of a better future as well) are necessary. If the sticks are in the stalemate, the carrots are in the contract.

NOTE

1. I am grateful to Dean Pruitt for help in eliciting some of these ideas.

7

SUPERPOWER STRATEGIES IN EFFORTS TO TERMINATE THE WAR IN BEIRUT, 1982–84

JUERGEN DEDRING

INTRODUCTION

THE MIDDLE EAST PROBLEM has been in the forefront of international attention for so many years that it seems difficult to treat this complex confrontation as an issue in which aspects of ripening and de-escalation can be studied. However, the long and painful history of the Arab-Israeli conflict may be analyzed in ways that reflect the ups and downs in regional tensions and wars and even more so the fluctuating roles played by the dominant international actors, the United States and the Soviet Union. The world community has been following the events in the troubled Middle Eastern region, awaiting anxiously even the smallest signs of a reduction of tension and a de-escalation in the levels of hostile interaction.

As one focuses on the strategies employed by the two superpowers at various points in an ongoing international crisis, it appears worthwhile to relate the behavior of the powers in question at the level of multilateral interaction, in this case in the United Nations Security Council, to the regional and local levels of interaction. Put differently, one asks whether the actions of the two actors in the U.N. context were consistent with the positions that they took in the volatile stream of Middle Eastern events or whether the aims of the two powers—assuming they sought to improve the chance for an easing of tensions, for an end to fighting, and for an opening toward negotiations and peaceful settlement of the long-standing dispute—were incompatible with their actions in the ongoing violent battle. The possibilities for several incongruities among the policies of the superpowers and within the policy pursued or declared by each of the two powers are considerable: *in abstracto*, there might be discrepancies in principal as well as in practical terms about the various sides or stages of the Middle East policy of each superpower; further, there might be fluctuations in the policy of each power over time in addition to the well-known and always open rivalry between the two powers that seldom allows a common approach.

As the theme of this project indicates, questions of timing and de-escalation are central to the researchers' probing. Timing, in particular, is of great significance on practical as well as theoretical grounds. In abstract terms, the timing of moves to de-escalate a critical situation and to seek its termination depends unquestionably on the relationship between the adversaries. Beyond that, it is reasonable to assume that international factors ranging from the local to the global level and including the multilateral dimension of international organizations affect in varying ways the timing of principal and less crucial moves in the evolution of the crisis. Last, not least, depending on the particular domestic political system, domestic factors also impinge on the conflict and its resolution (see Husbands's chapter).

The complexity of these interaction and interrelation patterns is such that the timing variable cannot be viewed as a one-dimensional factor but needs to be conceptualized as a multidimensional, with different actors ordering their time scales differently and changing them in divergent rhythms and patterns.

Similar assumptions must be made about international patterns as they seem to apply in the context of Middle Eastern politics: these are multilevel and multidimensional and give rise to different stages of action, resulting in a highly complex web of linkages across several dimensions. This condition applies to the local powers, Israel, Lebanon, and Syria, and much more so to the two superpowers that are distinguished strikingly in permeability versus rigidity of the decision systems. Together with the dynamic nature of all these relationships, that situation makes for a dense labyrinthian environment within which the search for explanation or interpretation will be seriously hampered.

The Middle East problem has given rise to a stream of journalistic and academic writings, as exemplified by one of the most recent convulsions in that troubled region, the invasion of Lebanon and the occupation of Beirut by the Israeli Defense Forces beginning in June 1982 and extending until 1984–85. The period to be considered here is defined by two junctures in the U.N. Security Council's involvement with that issue. Twice within less than two years, the two superpowers, together with the other members of the council, were called upon to vote on an identical proposal for the establishment of a U.N. peacekeeping force in Beirut. The remarkable feature of this sequence of votes was that the two superpowers switched positions 180 degrees and, although the United States vetoed the proposal in June 1982, the Soviet Union cast a negative vote in February 1984. This reversal of positions and defeat of a crucial U.N. initiative on both occasions gives rise to the first question: Why did both powers reverse their initial positions radically? The second question flows from the first in that the cohesion of the policy or policies of each power integrating the position taken at the United Nations with the direct involvement in the conflict itself either seems to be missing or inadequate. One would assume that in dealing with an issue of global importance—and the Middle East definitely is such an issue—the decision makers on both sides would try to have a unified strategy that would not only be consistent within itself but would also advance the underlying aims of each country.

Furthermore, going by the declaration of support for the principles of the U.N. Charter and for policies of peace and cooperation that are frequently issued by the two superpowers, their sincerity and commitment to the aims and work of the international organization cannot be questioned. That is to say, one must assume that the U.S. and Soviet votes in the Security Council reflected fully the overall policies of both powers. A careful analysis of the various dimensions of their entanglement in the Middle East problem—as exemplified by the battle over Beirut—may help clarify the puzzle over why the superpowers switched in their positions and whether and how that fitted into their overall policies toward Israel, the Arabs, and the resolution of that conflict. The emphasis here must be on the context of the crisis as much as on its progression. Only by juxtaposing the two aspects of the problem will one be able to detect the reasons for the erratic positions seemingly held by the two superpowers.

THE U.N. SECURITY COUNCIL AND THE OCCUPATION OF BEIRUT

Ever since the signals became clear that the Israeli government had decided to take matters once again into its own hands with regard to the presence of Palestinian activists under the PLO in and around Beirut and commenced its farthest-reaching penetration yet of Lebanese territory on June 6, 1982, the Security Council placed on its agenda this new outbreak of violence and essentially spent all summer 1982 in a marathon round of sessions to get a grip on a rapidly escalating situation. Owing to the structure of the Security Council, it was unavoidable that the perceptions and objectives of the two superpowers would determine the outcome of the council's deliberations because the U.S. and Soviet involvement in all aspects of the Middle East has been, and remains, one of the basic givens in contemporary international relations (see Rikhye's chapter).

As the Israelis rapidly advanced toward Beirut, the Lebanese capital, the future of Lebanon and the PLO as well as of Syria was uppermost in the minds of those charged with the maintenance of international peace and security under the Charter. From the beginning, the Security Council showed unanimity in the call for an immediate cease-fire and a complete withdrawal of Israeli troops from the heart of Lebanon. When the president of the council, in his capacity as representative of France, at the 2381st meeting on June 26, 1982, introduced a draft resolution[1] sponsored by his delegation, it could be expected that, in view of the unanticipated advance of the Israeli military into Beirut and the worsening conditions for Lebanese civilians and Palestinian refugees, the Security Council's search for ways to bring an end to the violence and suffering would be very persistent. But the French draft resolution, reflecting the deep concerns of France as the former administrative power in Lebanon, ran into trouble from its Western ally, the United States. The draft resolution, twice revised, demanded an immediate cessation of hostilities throughout Lebanon and the immediate withdrawal of Israeli troops as well as of Palestinian armed forces from Beirut. It also expressed support for the full-fledged sovereignty of Lebanon throughout its entire territory and, in that connection, requested the secretary general to station U.N. military observers in the capital to supervise the cease-fire. The secretary general was also to study any request by the government of Lebanon for the installation of a U.N. force that would take up positions beside the Lebanese forces as the latter tried to restore their control over Beirut and its vicinity. When the president put his delegation's draft resolution to the vote, it received fourteen votes in favor but failed adoption owing to the negative vote of the representative of the United States. There is little doubt as to why the U.S. vote was cast against the establishment of a new U.N. peacekeeping force that would have neutralized the battle zone in Beirut and put an end to the bitter fighting between the dominant Israeli forces and the inferior Lebanese and Palestinian contingents.

It is indeed noteworthy that the choice of the most effective and least biased instrument for peace and security in the arsenal of the world organization fell victim to the hidden objections of the U.S. delegation because the American delegate only took the floor after the veto had been cast. The explanation offered by the U.S. representative was unconvincing and seemed to cover other aims that might have helped to shed light on the true policy line followed by the administration in Washington.[2]

Before one returns to the circumstances under which this decision was taken in the Security Council, one should consider the episode in early 1984 when, in a replay of the summer 1982 events, the French representative made another effort to create a neutral and effective U.N. peacekeeping function in Beirut after the steadily deteriorating conditions in the city and its vicinity that involved inter alia rising casualties and deaths among the members of a multinational force that had been set up at the initiative of the United States in early fall 1982. Without paying attention to the fatal developments in the Lebanese capital during a period of little more than eighteen months, it should simply be noted that a French draft resolution, already revised several times,[3] was finally put to the vote at the 2,519th meeting on February 29, 1984. Under the draft, the council was to call once again for an immediate cease-fire, to request the secretary general to install the Observer Group Beirut, a small number of United Nations Truce Supervision Organization (UNTSO) officers stationed on an emergency basis in Beirut in June 1982, and to monitor compliance with the cease-fire in the Beirut area. The council was also to decide, in agreement with the government of Lebanon, to immediately constitute a U.N. force composed of personnel furnished by member states other than the permanent members of the Security Council. The draft further asked that member states refrain from any intervention in the internal affairs of Lebanon. After the French representative had introduced this text, the Soviet delegate announced that his delegation would cast a veto against the draft resolution because the French delegation had rejected the Soviet request for more time before the text would be voted on. In this tense situation, the council voted, and the draft received thirteen votes in favor and two votes against were cast, one of them by the Soviet Union (U.N. Security Council 1984).

Once again, an initiative that employed the best tool of the United Nations for defusing tension and de-escalating a conflict was defeated by one of the superpowers whose own priorities apparently conflicted with the thrust of the draft resolution. In this case, as in the first, one needs to study the context and the sequence of events before and during the time that the Security Council was dealing with the problem to arrive at a better understanding of why the Soviet Union reversed its vote of 1982 and switched to a position that defeated the initiative in the Security Council.

THE U.S.-ISRAEL RELATIONSHIP, 1982-84

The strength and intimacy of the relationship between the United States and the small state of Israel is well-known as well as self-evident. It is, however, equally self-evident that the interests and relations of a superpower reach much further and demand much greater discretion than those of a small state in the Middle East. It is also true that the stabilization of the area settled by the Jewish people in the Arab world has preoccupied not only the leaders of Israel but most other states and governments throughout the world. The Arab-Israeli relationship has long occupied center stage in world politics, and the events from 1982 through 1984 provide plenty of evidence that this preoccupation with the Middle East continues unabated—witness the uprising of the Palestinians in the Gaza and in the occupied West Bank since December 1987. Thus one must select from an abundance of data and events to try to bring out the particulars of the U.S. involvement in Israeli concerns.

Whereas the Carter administration could be considered sympathetic to the basic Palestinian cause, sympathy for the Palestinian movement diminished considerably with the arrival of the Reagan administration in 1981. As described and analysed in several articles (Binder 1985; Campbell 1983; Kreczko 1982–83; Mallison and Mallison 1983; Schiff 1983),[4] the focus of the new administration, which was spelled out by Secretary of State Haig, was exclusively on Israel and a new strategic consensus between the United States and its closest ally in the Orient. There is reason to believe that indications by the Israeli government under Prime Minister Begin and the new Defense Minister Ariel Sharon regarding growing Israeli restiveness about the increasing belligerence of the PLO cadres ensconced in Beirut and throughout the Lebanese territory were received with great understanding in Washington. But it is assumed that U.S. support for Israeli punitive operations was restricted to the southern part of Lebanon, which the Israelis had occupied in 1978.

It would add little to one's perception if one could establish more reliably whether the U.S. administration was informed in detail about the Israeli war plan, including the occupation of Beirut, or whether the Israeli leadership saw to it that the Americans were led to believe that it was merely planning to restore full control over the South Lebanese buffer zone to keep PLO cadres and weapons out of northern Israel. Once the Israeli troops had crossed the security zone and rushed further north, the U.S. government had opportunities to vent its displeasure in public and to cajole the Israelis through persuasion or threats to terminate the new war in Lebanon and to withdraw to the line that was commensurate with Israeli security needs rationally assessed and affirmed. Instead, the U.S. government was satisfied with words of mild disapproval and caution while it discreetly endorsed the Israeli plans.

After the onset of Operation Galilee, the U.S. administration was fully informed about the details of the Israeli strategy, and the U.S. representative in the U.N. Security Council joined the other council members in voting for several U.N. appeals for an immediate cease-fire. The decision makers in Washington concurred with the Israeli plan to expel the PLO forces from Beirut, if necessary to confront the Syrians on the soil of Beirut and in the Bekáa Valley, and to bring about a change of government in Lebanon that would result in an alignment, if not alliance, between the conservative Christian government to be set up in Lebanon and the conservative Israeli government under Begin.

Other aspects further strengthen this interpretation of American behavior during those critical weeks in Lebanon. While the U.S. policy makers refused to join the other Security Council members in a concerted and constructive effort to terminate the bitter fighting in and around Beirut, the planners in Washington were laying the groundwork for the Reagan initiative made public in the president's speech on September 1, 1982 (see Haass [1988], Kreczko [1982–83], Rosenbaum [1982–83], Siszo [1982], and Yaniv and Lieber [1983b]). This redefined U.S. plan for a comprehensive solution of the Israeli-Arab problem could not have been issued in the form it was presented had it not been for the successful execution of the Israeli plan to force the PLO cadres from Lebanese soil and for the success in bringing the young Phalange leader Bashir Gemayel to leadership in the new Lebanese government.

The main tenet of the U.S. proposal was the removal of the PLO as a party in the peace process and the notion that the Palestinians would accept living under Jordanian rule as a price for their freedom from Israeli occupation. What is striking in this phase of U.S. involvement in the Arab-Israeli struggle is not that American hopes for Jordanian and Palestinian willingness to consider the resumption of the Camp

David process were completely futile. There was indeed a slim chance that King Hussein would eventually take heart and embrace the U.S. initiative after soliciting enough Palestinian endorsement and Arab approval of such a new demarche. The truly astonishing feature in this episode is the blunt and unhesitating rejection of the Reagan initiative by the Begin government. Considering how much the U.S. plan had favored the Israeli side in the peace odyssey, it is still amazing that the Israeli leadership rejected the U.S. appeal for moderation, pressed its settlement campaign in the West Bank, and kept Beirut and half of Lebanon occupied, guided by an unrealistic vision of security in Eretz Israel. As the U.S.-Israel relationship showed, this was a case where the tail wagged the dog rather than the other way around.

The history of the next eighteen months from June 1982 through January 1984 is characterized by a deepening immersion of Israelis and Americans in the labyrinth of Lebanese politics. The Israelis pressed for an arrangement with President-elect Bashir Gemayel that would have clearly benefited the Israelis while burdening unduly the Lebanese side and refused in the meantime to withdraw from Lebanese soil. When Bashir Gemayel was assassinated very soon after his election (see also Barly and Salpeter [1984]), the Israelis exerted pressure on his brother Amin who succeeded Bashir in the presidency. The United States took it upon itself to provide protection and support for the Phalangist president and his weak cabinet and thus got drawn into the center of bitter rivalries and the religious, economic, and social ramifications of the clash of feudal lords and factionalism in Beirut and in Lebanon as a whole. The ill-fated multinational force, different from a U.N. peacekeeping force, was seen as partisan in the Byzantine world of Lebanese politics, as the United States also felt obligated to confront and attack Syrian positions in its pro-Gemayel campaign. The French eagerness to see a U.N. force established and its willingness to join the U.S.-sponsored multinational force is clear evidence that Lebanon could not survive without the active involvement of outside parties. There is no doubt that Amin Gemayel would have perished long ago had he confronted his domestic rivals and enemies without outside protectors. But there is also no doubt that the U.S. role in organizing the Western protective force composed of American, French, British, and Italian troops was bound to arouse deep hostility from various Lebanese factions, all of which rejected the U.S. linkage with the Israeli occupiers and the Phalangist enemies.

But the U.S. role in Lebanon during the years 1982 through 1984 must also be seen against the larger background of changing U.S. policies toward the Arab world. Ever since George Shultz replaced Alexander

Haig as secretary of state, the one-sided preoccupation with the political and military relationship with Israel has given way to a more diversified understanding of the Middle Eastern region that encompasses the crucial oil lifeline between the Gulf and the West and takes into account the deepening crisis in the war between Iran and Iraq. The U.S. balancing act of staying on good terms with the Israelis and a larger group of moderate Arab states at the same time became again a priority of U.S. statecraft. It comes as no surprise that such a difficult objective could not be implemented successfully.

The year 1983 reveals the rocky course that U.S. policy makers had taken when they sought to play the role of peacemaker and mediator in the multifaceted Middle Eastern politics. As they tried to draw moderate Arab leaders into the scheme of the U.S. peace initiative, they provoked the ire of both the Israeli hawks and the radical Arab states. Because the latter included Syria, which sought to resume a dominant role in the disintegration and reconstruction of Lebanon, U.S. policy was bound to collide with Syrian efforts. The year 1983 brought about a considerable change of political fortunes in Lebanon. Although in 1982 the United States had been able to establish itself in a controlling position over the future of Lebanon, by 1984 it had suffered major defeats at various levels of its military and political dealings regarding the critical issue of whether Lebanon would be controlled by Syria, by Israel, or by both.

It should be recalled that the U.S. Marines stationed in Beirut were struck by disaster when their quarters were bombed by either Shiite, Druze, or Palestinian terrorists on October 23, 1983, climaxing a period of growing turmoil in the worsening battle over the future of Lebanon. Although the U.S. government announced its determination to continue its military presence in Lebanon, it became clear at that juncture that the days of the U.S. presence in Beirut were numbered and that, sooner or later, under the impact of the widening chaotic conditions in Beirut and in view of growing demands by Congress, the U.S. troops would be removed from the dangerously exposed bridgehead in Lebanon.

The chronology of events after the attack on the marines depicts an accelerated deterioration in the U.S. ability to meaningfully affect the conditions in Lebanon. Once U.S. troops has been removed and stationed on U.S. ships off shore, the end of the U.S. role in Lebanon was signaled. Under these circumstances it was indeed desirable for the U.S. decision makers to substitute a new U.N. peacekeeping force for the U.S. troops as suggested by the French delegation in the draft submitted at the end of February 1984. Moreover, it also was seen as favorable to the aims of the Israeli leadership, which by that time had long abandoned the hope to control the Lebanese government and instead welcomed some effort to erect a *cordon sanitaire* in and around Beirut against the Syrians who complemented their newly gained political strength with a striking replenishment of their military capacity on Lebanese territory. Owing to the fact that the objectives and initiatives of both American and Israeli policy makers had encountered enormous obstacles in the Lebanese quagmire, the recourse to the international peacekeeping machinery was welcomed. It should be noted that the embattled Lebanese government under Amin Gemayel had long envisaged the stationing of a U.N. force in Beirut, but his reasoning was somewhat different from the American and Israeli calculations.

This short exposé of the main elements of the U.S.-Israel relationship in that crucial period helps to reveal the reasons for the otherwise seemingly inconsistent and erratic course of U.S. foreign policy regarding the defusion and de-escalation of the Lebanese crisis in 1982 through 1984. Whether the turnabout at the U.N. and in the Middle East was designed to terminate the conflict between the Israelis and the various factions in Lebanese politics or whether those startling moves derived from other policy objectives of the U.S. administration is a question that will be resumed once the relationship between the Soviet Union and Syria during those critical years in Lebanon has been examined more closely.

THE SOVIET-SYRIAN RELATIONSHIP FROM 1982 THROUGH 1984

Several basic givens stand out as one approaches the issue of Soviet policy in the Middle East and, in particular, the close relationship between the Soviet government and the administration of President Assad of Syria. As a superpower, the Soviet Union has always seen the Middle East as an area of foremost importance to Soviet policy makers. Moreover, it is self-evident that the Soviet Union, whose territory ranges close to the Arab world, would take a special interest in Middle Eastern developments because destabilization such as the Islamic campaign started by the new Iranian regime in 1979 and the turbulent events around Afghanistan must be perceived as threats to the future viability of the multinational Soviet system. The Soviet Union as one of the large producers of oil is less dependent than the West on the uninterrupted flow of oil from the Gulf, but the bipolar game of the two superpowers has a well-known dimension of rivalry in this resource-rich part of the world. Because much can be extrapolated from the pattern of superpower interactions worldwide, it is also fair to assume that action-reaction sequences occur frequently not so much because of a divergence of material aims but because stimulus and response are perceived as suspicious or even hostile when they come from the antagonist. In that sense, the U.S.-Soviet rivalry over the stakes in the Middle East is the result more of superpower antagonism than of concrete economic, military, or territorial goals. The basic policy of the United States has been to keep the Soviets out of the Middle East, and in response to that challenge, the Soviet policy has been to get a foot in the door and establish a concrete role in decisions affecting the future of the Middle East.

In view of these basic factors, it is possible to lay out the elements that provide the reasons for the Soviet-Syrian relationship. After the loss of the Egyptian connection subsequent to the deadlock and cease-fire after the Yom Kippur war in October 1973, when the president of Egypt decided to cast his lot with the United States, the Soviet link with Syria was its only steady tie in the quicksand of the Near East. The explosive dimension of the superpower entanglement over the October war, which brought them perilously close to a direct clash, illustrated to the Soviet leadership the inevitable risks to which any outside power would be exposed in the Israeli-Arab confrontation.

In the years leading to the Camp David Agreement of 1978 between Israel and Egypt, reduced Soviet policy options led to a precarious but determined embrace of the rejectionist front composed of Syria, Libya, and Iraq and to a solid backing of the rapidly emerging PLO. With these choices, the Soviet Union set itself up as a clear opponent to the United States in the aftermath of the Yom Kippur War. At the same time, it must be recognized that after October 1973 the Soviet approach was shaped by caution and risk avoidance in awareness of its inferior position in the Middle East. This caution applied in particular to the Israeli struggle against the PLO, the Syrians, and the Lebanese, the latter in particular suffering Israeli retaliation against Palestinian terrorist attacks. While the Israelis got ready to expand military operations into the heart of Lebanon and to wipe out the PLO as well as numerous Syrian contingents in and around Beirut, the hour of truth was rapidly approaching for the Soviet Union.

Recent studies (Spechler 1987, 115–43)[5] have strengthened the impression that the Soviet leadership under Breshnev was not meek and submissive but deliberately cautious in refraining from a direct or indirect response to the Israeli assault against Beirut. A review of the global situation then revealed a much more assertive posture taken by the U.S. government under Reagan since spring 1981 in a growing number of so-called regional conflicts and a decline in U.S. willingness to refrain from the use of force whenever its goals and objectives indicated.

The Soviet government was undoubtedly well advised not to take up the new challenge in Lebanon not only because it would not have been able to stay out of a major Israeli-Syrian war but also because a clash between the new U.S. government and the Soviet Union would have been likely and probably unavoidable. The Soviet reticence in approaching the critical situation in the Middle East was further due to a disillusionment with the Palestinians and the other rejectionists as useful players in the Middle East diplomatic encounter. Investment of Soviet military and political capital in the unpredictable fortunes of its Middle Eastern allies and protégés must have been seen by the Soviet leadership as unwise and thus as something to be avoided. The impression in Washington that Moscow was cowering under the threatening clouds over Lebanon and protesting only with words against the military campaign of the foremost ally of the U.S. in Lebanon was the price the Soviet leadership had to pay for its prudence.

The Soviet support for the French initiative in June 1982 was the complement to the policy of war avoidance. The Soviet decision makers also risked the displeasure of their allies in Syria by advising great caution and abstention from military clashes with the Israelis. The Soviet leadership must have been very uneasy as it held back its proxy in the terrible battle in Beirut and offered the PLO nothing but consoling words as it was driven out of Beirut and Lebanon.

Subsequent developments fully proved the wisdom of the Soviet policy of restraint. The Israeli forces got bogged down in a bitter urban struggle against Palestinian cadres and other enemies from which they could extricate themselves two months later only with considerable difficulty. The Soviet government, however, started quietly and rapidly to rebuild the Syrian armed forces, which had suffered major losses in numerous skirmishes with the Israelis. During a period where the Israeli military and political leadership together with the U.S. ally and protector were drawn deeper and deeper into the bottomless pit of Lebanese contradictions, the Syrians—and with them the Soviets—could prepare for the day after the Israeli and American withdrawal. Witnessing the growing dismay in both the Israeli and American publics with the conflagration and destruction all over Beirut and Lebanon, the Syrian and Soviet leaders knew that the massive involvement of Israeli and American troops was bound to come to an end.

Although the Syrians failed to engage the Israelis in any major way, they saw to it that the vulnerable American force was easily targeted and destabilized, safe in the knowledge that the United States would not retaliate against those assaults in any major way. A declaration of war by the United States was unthinkable, and massive bombardment of what were considered Syrian positions in the immediate vicinity of Beirut provoked disquiet back in the United States and, at the same time, achieved little in displacing the Syrians and their Lebanese friends and proxies.

By the end of the period under review, the Syrians had rebuilt their armed forces up to and beyond the levels of early 1982 and had gained a controlling influence over the political development of Lebanon, symbolized by the eagerness with which the Phalangist president sought to obtain the agreement or approval from the president of Syria. The Syrian dream to restore its historical territory including Lebanon had become a realistic option in spring 1984. The world could see that the military superiority and dynamic leadership that characterized the Israeli condition in 1982 had failed to penetrate the thicket of Lebanese rivalries and alignments and that by 1984 and 1985 the ability of Syria to play a decisive role in Lebanese and Palestinian affairs— in the latter case, the expulsion of the PLO from Syrian-controlled Tripoli was the key event— was fully restored and strengthened.

The decision of the Soviet Union to cast a negative vote against the renewed French initiative to establish a U.N. peacekeeping force in Beirut was a small gesture at the international level to the Syrian leadership that this veto was available to strengthen the Syrian hold over Lebanon. The hesitation expressed by the Soviet delegate in the Security Council when he asked for some more time from the French delegation showed that the Soviet government itself was not opposed to a U.N. force but that its Syrian ally demanded the Soviet veto. In that sense, the Syrian tail wagged the Soviet dog, offering a perfect parallel to the U.S.-Israel interplay. The losers, as in the first instance, were the people of Lebanon as well as the United Nations, once again ignored as an effective instrument in the maintenance of international peace and security (Dawisha 1982–83; Golan 1982–83; Hasan 1982; Hottinger 1983; Luard 1986; Neumann 1983–84; Olson 1984; Rustow 1984; Schahgaldian 1984; and Spechler 1987).

What lessons can one draw from this fascinating set of circumstances in which the superpowers switched sides and catered to the wishes of their proxies rather than to the mandate of the Security Council to seek a quick cessation of hostilities and to prepare the ground for a peaceful settlement of international disputes and situations?

THE SUPERPOWERS, THE UNITED NATIONS AND THE DE-ESCALATION OF CONFLICTS

The reputation of the United Nations, and especially its Security Council, in recent years can be measured by the number of times the organization is mentioned in the literature that was consulted for this chapter and by the frequency of errors or incomplete information about the deliberations of the Security Council when the council is mentioned. The picture emerging from such a review raises serious misgivings about the relevance and viability of the world organization for the superpowers and for the actors in the unending tragedy in the Middle East. It serves as one explanatory device that could expose the deeper reasons for the clearly inconsistent and contradictory policies and strategies guiding each of the superpowers in the crisis over Beirut. Why is it that the greatest powers of our time, committed under the U.N. Charter to guarantee and sustain the stability and peace of the international system and equipped with many powerful instruments to implement their priorities, not only have failed to apply their overwhelming power to extinguish another dangerous fire in the Middle East but, through their negative positions against peace-promoting initiatives, have exacerbated the critical situation?

The benign neglect shown by both the United States and the Soviet Union toward the peace capacities of the U.N. system initially grew out of the incompatibility of the ideologies and policies of the two powers as they vied and competed against each other in the simple framework of the Cold War. Strategies of each world power have been oriented toward denial and containment of the enemy. The decades of Security Council deliberations that have been dominated by this bipolar rivalry inevitably cheapened the tools with which the council was equipped in the Charter. By the year 1981, when the Reagan administration came into office, the Security Council had long lost the glamour of the original conception and states large and small felt free to accept or reject the will of the international community as expressed by the council.

It is no wonder that the new U.S. administration saw little use for the council unless it could be made an instrument of U.S. policy making, for example, during the early endeavors to bring about the release of the American hostages in Teheran or in the campaign from 1987 to 1988 to impose a unilateral arms embargo against the Iranian side in the war between Iran and Iraq. In that sense, it is correct to suggest that the veto cast by the two superpowers during the two related occasions was of little importance in the hierarchy of foreign policy objectives. As explained, neither power saw a need to justify its veto that blocked the consensus of all the other members of the council as they essentially exercised their prerogative. Had the negative decision been made at the highest level of the policy-making hierarchy, had it reflected principal and long-standing national priorities, their explanations in the council meetings would have been weightier. One cannot help but conclude that the opportunity offered by France, ally of the United States and friend of the Soviet Union, to protect the many suffering civilians in a once vibrant capital city and to seek nonviolent ways of resolving the clashing goals over the future of Lebanon and the future of the Palestinian movement was brusquely rejected. International law and the U.N. Charter contain numerous provisions for the pacific resolution of even intractable conflicts. The two superpowers ignored their special responsibility for world peace and instead sought short-term advantage in the confusion of Middle Eastern conflicts at the expense of the local population and the international community.

Can one reconstruct what motivated the American and Soviet decision-makers as they weighed the various options and likely consequences of their actions with regard to Beirut? For the United States, the de-escalation of the immediate confrontation was not of great importance as they shared with the Israelis the hope of driving the PLO cadres out of Beirut and, as the Israelis seemed to believe, into oblivion. I briefly touched upon the Reagan initiative of September 1, 1982, following the removal of the PLO troops from Lebanon. The overall thrust and the detailed scenario of the plan could not have been conceived without the execution of Israel's Operation Galilee, at least as far as its PLO dimension was concerned. Here, active opposition by the United States in the Security Council could be seen as inevitable and necessary to allow for its initiative of a comprehensive solution satisfying Israelis, Jordanians, and to some extent, also Palestinians on the West Bank and in the Gaza Strip. At the moment the U.S. plan was submitted and, even before, the chances to implement the plan were minimal because the PLO issue remained largely unresolved and neither the Israeli leadership nor the King of Jordan could be persuaded to endorse the U.S. plan. Realism was sorely missing not only in the defeat of the French initiative in the Security Council but also in the formulation and propagation of the Reagan initiative.

Ultimately, the United States lost severely in Lebanon and in its dealings with Syrians, Palestinians, and the Arab world at large and failed to educate the Israeli leaders to its point of view as to how peace could be achieved in the Middle East. Searching for intentions and strategies of the United States to de-escalate a big international conflict, one is left with the impression that U.S. foreign policy was ad hoc, short-term, and erratic. While the Beirut disaster was running its course, one opportunity to seek a cessation of hostilities by the interjection of an international peacekeeping force was rejected, and in its stead, a sharp escalation and expansion of the fighting was incurred. Inasmuch as the United States was and is a main player in the Middle East, it shares full responsibility for this outcome.

By February 1984, the signals were clearly pointing toward the emergence of Syrian hegemony over the remnants of a formerly independent and prosperous Lebanon. The Soviet Union saw a clear chance to assist its faithful ally in the extension of its effective rule over the future of central and northern Lebanon. Furthermore, the juncture of spring 1984 also offered an entry to the Soviet Union into the high stakes of the Middle East. Nobody could deny that with Syria's emergence as a potentially hegemonic power the role of its protector and supporter would also grow in status.

The interposition of a U.N. force as proposed by France would have hindered the hidden calculations of Syria and the Soviet Union about the likely power distribution in that part of the Middle East. It must be added that a redeeming feature, such as the Reagan initiative in the U.S. case, was not offered by the Soviet Union as a substitute for the rejected U.N. initiative. However, the resumption of full diplomatic relations between the Soviet Union and Egypt following the defeat of the 1984 French initiative for a U.N. peacekeeping force could be interpreted as an attempt by the Soviet Union to broaden its perspective toward the Middle East problem as a whole and to get involved in a renewed search for peace in the region through the revival of the idea of an international conference under the auspices of the United Nations in which the participation of the Palestinians would be settled pragmatically and not on ideological grounds. The evolution of the Soviet perception to that point took longer, but insight into the turbulence and unpredictability of Middle Eastern politics in general and the Lebanese situation in particular must have led the Soviet leaders to overcome the noncooperative orientation of the 1984 Soviet stance in the Security Council and to embrace a multilateral approach, thereby avoiding entanglements and defeats that had resulted from undue commitment to and support for the dependent ally in the region.

In the final analysis, both superpowers failed to develop general strategies that could contribute to the de-escalation of the Lebanese crisis at two critical junctures in that period. They not only missed the opportunity to impose a certain stability and a modicum of peace in the heart of Beirut under the auspices of the United Nations they both missed the chance to exploit a period of violent change for the implementation of long-held basic objectives regarding international order and the distribution of power in the region. They even failed to see that their compliance with the wishes of their proxies ran counter to the international mandate for peace and security and to the maxims and priorities of their foreign policies as world powers.

CONCLUSION

A few issues should be taken up that have been raised in the introduction of this chapter about the theoretical assessment of this case. Although it is easy to locate the Lebanese crisis, a full-fledged conflict, at a point where a de-escalatory move was initiated for the first time, the actors from whose vantage point the timing of that initiative appeared appropriate and promising, did not include one primary party, Israel. Neither is there certainty about whether the two superpowers were persuaded of the wisdom of the Security Council move initiated by the French government. This complication in the context of the two efforts at de-escalation should be seen as the most likely explanation for the failure of those moves. Despite the fact that the conditions for de-escalation appeared highly malleable, both in the context as well as on location in the rapidly evolving tragedy in Lebanon, the timing calculations of those actors who could affect the escalating situation were not only not synchronized but nearly diametrically opposed, so that the chance for success was nil. The period in which the de-escalation move was repeatedly pursued covered nearly two years, with a great gap of more than a year between the two concrete initiations in the Security Council.

These elements directly impinged upon the choices made by the various parties: focusing on the Security Council, the French government failed to include not only the dissenting superpower but also the local proxy in its de-escalating effort, thus revealing a strong misperception of the reality of U.N. decisions of this magnitude. It follows that the French strategies, overwhelmingly supported by members of the Security Council, offered a poor match for the conditions that prevailed at those junctures both in the Middle East and between the two superpowers.

This assessment underlies decisively the conclusions based on the historical review of that period. If the French knew that first the United

States and then the Soviet Union would refuse to join the other council members, in line with the wishes of their proxies, their demarche in the council was unwarranted. The question remains unanswered whether the sponsors really could not have known that the representative of the respective superpowers would defeat the adoption of a modest measure that in no way would have prejudiced the outcome of the Lebanese war between 1982 and 1984. It should be added in light of what has emerged from this exploration that the assumption of the state as a unified rational actor that is prevalent with much research in political science must be modified considerably, at least as pertains to this fascinating case from the troubled history of the Middle East in conflict.

The review of the two instances in the recent history of the Security Council has borne out some of the theoretical considerations put forward at the outset of this chapter. Although timing strategies can be pursued and studied with relative ease in a straightforward dyadic relationship that involves possibly some third party as mediator, the density, complexity, and multidimensionality of a prototypical intractable multilateral conflict such as the Middle East issue are bound to frustrate the analyst as well as the decision maker. In such a confrontation, which is acted out on several levels, in different locations, and under forever changing conditions by a large number of interdependent, yet to varying degrees autonomous, national, transnational, regional, and local actors, the observer-analyst is not able to develop a consistent notion of timing that would have theoretical or practical relevance for the "absurd theater" of the Middle East. If the outside observer fails to make sense of this huge puzzle, how can one expect the actors themselves to rise beyond their own biased perceptions to an all-encompassing awareness that could then become applicable for all actors simultaneously? If nothing else, this short case analysis should entice the student of international conflict to delve more deeply into the special arena of multilateralism where timing for de-escalation is extremely difficult to define, apply, and accomplish.

NOTES

1. Draft resolution sponsored by France (S/15255/Rev. 2). Spechler is in error when she claims that the draft was sponsored by the Soviet Union.

2. See the proceedings at the 2,381st meeting of the Security Council on June 26, 1982. It is surprising to learn that the activities at the United Nations are essentially

ignored in many of the sources listed in the References. For exceptions, see the articles by Hottinger (1983), Mallison and Mallison (1983), Sauvignon (1984–85) and Spechler (1987).

3. French draft resolution S/16351/Rev. 2. The discussion and vote on this draft resolution is completely omitted from the chronology in *Foreign Affairs*.

4. The book by Bavly and Salpeter (1984), although one-sided and poorly documented, also offers interesting details about the relationship in the Reagan presidency.

5. The paper by Spechler (1987) is very detailed and most convincing as regards the Soviet relationship with Syria.

8

FURTHER EXPLORATION OF
TRACK TWO DIPLOMACY

JOHN W. MC DONALD

WHEN DISCUSSING THE DE-ESCALATION OF INTERNATIONAL CONFLICT, one normally thinks about decreasing the scope or intensity of war. When using the word *war* one usually means a state of armed conflict between nations. Today's world, however, is different because most conflicts are not wars, in this sense of the word, but conflicts that take place within national boundaries rather than across national borders.

Research has shown that in 1987 (Sivard 1987–88) thirty-six conflicts were going on in the world in which more than one thousand people were killed. What is fascinating about this grim picture, however, is that only four of these conflicts were cross-border wars (Iran-Iraq, Libya-Chad, Thailand-Laos, Vietnam-China). The remaining thirty-two conflicts were internal, inside national borders, and were either called civil wars or wars of independence, depending on one's point of view (Lebanon, Angola, Ethiopia, Nicaragua, Kampuchea, to name a few).

The United Nations Security Council is the forum that most nations appeal to when they have been attacked by another state. Different rules apply to internal conflicts, however. The Charter of the United Nations, mainly for reasons of national sovereignty, prohibits the United Nations from settling disputes that are going on inside national jurisdictions.

ARTICLE 2, paragraph 7 of the Charter states, "Nothing contained in the present Charter shall authorize the United Nations to intervene in matters which are essentially within the domestic jurisdiction of any state or shall require the Members to submit such matters to settlement

201

under the present charter." This means that there is no international, intergovernmental institution in existence today that is in a position to provide advice, arbitration, mediation, or counseling services to the parties in dispute in these thirty-two countries. On occasion, individual nations have offered such political assistance, but such offers are usually rebuffed by the parties in power.

United Nations' agencies, such as the United Nations High Commissioner for Refugees (UNHCR), United Nations Children's Fund (UNICEF), and the World Food Program, or private international organizations, such as Cooperative for American Remittances Everywhere (CARE) and Church World Service, help enormously by providing economic assistance, such as food, shelter, and medicine, to some parties in conflict but only with the approval of the government in power. This assistance often reduces suffering in some quarters but does not help solve the basic causes for these conflicts.

Normal state-to-state or government-to-government diplomacy has shown itself, over the years, to be incapable of resolving the vast majority of conflicts in today's world. The resolutions that are "settled" are usually based on the relative power of the parties concerned and can become unsettled if power shifts. Currently, little effort is being made to reduce conflict by attacking the basic reasons for the conflict in the first place.

I believe that one greatly underutilized diplomatic tool that must be developed and used over the course of the next decade to first de-escalate and then to resolve international and national conflicts is the skillful application and use of Track Two (Montville and Davidson 1981–82), or citizen diplomacy. Track Two could become a powerful instrument for peace and change if its advocates focused particularly on those thirty-two conflicts that the world has basically ignored because they are internal crises and, therefore, not part of the world's global agenda. These conflicts cannot be ignored much longer, however, because of their de-stabilizing influence, their violence, and their potential flare into a cross-border war overnight.

Government-to-government, or Track One diplomacy, is power-based, formal, even rigid, official interaction between instructed representatives of sovereign states. Track Two diplomacy is a form of conflict resolution that is nongovernmental, informal, and unofficial. It is interaction between private citizens or groups of people within a country or between different people or groups from different countries, who are outside the formal governmental power structure. Persons involved in Track Two efforts have as their objective the reduction or de-escalation, of conflict within a country or between countries by lowering the anger, tension, or fear that exists, by facilitating improved communication, and by helping to bring about a better understanding of each party's point of view.

Track Two diplomacy should be viewed quite positively by Track One diplomats as a major tool in the world's search for peace and the de-escalation of conflict because it is more flexible, less structured, more innovative, and more deniable if it does not work. Unfortunately, Track One usually ignores Track Two completely or denigrates its efforts as ineffective and a waste of Track One's time. This reaction is unfortunate because much good can emerge from planned interactions between Track One and Track Two. Track One should recognize that Track Two is not designed or intended to supplant Track One, so no threat exists. In addition, Track Two diplomats recognize that if they are truly effective in doing their jobs and succeed in reducing fear and anger between the parties, this will help Track One get to the negotiating table and begin to formally resolve existing differences.

One of the principal reasons that interest in Track Two in the United States has increased so dramatically in the past few years, with particular emphasis on U.S.-Soviet, Central American, South African, and Northern Ireland's problems, is that Track One is seen as ignoring or rejecting ideas that responsible private citizens believe should at least be explored by their government. These same citizens have often turned to Track Two out of a sense of frustration, believing that doing something is better than doing nothing.

One excellent example of this phenomenon has been the work of the Natural Resources Defense Council (NRDC). This U.S. private citizens' environmental group was frustrated and disappointed at the U.S. government's refusal to join a nuclear testing moratorium begun by the Soviets in August 1985. The U.S. government said the ban could not be verified. NRDC negotiated and signed an agreement with scientists from the Soviet Academy of Science on May 28, 1986, permitting on-site verification at three sites in the Soviet Union and three sites in the United States. Over the following year, U.S. and Soviet scientists set up and jointly staffed and operated three seismic monitoring stations in eastern Kazakhstan, some 120 miles from the principal Soviet nuclear weapons testing facility, and three similar stations in Nevada. The purpose of this agreement was to prove to the U.S. government that it was possible to verify a comprehensive or very low-yield test ban treaty (Garelik 1987). This Track Two action has been successful because the results have encouraged the U.S. government to reopen discussions with the Soviets on ways to verify nuclear weapons tests.

Track Two diplomacy is not a new idea in the United States. In fact, as Ambassador Earle points out in his chapter, things got so bad in the early days of the Republic that President John Adams, in 1799, pushed through Congress what became known as the Logan Act, which makes it illegal for a private U.S. citizen to negotiate with a foreign government. This law has never been enforced, even though it could have applied, for example, to Jesse Jackson's January 1984 visit to Damascus, Syria, to attempt the release of Lieutenant Goodman, an American.

Joseph V. Montville, who conceived the phrase "Track Two" in 1981, did not intend for the Logan Act to apply because his focus was on citizen-to-citizen diplomacy not private citizen to foreign government negotiations. Since 1981, the phrase has caught on and now is used to encompass an enormous spectrum of events that are taking place every day, all over the world, always outside of formal, government-to-government Track One interactions.

Because Track Two, as a concept, has been growing so rapidly, especially in the United States, a certain amount of confusion exists about its meaning and its usage. An effort is made here to redefine Track Two by subdividing that phrase into four tracks to produce Tracks One, Two, Three, Four, and Five, and could now call the whole effort "Multi-Track Diplomacy."

The goal of this concept of Multitrack Diplomacy is to encourage Track One diplomats to move away from power politics, to open their collective minds and listen carefully and creatively to the new approaches and new ideas generated by the other four tracks. If Track One diplomats agree with some of these ideas, they should reshape their policies and become involved in these new approaches so that there can first be a de-escalation of fear and misunderstanding and finally, not just a settlement but a resolution of the conflict because the basic issues dividing the parties have been tackled, understood, and resolved.

Diplomatic efforts to de-escalate international conflict through multitrack diplomacy would be divided as follows:

Track One: Official government-to-government diplomatic interaction;

Track Two: Unofficial, nongovernmental, analytical, policy-oriented, problem-solving efforts by skilled, educated, experienced and informed private citizens interacting with other private citizens;

Track Three: Businessman-to-businessman, private sector, free-enterprise, multinational corporation interactions;

Track Four: Citizen-to-citizen exchange programs of all kinds, such as scientific, cultural, academic, educational, student, film, music, art, sports, and youth exchanges, to name a few;

Track Five: Media-to-media based efforts designed to expose and educate large segments of the population in conflict to the philosophy, ideas, culture, and needs of the other national, society, or ethnic group with whom they are in conflict.

As one moves further away from Track One, the ability to change Track One's thinking decreases. Conversely, the closer one gets to Track One, the more immediate impact one has on their thinking. If the proponents of each track learn to build on the track below them, they will gradually develop an enormous power base themselves. The proponents, collectively, will be able to force Track One bureaucrats to change their way of thinking into a more positive, problem-solving mode. If Tracks Two through Five are all working simultaneously in support of the same general goal, as is currently the case with U.S.-Soviet relations, then Track One is put under enormous pressure to reshape its thinking. It is indeed remarkable that the author of the phrase "The evil empire" had been to more summit conferences (four) with the Soviets than any other president in our history. Multitrack diplomacy played an important role in this connection.

A few examples of the work now taking place in the field of multitrack diplomacy may be helpful, keeping in mind that the basic goal of all tracks, separately or collectively, should be to reduce fear, anger, and tension between groups, tribes, cultures, or nations who are in conflict or on the edge of conflict, and to build understanding, hope, trust, and eventually friendship between the parties in conflict. All of these efforts are designed to bring Track One to the negotiating table to formally resolve the remaining issues that are still dividing the two groups.

TRACK TWO

This is the most difficult and the most sophisticated of the four tracks because it is the closest to Track One and is designed to identify the policy differences and the nonnegotiable issues that divide the parties in conflict and then try to impact their solution. This track is not for amateurs. It must be handled with skill, sensitivity, and confidentiality. Several outstanding ongoing programs should be mentioned as examples of what can be done.

The Dartmouth Conference

In 1959, President Eisenhower asked Norman Cousins if there were some way that he could arrange to get private Soviet and American citizens together to discuss U.S.-Soviet relations. He finally succeeded after eighteen months of effort, and the first such nongovernmental citizen-to-citizen meeting between these two great powers took place at Dartmouth College in October 1960. Participants change over the years, depending on subject matter, but these meetings have been taking place regularly, outside of the public eye, for the past twenty-nine years.

All of the expert participants on both sides have informal, unofficial ties with their governments, but they can act on their own and without formal governmental blessing or instructions. When they meet they exchange information and ideas, and each group knows how to listen carefully to the other side. In the 1960s, the idea of a renewed trade relationship was discussed, which paved the way for the 1972 trade agreement between the two countries.

In November 1983 at a meeting in Moscow, the Soviets indicated that a red line ran along the Syrian border, and if this were crossed by U.S. or Israeli planes, the Soviet-manned air defense forces in Syria would be activated. Word was passed back on the U.S. side and the red line was not crossed.

The Regional Conflicts Task Force of the Dartmouth Conference, chaired on the U.S. side by Hal Saunders, former assistant secretary of state for Near Eastern and South Asian Affairs, has been meeting for years with Soviet experts in spite of the fact that U.S. Track One policy has generally discouraged, if not forbidden, official discussion with the Soviet government since 1967 about their role in the Middle East. I am convinced that these Track Two efforts encouraged the U.S. government in the past two years to rethink its official position on the Soviet role in the Middle East peace process to the extent that the United States is talking once again about cochairing a Middle East peace conference with the Soviet Union.

UNA-USA

Beginning in the late 1960s, the United Nations Association of the United States and the United Nations Association of the Soviet Union have held yearly meetings in the United States or the Soviet Union to discuss, citizen-to-citizen, policy issues dealing with their respective views of the United Nations and the problems up for discussion each year at the General Assembly. This regular interaction has proven most useful over the years to both parties.

Problem-solving Workshops

Over the past twenty years, Dr. John W. Burton has evolved a theory about the resolution of deep-rooted conflicts that involve deep feelings, values, and needs that cannot be settled by an order from some outside authority, such as a court or a government (Burton 1987). He argues that most conflict is about the need for recognition and identity and that his Track Two problem-solving workshop provides the mechanism for dealing with these underlying conditions. The workshop brings five or six nongovernmental representatives from each of the parties in conflict together around a table with the interaction stimulated but controlled by a panel of five or six extensively trained and experienced facilitators. The facilitators ensure that there is no power bargaining, that there is a thorough analysis of the issues by the parties themselves, and that the parties come up with options that meet their own requirements. Two examples of the work that Dr. Burton and Dr. Edward E. Azar have carried out will demonstrate the power and potential of these policy-changing, Track Two, problem-solving workshops.

The Falkland/Malvinas Islands (Bendehame and McDonald 1986). In September 1983, one year after the Falklands War, John Burton and Ed Azar were able to convene for five days at the University of Maryland, British Tory and Labour leaders from the House of Commons and Argentinian parliamentarians, with facilitators, using the problem-solving workshop technique. In April 1984, they met for a second time. The makeup of the Argentinian team was different because of elections, and the chairman of the Foreign Affairs Committee of the Argentine Parliament headed this delegation. These were in-depth discussions, and the gradual building of a trust relationship took place. The British then visited the Falklands and Argentina. In February 1985 in a third meeting, the Falklands were represented. At this informal conference where the participants were meeting privately and on their own, they agreed on twelve points including an agreement to discuss "shared sovereignty." At the end of this last session, all of the participants were extremely optimistic that the resolution of this conflict was fast approaching. A few days later on February 27, 1985, the *Guardian* carried a major story about the meeting and printed the twelve points of agreement! One of the Labour members of the workshop, for domestic political reasons, had violated his sworn confidentiality and given the story to the newspaper. This publicity forced Prime Minister Margaret Thatcher to first deny and then oppose everything in those twelve points. There has been no progress on the Falklands since.

Lebanon. In May 1984, Burton and Azar (Azar 1986; Azar and Burton 1986) used the problem-solving workshop approach on the Lebanon conflict. They invited five Lebanese Muslims and five Lebanese Christians to come to the University of Maryland for five days. By the end of the first day, it was clear that the two groups were irreconcilably divided. The Muslims were convinced that the Christians wanted to divide Lebanon in half and have the southern half of the country become a part of Israel. The Christians, on the other hand, were convinced that the Muslims wanted to divide Lebanon in half and have the northern half become part of Syria.

After five days of sometimes angry and bitter interaction, and with expert facilitators, the participants were surprised to find that in fact they all had a common goal—they all wanted to keep Lebanon intact as a nation! With this basic issue decided, they agreed to work together toward this common objective.

In October 1984, the group met for a second time. There was one person on each side from the first meeting, for continuity. The other members were more senior representatives of the various sects. They started their discussion based on the previously agreed premise and spent their five days developing a total of twenty-two recommendations for action that would have to be achieved to reach their goal—to keep Lebanon intact as a nation.

These twenty-two points, taken together, could form the basis for a new Lebanese Constitution. Such a document will have to be adopted before there is peace in that war-torn land.

LANAC

The Lawyers' Alliance for Nuclear Arms Control (LANAC), mentioned in Earle's chapter, is another fine example of sophisticated Track Two, U.S. citizen-to-citizen interaction with Soviet representatives directed toward helping Track One make policy changes that would reduce the potential for international conflict.

Soviet-American Working Group

Historically, the leadership of the Soviet Union and, before the revolution, the Russian czars, resolved conflict, whether internal or external, by the use of force. Even Gorbachev, in 1989 alone, sent in the tanks and armed forces on four different occasions to try to resolve conflicts within the Soviet Union.

In May 1989, a small first step was taken in the Track Two arena that could have a long-term impact on this practice. A "letter of intent" was signed by three U.S. private, not-for-profit organizations (Search for Common Ground, the National Institute for Citizen Participation in Negotiation, and the Iowa Peace Institute), and three semiprivate institutions in the Soviet Union (Institute for the USA and Canada, Literaturnaia Gazeta, and the Soviet Peace Committee).

The parties agreed to establish a joint Soviet-American Working Group for the Analysis and Resolution of Conflict. The Working Group will undertake some or all of the following: to collect information; carry out research and analysis; conduct seminars; develop materials; sponsor training programs; develop evaluation instruments; develop conflict resolution models; and disseminate findings through meetings, reports, and publications. The Working Group will develop a two- to five-year plan and will explore the possibility of establishing a joint Soviet-American Center for the Analysis and Resolution of Conflict in Moscow. The potential for change here is enormous if the Americans can prove there are ways of resolving conflict other than through brute force.

On November 5, 1989, the agreement was signed in Moscow to create such a center, which will focus on internal Soviet conflict. Training will start in Moscow in March 1990. These examples of Track Two diplomacy give some idea of the diversity and the potential this diplomatic tool offers to Track One.

TRACK THREE

The private business sector has basically been overlooked as an instrument for change in the peace and conflict resolution process. In fact, business will probably be surprised to learn what a major role it is playing in the de-escalation of conflict.

Armand Hammer is, of course, a classic example of how a single citizen has been able to help keep the doors of the Soviet Union at least slightly ajar to hear U.S. voices over the decades. In the last several years he has played an important role in encouraging commercial interaction between the United States and the Soviet Union.

John Chrystal, a bank president in Des Moines, Iowa, is another living example of the role an individual can play over the years. Chrystal's ties to the Soviet Union go back to September 1959 when Nikita Khrushchev visited the Iowa farm of Chrystal's uncle, Roswell Garst. Chrystal has been to the Soviet Union dozens of times over the past thirty years and has always been able to do business with the Soviets. He brought back the news to Iowa in July 1989 that perestroika offered Iowa an enormous opportunity to do business with the Soviets in the field of agriculture. Soviet farmers lose 25 to 30 percent of their crops between the farm and the table, and Iowans can help solve that problem.

Another Track Three example is in the making in Iowa. In the summer of 1987, a group of concerned businessmen in Des Moines created an organization called Business for Peace. Over one hundred chief executive officers now belong. Their consensus statement says in part: war does not work anymore; the arms race must be halted; the number one item on today's foreign policy agenda must be multilateral disarmament. They state that business has learned that its own well-being depends on a global economy. They are currently negotiating with the Soviets to send a Soviet businessperson to live in Iowa, and they will send an Iowa businessperson to Moscow to live there. This arrangement is designed to stimulate business relations on a business-to-business approach outside the bureaucracy of both governments.

The multinational corporation community, long maligned by many Third World countries as being responsible for conflicts, has turned itself around in the past twenty years and is now a very constructive force in the broad development picture. As long ago as 1977, the International Labor Organization (ILO) completed a major research study in which it showed that multinationals have taken the lead in social policy in the Third World: their wages, working conditions, training and general employment practices are better and more generous than nonmultinationals operating in developing countries in all parts of the world.

Not only can the corporate sector help to stimulate economic growth and development it can also attack and help solve those economic problems that an existing conflict has caused and can begin to rebuild what has been destroyed. It is able to create new jobs, attract capital, and improve the standard of living in a community.

One of the most dramatic examples of the role of the private sector is that developed by Dr. Brendan O'Regan. His Co-operation North (Montville 1988), a joint Northern Ireland-Irish Republic organization, through research, consultation, and information exchange has been responsible for job creation, the establishment of joint ventures, business expansion, and trade in that troubled part of the world. He believes strongly that a positive work environment and a job for the individual, in and of itself, will help the peace process and de-escalate conflict.

In 1987, Dr. O'Regan founded the Center for International Cooperation, in Shannon, Ireland. This center, which has major corporate sponsors, aims to promote expanding economic relationships between the Soviet Union, Eastern Europe, and the West, as well as between individual nations and the Third World.

In April 1988, 500 American business people from 315 corporations, banks, and associations met in Moscow with 350 Soviet business people. An American trade consortium and a Soviet foreign economic consortium were formed, and 7 American corporations, including Ford and Johnson & Johnson, agreed to develop joint ventures (Alexeyev 1988). The opening of a McDonalds in Moscow will have an important position impact on the Soviet business community.

More will be done as business realizes it has a major role to play in peace building and the reduction of conflict. A person with a job, food, shelter, health care, and access to education and training is far more apt to explore future options in a peaceful way than to fight and die over those options.

TRACK FOUR

Citizen-to-citizen exchange programs with many countries have become very popular in the United States, with a particular upsurge in the past five years. Probably the best known and certainly one of the most popular exchange programs in our history has been the Fulbright Program, named after Senator Fulbright, who authored the bill in Congress that established the program in 1946. Since that time, some 24,000 American scholars and academics have lived and done research abroad under this program, and 25,000 foreign scholars have studied here in the United States. In the early years of the program most Americans studied in Western Europe. The Fulbright Program has truly been an outstanding example of citizen exchange because not only have the individual professors benefited but literally hundreds of thousands of their students have also benefited.

A far more modest and one-sided exchange has taken place over the last four years in a small town in northeast Iowa. A group of concerned citizens invited twenty young people from Northern Ireland to visit their community for the summer. What was of interest was that half were Catholic and stayed in Protestant homes whereas the other half were Protestant and stayed in Catholic homes. This has been a very successful learning experience for everyone involved in the project.

These exchanges are invaluable in their ability to change the perceptions and the way of thinking of one people about another people. The ping-pong team exchanges in the early 1970s dramatically humanized the Chinese in U.S. eyes and eventually led to a fundamental change in U.S. attitudes towards the People's Republic of China.

The Esalen Institute Soviet-American Exchange Program in San Francisco was one of the earliest and most effective in this field because of the high intellectual quality of the exchanges they organized. The Esalen Program has brought together U.S. astronauts and Soviet cosmonauts as well as scientists, physicians, and writers. In 1986, Esalen organized a tour of the United States by Abel Agenbegydn, Gorbachev's most prominent economic advisor, at the latter's request.

Neve Shalom—Wahat Al-Salam, the Jewish-Palestinian village in Israel, is another example of effective Track Four effort. The village demonstrates that two peoples can live together in mutual respect and peace. The village has a School for Peace that holds four-day workshops to train the youth of both faiths how to live together and value each other.

The Iowa Peace Institute has carried out a unique and highly successful experiment in Track Four. In December 1988, the institute brought to its headquarters in the town of Grinnell a Soviet family, Alexander and Olga Khomenko and their four-and-a-half-year-old daughter Xenia. The Khomenkos were provided a furnished house, a car, and money for expenses and, although they were both teachers of Russian as a second language, they were not given an opportunity to teach. Instead, they developed a slide show about the Soviet Union and traveled all over the state of Iowa for seven months, spending one week in each community, talking and answering questions about what it was like to be a Soviet. Iowa was fascinated with the family. They were interviewed by fifteen TV stations, twenty-nine radio stations, gave over fifty press interviews, and spoke personally to over twenty thousand citizens in the state. What they achieved that was so impressive is that they changed the face of the enemy in the eyes of the people they were in touch with. After all, the Soviet Union has been the enemy for over forty years, yet for the vast majority of Iowans these were the first Soviets they had ever seen, let alone talked to. They could not believe their eyes. "Why, they are just like us," was the most commonly heard expression. Hundreds of Iowans just wanted to come up and touch the Khomenkos. It was a remarkable experience for all concerned and proved yet again the power of citizen exchange.

Sometimes exchanges can take place over a two-year period and get started in unusual ways. In 1988, the Iowa Peace Institute hosted a group of Soviets for one week. One member of the group was the manager of a farm collective in the Ukraine and was most impressed with what he saw and learned about farming in Iowa. In February 1989, totally out of the blue, the institute received a letter from the farm manager directly inviting the institute to send fifteen young Iowa farmers to work on his collective along with Soviet youth for three weeks in August. The institute staff was delighted but skeptical because the manager said that he would take care of all expenses if the institute would get the young people to Moscow and back to the United States. This was glasnost in action! It worked. Nineteen young Iowa farmers, average age eighteen years, spent the most fascinating time of their lives in the Soviet Union. The Iowa Peace Institute hosted fifteen young Soviet farmers in 1990, following the same model.

It is impossible even to begin to identify the citizen exchanges taking place now or the Sister Cities programs that have been started in the past ten years because they are so numerous. Several successful programs come to mind as examples: the Peace Child Foundation, Ploughshares, Peace Links, International Peace Walks, the Center for U.S.-USSR Initiatives, Beyond War, the Center for Soviet-American Dialogue (Melnikov and Potapov 1988), and Chautauqua.

Citizen exchange programs and the continuing efforts to understand other cultures and ways of thinking are extremely important to the whole idea of multitrack diplomacy. In many cases, this is a citizen's first exposure to another country, to another way of looking at the same problem, and it can have an enormous impact on that citizen's thinking about the future. The vast majority of experiences are positive and usually stimulate a desire to do or learn more about the country visited. Exchanges of all kinds should be encouraged.

TRACK FIVE

Media-to-media-based efforts are the foundation stone for citizen-to-citizen diplomacy. This is where it all starts, at the very basic level of learning about another culture. The principal purpose of these media efforts is to humanize the "enemy." The media can demonstrate most effectively that the "enemy" is, in fact, a normal human being without horns or a tail or yellow skin (as in the case of the Japanese "yellow peril" of World War II). The resultant reduction in fear, anger, distrust, and misunderstanding can provide an educational base on which the other tracks can build.

"Spacebridge" television programs, developed by Beyond War and Search for Common Ground, Ted Turner's programs developed by his Better World Society, and Phil Donahue's broadcasts from Russia in 1987 and Israel in 1988 are just a few examples of the organizations that have been very effective Track Five innovators. Newspaper articles, magazines such as *Citizen Diplomat* and the April 1987 *People* magazine, as well as the various books on citizen diplomacy are impacting everyday thinking.

Ted Turner's CNN television network began to explore the concept of multitrack diplomacy in 1989. They developed thirty, five-minute segments separately, each focusing on a different area of national or international conflict, and the approaches that might be used to bring some resolution or at least reduction of that conflict. They aired these segments separately at the end of 1989 and in 1990 had a two-hour documentary combining these various segments. What is exciting is that a major television network is prepared to spend time and money to bring this concept of citizen diplomacy to the American public's attention. Certainly, the two-hour documentary will be picked up by other nations as well.

Yet another Track Five approach is being carried out by Louise Diamond, demonstrating that you do not have to be a multimedia giant to make an impact by educating a large group of citizens about a particular conflict. During 1989, she produced a one-hour documentary video film entitled "Many Voices, One Song: Everybody's Promised Land," which tells the human story of the Israeli-Palestinian conflict and explores possibilities for its resolution. The power of the video comes from the fact that it is the people who are talking not politicians. She interviews an extended Palestinian family on the West Bank and an extended Israeli family living in Israel. The interviews all took place in 1989 and reflect the fears and hopes and aspirations of the next generation in a very balanced fashion. Ms. Diamond took the documentary to

Iowa as a guest of the Iowa Peace Institute and during the last two weeks of September 1989 showed the film to hundreds of Iowans. She then led discussion about that conflict, always striving to build the knowledge base about that tangled and often misunderstood part of the Middle East. She plans to return to Israel and show the film to Israelis and Palestinians alike.

Track Five is a slow process and Americans are a very impatient people, but Track Five is essential if one wants to start the process of changed perceptions on a large scale. We did, after all, change our national perceptions about China in the early 1970s in two to three years. There certainly has been a shift in our attitude toward the Soviet Union since the 1985 Geneva summit. It is also fair to say that the Chinese and the Soviets think differently about us today. It is sometimes more difficult to change the attitudes of relatively small groups of people, like the Catholics and Protestants in Northern Ireland or the Tamils and Sinhalese in Sri Lanka, who are territorially linked, than it is to change the thinking of large populations like those in the United States and the Soviet Union who have not been "enemies" for such long periods of time and who are physically separated from each other.

GUIDELINES TO NEWCOMERS TO TRACK TWO DIPLOMACY

Because Track Two is the most difficult of the four Tracks and requires the most sophisticated diplomatic efforts, I have developed "Guidelines for Track II Diplomats" (1988) designed to help those individuals who are interested in seriously exploring the possibility of becoming involved in third-party de-escalation of ethnic or sectarian conflict. The guidelines are divided into four phases; each phase builds on the previous phase and should not be viewed as negative, oppressive, or restrictive. The phases are designed to focus the newcomer's attention on the serious nature of the subject. Third-party de-escalation is an extraordinarily sensitive, sometimes life-threatening issue, and requires extensive knowledge of the process. These guidelines should also prove useful to those persons interested in Tracks Three, Four, and Five because of the insights they offer to any prospective citizen diplomat.

Phase 1. Exploration of Subject and Self

If you are serious about this form of Track Two diplomacy you must become knowledgeable about the subject. The field is relatively new, however, and only a handful of books deal with citizen diplomacy. Become familiar with them and even discuss your interests with some of the authors, if possible. Inform yourself about the role of a facilitator and how that differs from an arbitrator, a mediator, or a Track One diplomat. Study intercultural communication and recognize that Americans have their own cultural biases. Be aware of what is possible and what is not possible to achieve in this general field. Know the difference between conflict management and conflict resolution and understand "win-win" compared to "win-lose" as well as the value of consensus. Become familiar with the literature on the art and science of negotiation, both at the national and the international level.

Once you are familiar with literature, take a look at yourself. Do you have some of the attributes that make a good facilitator? As a Track Three or Four person, you should at least be aware of these characteristics.

Compassion. Compassion, sympathy, enthusiasm, and the desire to want to help your fellow citizens are fine, in fact, necessary, but they are not nearly enough.

Patience. Americans are a very impatient people. Recognize that and do not try to impose your sense of time or schedule on an ongoing process.

Humility. Modesty and humility do not come easily to Americans, who often think they have all the answers to the world's problems. Recognize that you can learn from other nationalities.

Good faith. Honesty, integrity, and good faith are essential elements in trying to establish a trust relationship with all of the parties involved. This takes time to achieve.

Personal interests. Be careful of your own ego. Do not seek to advance your own interests at the expense of other parties involved. A facilitator should be neutral.

Know yourself. Are you a creative person? One of the strengths of Track Two diplomacy is that it encourages an innovative and unconventional approach to old problems.

Qualifications. There are no automatic credentials for entering this sophisticated field that, once met, make you a Track Two facilitator. Personal integrity, intelligence, expertise in related fields, extensive experience in cross-cultural dispute resolution, and common sense will all help to build your credibility. The building of credibility is a gradual and ongoing process and is essential to the establishment of a trust relationship.

Phase 2. Analysis and Involvement

Having passed through Phase 1 successfully, you now have to analyze your own interests and prepare your involvement in the Track Two process. The following points must be considered:

Focus. It is more useful to focus on one conflict and develop expertise in that area than to move from conflict to conflict. Try not to overload the channels of communication, however. Be aware that the Soviet Union, Northern Ireland, South Africa, and Central America are currently very popular Track Two subjects for U.S. citizens.

Communicate with others. No matter what conflict you want to focus on, remember, many have been there before you. Find out who they are, get to know them, learn from them. Perhaps you should join ranks and work together rather than going it alone. Others can teach you a great deal.

Knowledge of the subject. Once you have decided on the area you wish to pursue, immerse yourself in the subject. Read widely, identify the issues and the different points of view, talk to knowledgeable persons in this country, and become familiar with the history, religion, culture, mores, and even the language of the groups with which you will be interacting.

Develop a plan. Carefully think through your aspirations and your potential role, and then develop a written plan that identifies your goals and methods. Goals should be realistic and should be projected over a five-year period.

Define the process. Make it clear from the beginning that you are not speaking for or representing the U.S. government but that you are acting on your own or as a part of a nongovernmental group or institution.

Institutional support. Try to obtain some form of institutional support. Having the backing of a university or foundation or a nongovernmental organization will considerably increase your credibility and effectiveness. Free agents or individuals are discouraged by all parties.

Equality. Experience has shown that interaction among people of equal status is often more effective than when the disparities are too great. Equal status will also make access and credibility easier.

Agenda for solutions. A newcomer's agenda for a "solution" probably has been thought of and rejected years ago. Do not try to impose your solutions on their problems, but try to work with them to take small steps that may lead to their solution.

Commitment. Any conflict you may become involved in will probably have been going on for years or decades, if not for hundreds of years. Outsiders are often not welcome, and certainly, newcomers who arrive, wave the magic wand of their "solution," and then depart are even less welcome. Your presence must be seen as a commitment, which will take time, human resources, money, and patience. There are no quick, easy solutions left.

Timing. The timing of your initial entrance onto the scene is most important and should be carefully considered and coordinated with others who are operating in your subject area. It is preferable if one starts to become involved during a lull in the conflict, rather than when anger and emotions are at a high and intemperate level. You can afford to be patient to pick the right time because the conflict is probably an old one, and your entry is not going to resolve the conflict.

Phase 3. Follow-through

An understanding of the principles as well as the ethnical standards defined in Phase 2 are essential to your success. Now that you have started down the facilitator's challenging path, what are some of the specifics that you should recognize, if you do not want to abort your efforts early in the process?

Contacts. Well before you leave the United States, contact the parties concerned. They must provide you with some signal that they agree to your involvement and the timing of your arrival. Actually, the development of a joint venture, where all parties have equal status, will give the project more credibility.

Personal Safety. I recommend that on arrival in a country you advise the U.S. Embassy of your presence and the length of your stay. You might even call on the embassy political officer for a briefing on the current situation. This arrangement should not be viewed by you as an infringement on your privacy or a constraint on your freedom of movement but as a safety precaution designed to protect your person.

Promises-promises. Do not raise unjustified hopes in the hearts and minds of the participants about rosy conclusions to be reached, monies forthcoming, projects to be launched, and so forth. False promises and raised expectations are far worse than no promises at all.

Confidentiality. Off-the-record interactions are absolutely essential to success—this means no press releases, press conferences, speeches, articles, books, or media coverage about your role. Even if some modest success is achieved, it can be nullified immediately by premature, unilateral publicity. Confidentiality by all parties is critical to success. If progress is made, at some appropriate point a joint communiqué can be negotiated and released by all parties simultaneously. Unilateral publicity, by whatever party, is always destructive. This characteristic specifically would not apply to Tracks Three, Four, and Five.

Phase 4. Disengagement and Aftermath

Once you have completed a segment of your long-range goal, you must realize that no ethnic or sectarian conflict will ever be "resolved" by one event in the scheme of things. What are your next concerns?

Reentry problems. A Track Two practitioner must be particularly sensitive to what is known as the *reentry* problem. This problem occurs after the involved parties have left their homelands to participate in Track Two meetings designed to foster greater understanding and reduce fear and tension and then are ready to return to their constituencies and homes after the interaction is over. This return, or reentry, into what could be a hostile environment can be dangerous to the participants and must be carefully discussed in advance; the reentry must be well managed to ensure the minimum of danger to the returnees.

Handling of success. If your actions, over time, bring about some forward movement, some progress or small success in the conflict you are working with, you should, as appropriate, inform your government. You should not view this suggestion as a restraint on your efforts. The government representative you contact, either in-country or in Washington, D.C., may in fact be in a position to provide you with information or be of other help to you.

Costs. Track Two facilitators should operate on a *pro bono* basis at no cost to the participants. There should be no conflict of interest between the facilitator and the other parties.

Track One–Track Two relationship. The interrelationship between the two tracks can be a sensitive one. Track Two facilitators do not want to feel pressured or unduly constrained just because they happen to be exploring a policy that Track One opposes. Track One, on the other hand, likes to be kept informed about what is going on. Track Two facilitators must recognize that if their initiative is successful, Track Two will probably have to merge with Track One. It is governments, after all, who are responsible for negotiating, signing, and ratifying treaties and other formal documents that may be needed to seal a successful Track Two initiative.

CONCLUSION

The de-escalation of international conflict is not the end game of the peace process but really one of the first steps that has to be taken on the road to peace.

Effective use of multitrack diplomacy will destroy the need for an enemy, will identify the nonnegotiable issues, such as ethnic identity or religion, and can lead to the gradual building of a trust relationship between two peoples. When that happens, then Track One negotiations can formally solidify the agreements that have been evolving.

History shows that the most violent conflicts can be resolved. Franco-German rivalry began in the ninth century with the breakup of Charlemagne's empire and culminated in three major wars between 1870 and 1945. These two former enemies have now been allied for forty years. The creation of the European Coal and Steel Community formally started the Franco-German Alliance. This grew into the European Economic Community and has now bound those two ancient enemies inextricably together. Today's relationship was created through the effective use of citizen diplomacy in the decade following World War II and is probably the greatest success story that multitrack diplomacy has ever achieved. If peace can be achieved between these two enemies, then the skillful application of multitrack diplomacy to any conflict, including the thirty-two internal conflicts mentioned earlier, can bring about first, a de-escalation and then, an eventual resolution of that conflict.

9

PRIVATE INTERVENTION IN PUBLIC CONTROVERSY
Pros and Cons

RALPH EARLE II

A S THE YEARS GO BY, the world seems to be faced with an increasing number of international crises, minor and major, in which private negotiations are used, will be used, or could be used to de-escalate the tensions. That stated, several questions come to mind. How new is the role played by private negotiators? What success, if any, can these negotiators claim? What are the drawbacks? Have they hindered public, or governmental, policy? Finally, to what extent, if any, should private negotiators be used or permitted to act?

Before these questions are addressed, a working definition of private negotiations is necessary. In general, private negotiations include those interventions conducted by an individual or group that occur outside the purview of official government-to-government negotiations. Such actions include efforts by private citizens or groups as well as public officials or public figures to influence an international event or to exchange information that is relevant to a particular international crisis.

This definition is exceedingly broad, so in this chapter I will focus only on efforts by public officials and public figures. For purposes of clarity, I will explore the background and some relevant examples before the analysis and the conclusion.

Although recent events have shown increasing activity among public figures and public officials acting independently in international situations, this is not a new phenomenon, at least not in the United States. In fact, early in U.S. history such activity was of sufficient concern that the Congress passed and the president signed into law a statute that was designed to eliminate the role of private persons in international problems. This statute is known as the Logan Act.

In 1798, the United States was engaged in an undeclared naval war with France in which a number of Americans had been taken prisoner. George Logan, a private American citizen, traveled to France to attempt to secure their release.

While in Paris, Logan met with a number of French officials, including Foreign Minister Charles Talley; as a result of Logan's entreaties, the prisoners were released. When Logan returned, President John Adams denounced the "temerity and impertinence of individuals affecting to interfere in public affairs between the United States and France" (Kearney 1987, 294).

The next year, Adams proposed and pushed through legislation titled "An Act to Prevent Usurpation of Executive Functions," designed to forbid private negotiations in foreign governmental affairs. Originally enacted in January 1799, the act currently reads:

> Any citizen of the United States, wherever he may be, who, without authority of the United States, directly or indirectly commences or carries or carries on any correspondence with any foreign government or any officer or agent thereof, with intent to influence the measures or conduct of any foreign government or of any officer or agent thereof, in relation to any disputes or controversies with the United States, or to defeat the measures of the United States, shall be fined not more than $5,000 or imprisoned not more than three years, or both (U.S. Code, Title 18, Section 953).

However, President Adams's goals and wishes to the contrary, private activity in the field of international relations has not ceased. Today the Logan Act retains, for all intents and purposes, solely symbolic meaning because no one has ever been successfully prosecuted under its terms.

In fact, over the past two hundred years there have been many attempts by other persons to intervene in (and sometimes create) international crises. The results have ranged from successful to destabilizing, depending on the issue and the timing involved. Some, in fact, have proved both successful and destabilizing.

Consider, for example, the Reverend Jesse Jackson's 1983 excursion to Beirut where he successfully negotiated the release of the downed A6E bombardier Lt. Robert Goodman. After Reagan administration attempts to free the bombardier, downed in December 1983 by a Syrian

SA7 during a U.S. air raid of Syrian antiaircraft sites, had failed, presidential candidate Jesse Jackson prepared and executed his own agenda. He sent a letter to Syrian Foreign Minister Abdel Halim Khaddan offering to meet with him to discuss Goodman's release. In response, on Christmas Eve, Syrian Ambassador Rafic Jovejati invited Jackson to Damascus; two days later Jackson announced his intention to travel to Syria with a delegation as "an ecumenical body of ministers making a moral appeal" for Goodman's release (Coleman 1983).

The White House reacted gingerly: "At the President's direction, diplomatic efforts are now underway to secure Lt. Goodman's release. History has proven that efforts of this type have a better chance for success when they are not politicized" (Coleman 1983).

The following day, Sol Linowitz, U.S. envoy to the Middle East during the Carter administration, criticized Jackson's intentions, saying that he would "muddy up" diplomatic attempts to free Goodman and warned Jackson that he should allow "established government authority" to proceed without his intervention (*Washington Post*, December 27, 1983).

Jackson responded by stating that he was "simply making a moral appeal to [Syrian President] Assad to set the man free" (*Facts on File* 1983, 1975). As before, U.S. government officials proceeded cautiously saying, "We have no objections to private Americans seeking Lt. Goodman's release on humanitarian grounds; it is important however that there not be a plethora of negotiators and negotiating positions" (*Washington Post*, December 27, 1983).

On December 28, Jackson announced that he would not undertake the mission if President Reagan asked him not to. He added that the president had not been returning his phone calls. Reagan said later that the rebuff was an effort to avoid putting an "official imprint" on Jackson's mission.

Finally, on December 29, Jackson, along with fellow ministers, his sons, and journalists left the United States for Syria on a self-described "pilgrimage." Once again, the White House emphasized that Jackson was traveling as a "private citizen, not as a government representative. It is important that we don't send conflicting signals" (*Facts on File* 1983, 976).

Once in Syria, Jackson met with Goodman, members of the Syrian Foreign Ministry, and finally, with Syrian President Assad. The White House spokesman now reacted more sharply than before, saying, "There is a strong consensus that Syria is using Reverend Jackson to inflame American sympathies for Goodman's release on Syria's terms"; these "terms" included halting American reconnaissance flights over Syrian-held territory in Beirut (*Washington Post*, January 3, 1984).

On January 3, 1984, one month after Goodman's capture, Jackson accomplished his mission; Goodman was released unconditionally and unharmed and permitted to fly in an Air Force C-141 en route to Athens and then home, where he and his "rescuer" were greeted as returning heroes.

President Reagan, in turn, had nothing but praise for Jackson's "success." "Jesse Jackson's mission was a personal mission of mercy," he continued, "and he has earned our gratitude and admiration" (*New York Times*, January 5, 1984).

Others were not so kind. The *Washington Post* called his mission "lucky, mischievous, irresponsible, and an intrusion into sensitive foreign negotiations" (*Washington Post*, January 4, 1984). George Will branded Jesse Jackson "a political harlequin who is preoccupied with stunts and contemptuous of the national interest" (*Washington Post*, January 1, 1984). Interestingly, as recently as July 1988, when it was suggested that the Reverend Mr. Jackson might play a role in the release of some of the American hostages in Lebanon, presidential candidate George Bush denounced Jackson as a "loose cannon" (Bush interview on NBC-TV *Evening News*, July 28, 1988).

Other private negotiators, such as former Representative George Hansen (R-ID), have not been as successful in their missions.

In 1964, Hansen was elected to Congress in Idaho's 2d District. Hansen quickly established himself as a staunch conservative, earning a perfect 100 rating from the conservative Americans for Constitutional Action and a 0 rating from the Americans for Democratic Action. Although he had two unsuccessful runs for the Senate, he held considerable influence into the 1980s.

In July 1979, Hansen traveled to Nicaragua with fellow conservative Representative Larry MacDonald to meet with the dictator Anastasio Somoza. During their stay, they denounced the U.S. press coverage that had "distorted" his popularity and assured Generalissimo Somoza that the United States stood behind him. Such was not the case, and two weeks later Somoza was overthrown.

Again in November 1979, Hansen defied the wishes of President Carter and flew to Teheran in an attempt to win the release of the recently seized American hostages. While in the Iranian capitol, Hansen met with twenty hostages and gave round-the-clock interviews to an eager world press corps, but he returned empty-handed.

Members of the Carter administration attacked Hansen for inserting himself into matters for which he had no responsibility or expertise.

State Department spokesman Hodding Carter said, "It is not useful to confuse a situation already confused by raising a specter that there may be more than one voice negotiating for the United States government." White House spokesman Jody Powell said, "Hansen's activities have not been helpful" (*Washington Post*, November 27, 1979).

Fellow members of Congress frowned on Hansen's activities as well. Speaker O'Neill stated that "[Hansen] was out of bounds as far as a member of the House is concerned. As far as any deal he would make, he is not in a position to deal, that is for the United States government." Millicent Fenwick (R-NJ) called Hansen's trip "dangerous" and "irresponsible" (*Washington Post*, November 27, 1979).

Fortunately, Hansen's efforts did not prove significantly destabilizing, although they may have potentially been so. Other private interventions, however, have not been so innocuous. As stated previously, some private interventions can prove both successful and destabilizing as witnessed by the actions of representatives of Richard Nixon in 1968 and Ronald Reagan in 1980.

In the first case, in the fall of 1968, although presidential candidate Richard Nixon was leading Democrat Hubert Humphrey by over a dozen points in public opinion polls, the Nixon camp knew that the Democrats held a potential "trump card"—a cease-fire in Vietnam. They reasoned, probably correctly, that a cessation of hostilities in Vietnam would give Humphrey the victory.

In an effort to achieve such a cease-fire, President Johnson had directed a U.S. delegation led by Averell Harriman and Cyrus R. Vance to begin confidential negotiations in Paris with the North Vietnamese. At the same time, Johnson was seeking to assure the South Vietnamese government and its President Thieu that he, Johnson, in the face of widespread student riots and demonstrations across the United States, would not simply search for a way to withdraw unilaterally from Vietnam.

In early October 1968, Johnson had secured with President Thieu a joint statement of support for the negotiations. However, shortly thereafter, Thieu abruptly withdrew his support. According to Seymour Hersh's *The Price of Power*, Jack Valenti, one of President Johnson's closest confidants, reports Johnson as saying that "hard information had come to him that representatives of Nixon reached President Thieu and urged him not to accept" any last-ditch negotiations, suggesting that he would receive preferable treatment if Nixon won the election. Nixon was also using the U.S. press as a messenger to Thieu; columnists Joseph Kraft and Walter Lippman continually wrote that Nixon would be freer and able to do more to end the war than Humphrey (Hersh 1983, 17).

It is, of course, unknown whether Harriman and Vance could have reached a settlement in time for the election. But, if in fact Hersh's book is accurate and members of the Nixon campaign did interfere with attempts to stop the fighting in Vietnam and indeed may have contributed to prolonging U.S. involvement in Vietnam, some system needs to be intact and functioning that can monitor and prevent this kind of private intervention.

Twelve years later in 1980, a similar problem faced President Carter in connection with the American hostages held in Teheran. Then, too, it was a presidential election year and, like Vietnam during the Humphrey-Nixon race, the hostages and their fates were a crucial campaign issue.

According to Abolhassan Bani-Sadr, former president of Iran now exiled in Paris, in October 1980 the Iranian government was ready to negotiate with the Carter administration for the hostages' release. Bani-Sadr, in an interview with Flora Lewis of the *New York Times* said that following the Iraqi invasion in September 1980, the Iranians were desperate to restore relations with the United States in order to acquire spare parts for the many weapons purchased from the United States by the Shah. "We had only 5–10 days' supplies," he said (*New York Times*, August 3, 1987).

But in October, the preliminary discussions came to an abrupt halt. Khomeini made a new demand, which was later dropped, for a 24 billion dollar guarantee. Bani-Sadr claims he knows the reason for the turnabout: "My aides found out it was because the group in charge of hostage policy, Hashemi Rafsanjani, Mohammed Beheshti, and Khomeini's son, did not want Carter to win the election. There was a meeting in Paris between a representative of Beheshti and a representative of the Reagan campaign." In addition, there was a subsequent meeting in Washington, according to Bani-Sadr, of an Iranian envoy with three Reagan workers, Richard V. Allen and Robert MacFarlane, both later National Security advisors, and Laurence Silberman, subsequently ambassador to Portugal and now a federal judge. (*New York Times*, August 3, 1987).

Allegedly, in these meetings the Reagan representatives persuaded the Iranian government not to release the hostages before the November election and that the Reagan campaign would supply arms if the hostages were released later. As is well known today, the hostages were, in fact, released simultaneously with Reagan's inauguration.

It was subsequently learned that arms did start going from Israel to Iran in the first half of 1981. Bani-Sadr said there were three shipments before he was ousted in a coup in July 1981. Although U.S. officials have admitted that they knew about the arms shipments, it is unclear whether the United States was directly or indirectly involved. In any event, if Bani-Sadr's charges are true, it would mean that the private intervention of Governor Reagan's three agents resulted in months of additional incarceration for the hostages (and may have changed the results of the 1980 election).

All of these examples demonstrate that efforts at private negotiations are not new. Although some attempts have proven successful, this success has not always been in the interest of the U.S. government or in that of the people directly affected. It is also clear that, although there is federal legislation relevant to this issue, actions by private citizens are often difficult to monitor and, even when publicized, nearly impossible to prevent.

Having explored a small sampling of the private interventions in the past, it is time to attempt an analysis, more in the abstract, of the advantages and drawbacks presented by the use of private negotiations. First, a few words about my own background are appropriate.

I have spent a large portion of my professional life in the U.S. government. Most of that time, nearly ten years, was spent negotiating with representatives of foreign governments. That period included extended negotiations with Spain over the renewal of the U.S. basing rights agreement, more than three years dealing with U.S. NATO allies in Brussels, and almost seven years negotiating a strategic arms limitation treaty with the Soviets.

In contrast, recently, in a private capacity, I had the opportunity to travel to Moscow as a member of a delegation of American lawyers and meet over a period of ten days with Soviets to discuss substantive concerns currently formally at issue between the two governments in Geneva. Not only were the issues similar, but a number of the Soviets with whom we met were the same people with whom I had had previous official dealings.

As a result of these separate experiences, I have seen, firsthand, both government and private negotiations. It is on the basis of this experience that I compare the merits and demerits of private, as opposed to government, intervention in international controversy.

However, before such comparisons are made it is relevant to understand the structure of public, or government-to-government, negotiations. First, they are highly stylized—a pattern of behavior has been established and is maintained. Formal talks tend to take place on the same days of the week at the same hour and at the same location. Even the seating arrangements become codified: in bilateral discussions the sides sit across from each other with members of each delegation sitting in descending order of rank from their chief in the middle; in multilateral negotiations the parties sit around a table in alphabetical order from the chairperson (here even language can create a minor seating controversy, e.g., "United States" or "Etats Unis").

Second, official negotiations are not only physically stylized but also substantively stylized. Positions put on the table at SALT were always consistent with an implementing of instructions received from one's capital. All these instructions (at least on the U.S. side and presumably in the Soviet case) were a result of extended preparation, discussion, and negotiation within the bureaucracies.

In fact, in SALT I and SALT II whole committees were formed in Washington at various levels to deal with SALT issues: for instance, the assistant to the president for national security affairs, Henry Kissinger, chaired the Verification Panel, (whose membership included the Secretaries of Defense and State) created solely to deal with SALT. This microcosm of the bureaucracy, which also included the chairman of the Joint Chiefs of Staff, the director of the Arms Control and Disarmament Agency (ACDA) and the director of Central Intelligence, was then replicated on a slightly lower level in the delegation itself, where the same issues as decided in Washington were in Geneva reconsidered for implementation, and in certain particularly contentious areas, were redebated and, occasionally, renegotiated.

A third facet of the official negotiations and their conduct is the influence of outside pressures. As seen in the examples discussed earlier here and in Husbands's chapter, domestic politics play a major role in the formulation and implementation of international policy. This influence can be manifested in overt or covert fashion.

A clear example of this interaction was the impact of the Republican Right during the 1976 and 1980 presidential campaigns. It was clear in early 1976 that a SALT II agreement was achievable that year, but Ronald Reagan's challenge to President Ford forced the White House to defer progress. In 1980, it was again clear that the probable Reagan challenge to President Carter (exacerbated by the Afghanistan invasion) resulted in nonratification of SALT II and Carter's slowing of other U.S.-Soviet negotiations, including the Indian Ocean discussions and comprehensive test ban negotiations. Put simply, even the chief executive of the United States is restrained by public, political, and congressional points of view.

A final problem with government-to-government negotiations is their slow pace. This is particularly the case when many important agencies and people are interested, as in the SALT negotiations. There, it was not only ACDA that was involved on a daily basis but also the Departments of State and Defense as well as the Joint Chiefs of Staff, the intelligence community, and the White House; the problem was magnified because the chiefs of each of these agencies chose to be directly involved. Consequently, it was very difficult, if not impossible, to respond rapidly to Soviet proposals. Given the fact that Soviet responses were at least as dilatory as our own, it can be reasonably assumed that their bureaucracy was as cumbersome as our own.

One comment in favor of official discussions must be said: the positions taken have been thoroughly analyzed and considered; therefore, it is virtually impossible to "give away the store," or for the store even to be jeopardized. The other side is at least generally aware of the process of supervision and can, therefore, be confident that the U.S. stated positions are authoritative.

It is no secret that official negotiations can be slow, detail-oriented, and prone to influence by outside factors. Although these characteristics are not necessarily drawbacks (in fact, they are essential to some extent) their very nature does offer some advantages to more private negotiations.

First, in the absence of official formality, actors can often maneuver more rapidly. Free from the strains of bureaucratic infighting, private negotiators need only be concerned with the issue at hand. Because they are not official representatives of the U.S. government, they are not in positions to promise anything to those with whom they are negotiating. Additionally, less time is spent waiting to arrive at a common understanding.

Second, private intervention offers an ideal opportunity for information exchange—something that, when done on an informal basis among public figures on opposing sides of the table, can often facilitate more efficient and, therefore, possibly more effective negotiating when the actors return to their formal setting. I often say that no one can be taught how to be a good negotiator; however, one can be taught how not to be a bad negotiator. Private and informal discussions offer an excellent classroom with the prices paid for mistakes much lower.

Finally, private negotiations within public ones, although rarely successful, can offer the opportunity for a break from the formality, which can often lead to more comfortable, "off the record" discussions. Although it is important not to expect overnight breakthroughs from a "walk in the woods" type of discourse, such conversations can provide useful insights into where the other negotiator, free from the demands of official rhetoric, may stand.

I witnessed many of these advantages on a trip to Moscow. In May and June 1987, I spent ten days in Moscow as part of a delegation from the Lawyers Alliance for Nuclear Arms Control (LANAC) at its annual meeting with members of the Association of Soviet Lawyers. The American group included a number of former government officials, including a U.S. senator, State Department legal advisor, a Cabinet member, and a frequent official consultant on negotiations.

The formal Soviet delegation had few former officials but brought to our discussions as the occasion warranted the de facto chief of the Academy of Sciences, the head of their space agency, and the chief of their arms control department along with one of their principal representatives on U.S.-Soviet relations. In short, the two groups were experienced and knowledgeable but fully conscious that the talks were informal and without official status.

The principal issues discussed were clarification or amplification of the 1972 Antiballistic Missile (ABM) Treaty and its impact on planned and future testing of space weapons. The goal was to have an informed and objective dialogue about what is and what is not permitted in testing futuristic weaponry, such as lasers. The discussions were of particular interest and benefit given the controversy surrounding the Strategic Defense Initiative, the ABM Treaty, and the U.S. government rejection of Soviet overtures for formal discussions on the subject.

Whereas my government experiences had been, as noted, stylized, heavily instructed, influenced by outside pressures, and slow, our discussions over ten days in Moscow were quite different.

For example, most conferences become somewhat stylized, but this was not true of our Moscow talks. Americans and Soviets sat in an unstructured order, they seldom were in the same seat in consecutive sessions, and participants would, upon occasion, leave the table to carry on a private discussion at the back of the room. Moreover, because the Americans and the Soviets had not coordinated their respective "positions," the discussions were completely freewheeling, with almost as many intradelegation arguments and disputes as there were interdelegation differences. Part of this "freedom" stemmed from the fact that each delegate was on his or her own and had neither the duty nor the responsibility to represent and report to a senior entity or outside interest.

Another difference from my government experiences was the speed with which matters advanced. Either side could answer a question contemporaneously—we did not have to wait for months for a response; as a result, the discussions moved along rapidly. At the same time, comments and responses were obviously less thorough and, in some instances, quite superficial.

On balance, however, they were worthwhile as both groups acquired a better understanding of the relevant issues and the underlying facts, and each group came to understand far better the concerns of the other. Progress was made, which, conceivably, can help form a basis for more thorough and significant negotiations when the two governments agree to talk officially.

Of course, certain issues or negotiations are more receptive to these advantages than others. Of the three levels of private negotiation considered in this chapter—those among former public officials (such as myself), current government figures or representatives (Hansen), and private negotiations within public ones (Jackson)—this would most certainly seem to be the case.

International terrorism that involves taking hostages is one area where private actors have enjoyed some success, as exemplified by the Jackson case. It seems likely that this success is partially owing to the fact that private citizens cannot "deal" with terrorists and, therefore, cannot violate any set national policy. Unfortunately, as witnessed in the case of Terry Waite, such attempts are not without their dangers and are certainly not as simple as some might hope.

Arms control offers an area where private intervention can play a role but not one as tangible as that presented by Jackson. Public figures acting on their own behalf, as I experienced in Moscow, can facilitate discussion and increase awareness. These, in turn, can expedite the process when those actors return to a more formal setting. As previously stated, private conversations within public negotiations also can provide useful information when the players return to the table.

Finally, another area of international conflict in which private negotiations can play an active, if not visible, role is that of regional crisis, such as those witnessed in the Middle East, Central America, or South Africa. As in the case of arms control, such interventions can provide useful insights and contacts that can be put to use by the actors at a later date.

Whatever the advantages, there are serious drawbacks in private action that should not be overlooked. First, it is too easy for private negotiations involving public officials or figures to appear to be representative of U.S. policy. When that distinction is not drawn clearly and understood explicitly by the other players in question, long-term damage to U.S. negotiating posture can result. For example, although Representatives Hansen and MacDonald's inaccurate assurances to Somoza that he had U.S. support caused few problems in the short run, such actions often confuse and alienate foreign leaders who cannot appreciate why the U.S. government does not better control or monitor the statements of its "representatives." In the long run, distrust of official U.S. negotiators increases as the international community ponders exactly to whom they are to listen.

Second, and assuredly the most destabilizing form of private negotiations are those of the sort allegedly undertaken by representatives of Nixon and Reagan. National interest, for lack of a better term, does suffer when public figures intervene in ongoing official negotiations and turn the tide in their own favor for their own purposes. Such direct interferences are destabilizing on both an international and national scales. In the future, they invite foreign players to wait for the best offer—from whomever it may come. Domestically, they increase distrust and distaste for government in general. In the final analysis, no one benefits.

Based on the examples cited and my personal experiences, I offer these conclusions:

1. Private intervention in international controversy can, on occasion, be helpful in the short run but should not be approved as standard operating procedure.

2. Private intervention should, to the extent possible, be barred from application to major international disputes without prior government approval or coordination. A private individual can be used as part of a larger program (e.g., John Scali's role in the Cuban Missile Crisis, but compare Richard Secord's and Albert Hakim's roles in the Iran weapons scandal).

3. Skilled, experienced private citizens can, even without government sanction, be helpful in exploring major issues as long as there is *no* suggestion that they have official authority and they do not seek to reach conclusions.

4. Whoever undertakes to discuss important issues with representatives of foreign governments should be thoroughly familiar with the facts underlying those issues and should have made as objective an analysis as possible.

5. Such persons should also have carefully studied the views of the other side concerned and continually take that perspective into account.

Private intervention in international crisis is a phenomenon that will continue and may easily expand. If the U.S. government wishes to benefit from such activities, it must monitor them more closely, cooperate where appropriate, and take steps, as necessary, to prevent those that are undesirable for any reason, particularly those that have the potential to undermine U.S. international relations.

PART THREE

CONCLUSION

10

THE TIMING OF RIPENESS AND THE RIPENESS OF TIMING

JEFFREY Z. RUBIN

THE TROUBLE WITH SOCIAL SCIENTISTS is that they refuse to leave well enough alone. A new concept is introduced, enjoyed, and appreciated for a while, then subjected inevitably to the kind of close, critical analysis that causes the concept to dissolve before one's very eyes.

So it is in the case of *timing* and *ripeness* in the study of conflict. Here are two perfectly reasonable conceptual hooks—the former arguing for the importance of doing things in one sequence or at one point rather than another, the latter being so bold as to argue that there is a *right* time. Yet after months of study and careful analysis, in the collection of papers assembled in this volume we are in danger of concluding that the role and effectiveness of ideas about timing and ripeness "all depends" on certain circumstances. In other words, the very unusual and provocative quality about these concepts is about to be snatched away from us, almost before our very eyes.

Without a doubt, timing and ripeness are important concepts in understanding conflict. To dismiss either concept on the grounds that its place "depends on circumstances" is to do a disservice both to the field of conflict studies and to the concepts themselves.

To begin with the concept of ripeness: how bold and provocative an idea, arguing that, like the maturation of some fruit of the vine, there is a certain *right* or *best* moment to pluck a conflict or to wait—as one might do with a ripe Turkish fig—for it to drop into one's lap. To pluck the fruit of a conflict too soon is to risk the greenness that comes from insufficient motivation on the part of one or more of the interested parties; without the motivation to take their dispute seriously and to do whatever may be necessary to bring about a settlement, the disputants

237

are unlikely to engage in the exchange of views that can create a negotiated agreement. On the other hand, to wait too long, beyond some
point of optimal ripeness, is to risk finding that one or more of the
parties involved is by now so deeply entrenched in its positions that
little opportunity remains to reach agreement. Positions may have been
taken in Track One diplomacy, perhaps before the watchful eyes of
various constituencies and publics (as dutifully recorded by the media)
that are so extreme that their partisans believe they are now locked into
these positions, unable to budge without endangerment.

One of the most interesting aspects of Kriesberg's introductory
chapter on timing emerges in his discussion of possible "timing errors."
If we can agree that is generally wise to attempt de-escalation when the
timing is right and to avoid de-escalation when the timing is not right,
then that leaves the two other possibilities as potential "errors": failing
to attempt de-escalation when the timing is right and attempting de-
escalation when the timing is not right. Most likely, *neither* of these
actually constitutes an "error." Thus I believe in the existence of multiple "ripe moments" so that missing out on one now does not eliminate
(and may even make more attractive) the next opportunity. On the
other hand, there is no such thing as a "wrong time" to attempt de-
escalation. The worst that can happen is that no agreement results and,
perhaps, the disputants take a bit longer than they might have otherwise
to achieve the hurting stalemate that predisposes them to negotiate. In
some sense, there is a tautology here: a ripe moment exists, by definition, when efforts at de-escalation are successful!

Ripeness is a perfectly reasonable and helpful hook for understanding the nature of conflict. It suggests, quite correctly, that the life
cycle of a conflict—whether this be conflict between individuals, groups,
or nations—consists of blips and bulges rather than a straight line.
Conflict varies in intensity over time, and such changes in intensity
create opportunities for movement. To ignore the plausibility of such a
concept, and to fail to understand the opportunities and limitations it
implies is to miss out on a conceptual gold mine. The time for analysis
of ripeness is *now*.

As several of the volume's contributors point out, of course, ripeness can also be a trap. One side can turn to the other and justify its
own intransigence on the grounds that the conflict is not yet ripe for
settlement. Moreover, each side can successfully delude itself into believing that, if only it waits a bit longer, thereby allowing circumstances to
change more in its favor, then the *right* moment for movement can be
achieved. In his book, *Prisoner Without a Name, Cell Without a Num-*

ber, Argentine journalist Jacobo Timerman (1981) describes the dilemma confronting Argentine citizens who were opposed to the military junta but were also reluctant to "stand up and be counted" before the right time. Many of these people seemed to reason more or less as follows: "I've gone along with the government for so long that when the moment does come for me to stand up in opposition, it is important that it be exactly the right time. By continuing to work *with* the system, rather than in opposition to it, I can increase my stature and responsibility, thereby making it more likely that when I *do* intervene in opposition, I will be effective." This is the well-known rationalization that has led people for thousands of years to hesitate about "coming out of the closet." The longer they procrastinate, the more impactful will be their eventual emergence, or so they would have themselves (and everyone) believe; but procrastination begets further procrastination, and coming out of the closet eventually becomes all but impossible.

A danger inherent in the notion of ripeness, therefore, is that people can delude themselves and others into believing that tomorrow is better than today, even though this means trading off a present certainty against an unpredictable (and, therefore, possibly rosier) future.

Yet another possible danger is the use of ripeness as a club. "Look," the strategist argues, "the time to do something is *now*. The moment is ripe, and you'd better seize it. In fact, if you fail to do so, this narrow window of opportunity before us will disappear, either never to appear again—or not for a very, very long time." Many of the principals in the ongoing Middle East drama of the last several decades have proven themselves masters at this gambit. If we could have a dollar for each time that King Hussein, Yasir Arafat, Anwar Sadat, Menachem Begin, and many others have asserted (with a sense of great solemnity) that the ripe moment is now (and, by implication, not to come again until the next total eclipse of the sun!), we would all be considerably wealthier than we are.

Note that these arguments in no way diminish the importance or validity of the concept of ripeness. Rather, they make clear that the concept is of such shared significance that it invites use as an effective stratagem against others, as well as a device for fooling ourselves.

The primary difficulty I see with the idea of ripeness is that it implies a form of passivity that makes neither conceptual nor practical sense. If there really is a right, or ripe, moment to address a conflict, that might suggest that one must wait for this moment to arrive before moving ahead. But to wait for the right moment is often precisely the wrong thing to do. Rather, analysts and/or practitioners need to continue to look for ways of *creating* ripeness. If those tomatoes are not ripening fast enough to suit us, then perhaps we will just have to pluck them and ripen them artificially; they may not taste quite as sweet as they would have had they been allowed to ripen in the sun's natural rays, but this disadvantage is more than offset by the fact that we have seized control of nature and have helped it along to suit *our* needs and tastes.

Much of the analysis of timing and de-escalation in this volume assumes more of a passive, cautious approach than I believe either to be necessary or practicable. Thus, some of the contributors have argued that timing is purely subjective, and therefore, the time that seems right to one party may seem quite wrong to another. In response, these authors have tried to understand better the conditions that contribute to timing, be these conditions in the international environment or domestic considerations. Only if these conditions are favorable is the timing right for de-escalation of international conflict.

The challenge, however, is to *create* these favorable conditions rather than wait for them to appear. How, then, can one proceed to ripen artificially those vine-grown fruit? What hints along these lines are to be found in the pages of this ambitious volume?

First, as Zartman and Aurik and others observe, one can make judicious use of sticks and in this way bolster a decision to "come to the table." "Threats," they write, "are . . . useful in tightening the jaws of deadlock, making the stalemate more painful and future alternatives more attractive." The underlying idea, presented here and in other chapters throughout the volume, is that of creating a "hurting stalemate": an impasse that is so unappealing to each side that, rather than attempt to continue in its efforts to dominate the other, each prefers the alternative of negotiated settlement. Each side is, in effect, led to the edge of a great abyss, contemplates its broken body down below, then chooses negotiated agreement instead.

But if a hurting stalemate is one way to help create the ripe moment, then what does one do once such a stalemate exists? Here, too, Zartman and Aurik's observations are to the point. "What is crucial to making the deadlock productive," they write, "is the positive exercise of power to provide incentive to a better alternative." Thus, if sticks are to be used to lead the protagonists to a stalemate, carrots are there to show the way toward agreement.

The use of carrots, of course, implies that the purveyor of these rewards is in a position of some greater relative power—like the United States in the Middle East—and hence, has access to incentives that one or more of the targets of influence (in the case of Camp David, Egypt and Israel) finds attractive. A third method of creating the ripe moment also relies on incentives, except that these are in the form of information about underlying interests—information that, once exchanged, helps make possible new ways of moving toward agreement. The power here resides in the value of a good idea rather than the infusion of economic or military aid. Jack Sprat and his wife have a potentially intractable dispute, as long as each operates on the basis of *how much* of the meat each wishes to have. But as soon as the discussion shifts from how much to *how come* (that is, to the reasons underlying each demand), the parties discover that there is really no conflict at all. One wants fat, the other lean, and the rest of the story is history. The point is that ripeness can also be created by putting forward an idea (often represented by greater understanding of underlying interests) that makes possible the bridging of conflicting points of view.

A fourth approach to creating ripeness involves *inaction*, that is, deliberately deciding to do nothing. The passage of time often has the effect of changing elements in such a way that a new reality emerges, one that may make negotiation look more promising than before. If two sides are hurting, but not quite enough to take their conflict seriously, the passage of time may increase the cost to such a point that the equation changes in favor of negotiations.[1]

Yet another class of approaches that can be used to create ripeness involves pie-expanding solutions. Stated most literally, if each demands three-quarters of the existing pie, and neither is willing to budge, then this constant sum conflict does not easily lend itself to solution. But if some new pie can be found, increasing the resources under division by 50 percent or more, then each can have as much as he or she aspires to—perhaps even more. To be sure, not all conflicts lend themselves to this nonconstant sum transformation, but many do. In addition, there is always the matter of *where* these increased resources are to come from; it is here that third parties can often help.

A particular form of pie expansion deserves special mention because it is not tangible resources that are added but new analysis of an old problem. Often, protagonists find themselves locked in a stalemate because they have run out of ideas. They have each committed themselves to a belligerent, confrontational posture from which it now appears impossible to budge. Perhaps this commitment has been made in front of various observing audiences, thereby increasing pressures to avoid looking weak or foolish in the eyes of these audiences—in other words, to save face. Under these circumstances, the introduction of a "decommitting formula" can make all the difference. As described by Pruitt and Rubin (1986), this formula transforms a conflict by defining it in different terms.[2] In so doing, the basis is created for moving out of stalemate toward a settlement of differences.

Yet another important, if neglected, way of creating a ripe moment is through the systematic extraction of small, constructive, and irreversible commitments. If parties in a stalemate—hurting or otherwise—are reluctant to move toward negotiation, then the ripe moment can be created by developing a set of commitments that are deliberately designed to be irreversible. One side might take the initiative and make a unilateral, largely symbolic concession on some issue; it is important that this concession be small and in no way endanger the initiator. This concession would be coupled with a request that some equally small but irreversible commitment be made by the other side. Even if this is not forthcoming, the first party (in keeping with Charles Osgood's GRIT proposal [1960]) might offer to make a second unilateral overture, again tying it to the expectation that this will be reciprocated.

Once such reciprocation has taken place, a process is set in motion that—through the psychology of overcommitment—can assume a life of its own. Thus a series of such small, constructive commitments can create a rhythm of concession making that is *entrapping*. Each side comes to feel that it now has too much invested in this new process (or rhythm) or movement toward agreement to give up. And the more concessions each side makes, the more each side has invested in this process, which makes it increasingly important that the process be continued (Brockner and Rubin 1985).

A final, and extremely important, method for developing the ripe moment involves the judicious introduction of third parties. This approach has received considerable attention in this volume, as a number of contributors have commented on the role of various third parties (ranging from the secretary general of the United Nations to the two superpowers to private citizens to members of the private business community) in moving disputants over the hump of stalemate. Needless to say, any and all of the suggestions advanced, as applied by one or more of the antagonists themselves, can also be applied by a third party. Indeed, some of these suggestions are probably best put to use by a person occupying such a relatively dispassionate, external role. For example, although each side is capable of making a series of small, irreversible, constructive commitments, such concessions are probably more likely to be forthcoming when requested by a third party. The same can be said of introducing a decommiting formula and, often, the introduction of rewards and punishments as well. Moreover, third parties not only can help to create ripeness, their introduction (at the behest of the disputants) *reflects* the motivation among the disputants to move toward agreement *now*. In other words, the invitation for third party intervention often signals the very ripeness that third parties, under other circumstances, set out to create.

Third party intervention is not without its risks, and I would caution disputants against automatically turning to outside intervenors for assistance. For one thing, such intervenors may prove to be incompetent; they may render an already bad situation even worse through ineffectual intervention. Second, they may have their own axes to grind, in the form of vested interests that, although remaining undisclosed, nevertheless guide the third party's particular point of view. Finally, third party intervention risks taking the initiative toward settlement out of the disputants' hands and placing it with someone else. Ultimately, if an agreement is to be reached that has a chance of enduring, it is important that the disputants create an agreement that makes sense to *them*, that is "owned" by them, to which they feel responsible because they have devised it.

The preceding listing of ideas for creating ripeness is partial at best. It is meant to suggest a line of analysis that, I believe, is warranted—both conceptually and for good practical reasons. Several of the contributors to this volume have deliberately chosen to address this matter of actively creating the ripe moment. Other contributors, however, have managed to elude this important task, and instead have focused on the factors that contribute to the establishment of the timing necessary for de-escalation of conflict. To the extent that these contributors have avoided the topic of ripeness and analysis of the ways in which ripeness can be created because they find the concept too colorful, broad, or vague, I wish gently to demur. Ripeness *is* a meaningful concept, worthy of analysis in its own right. Moreover, the ripe moment (or the several ripe moments) *can* be engendered, if only analysts and/or intervenors are sufficiently imaginative and resourceful. To discount the notion of ripeness on the grounds that it is subjectively experienced, and differentially so, by the parties to a conflict is to ignore its importance to the protagonists. Ripeness is not a fiction but a reality. Moreover, even if ripeness were a fiction, because the concept has shared meaning for the disputants, it is an important part of the emerging relationship between the parties to a conflict.

Having said this, it is, nevertheless, of interest to consider the range of factors that have been outlined in this volume as "contextual features" that help establish the conditions necessary for ripeness or advantageous timing. Granted, the line is a fine one, but one should distinguish efforts to create ripeness from concern about the surrounding, contextual conditions that make ripeness more or less likely to occur.

First, several authors have rightfully pointed to the role of domestic considerations, arguing that unless intraorganizational, intranational negotiations proceed toward a single unified position in favor of agreement, there can be no condition of ripeness.

Second, several contributors have argued that the timing of negotiations must be pegged to the current climate of the international environment. Particularly interesting in this regard is Hopmann's suggestion of a curvilinear relationship between external tensions (what he elsewhere refers to as one aspect of the international environment) and ripeness. The timing may be right *either* when external tension is very small *or* very large; in the former instance, there is little difficulty to interfere with the disputants' efforts to achieve a negotiated settlement; in the latter situation, a hurting stalemate is the result—which, in turn, motivates negotiated agreement.

A third, extremely important consideration that is cited by several authors is power equality. As Haass observes, rough parity is required before a conflict is ripe for settlement, and this is so for two reasons: if power is distributed asymmetrically, the more powerful will likely feel little inclination to negotiate, whereas the less powerful will be concerned that any negotiation under these asymmetric auspices will lock its inferior position in place. It is when parity exists, in one form or another, that the conditions necessary for a hurting stalemate are most likely to exist.

A fourth consideration, of particular relevance in the international domain, is the presence of leadership that is *either* very strong *or* very weak. As Haass writes, "Political leaders must either be sufficiently strong . . . to permit compromise or sufficiently weak so that compromise cannot be avoided." Thus, leaders must be able to move their constituencies toward negotiated settlement, either by dint of their authority to do so or because they have little possibility of doing otherwise.

Another factor that is cited by a number of the authors can be called simply "good luck." The time was right for the little Dutch boy to prevent a terrible flood from descending on the lowlands of Holland simply because he chanced to be on the scene (with an available thumb) when the dike happened to break. It is not enough for the disputants to be motivated to work toward settlement. There also must be some reasonable degree of good fortune—in the form of no untoward or unanticipated events that could prove disruptive. No matter how well intentioned Chinese and Soviet diplomats may have been about improving diplomatic relations between their two nations, and doing so now, the events of 1989 in China surely have altered any such plan.

A sixth contributing factor to conditions of ripeness, also of great importance, is described in Zartman and Aurik's chapter as the concept of *requitement*. This is the belief that the other side is likely to reciprocate one's own initiative toward agreement. It goes hand-in-glove with the earlier observation that one way of creating ripeness is for one side to take the initiative and make a series of unilateral, constructive commitments. Zartman and Aurik's qualifying comment is well taken, namely, that such unilateral initiatives are especially (or only) likely to be pursued if the initiator suspects that there is some hope of requitement.

A final, extremely valuable suggestion emerges in Haass's chapter when he observes that for the ripe moment to exist, the disputants must know what to *omit* from their upcoming deliberations as well as what to include. "Modesty of scope," he writes, "can be an essential component of reaching an agreement." If one believes, as I do, that there is no single ripe moment but many such opportunities in the life history of a conflict, then it is reasonable to acknowledge which issues are to be included this time around—and which are perhaps best left for a later time. As observed earlier, the passage of time (as a result of strategic inaction, for example) can make a conflict ripe for settlement but can also turn a situation from bad to worse. In his introduction, Kriesberg points out that the Camp David Agreement of 1978, by focusing on some issues but not others, may have made subsequent settlement of some truly thorny issues (like Palestinian autonomy, the fate of Jerusalem, etc.) not easier but more difficult. Still, Haass's point is well taken: the wise negotiator should know what to omit from the present negotiating agenda as well as what to include.

A subtle confusion has emerged in a number of the papers between timing and de-escalation. As Kriesberg observes, "De-escalation efforts are especially likely when a conflict has rapidly escalated and violence has broken out." In other words, de-escalation is related to timing: some times are better than others as points to initiate efforts at defusing an intense conflict. Although I entirely agree with this observation, it has led a number of the contributors to focus less on matters of timing and more on the factors that contribute to the de-escalation of conflict. An immense literature has emerged over the last two decades or so in the areas of negotiation and third party intervention. This literature largely addresses the matter of de-escalation of conflict through these two major sources of dispute settlement. Largely neglected, however, has been the study of timing, the sense that there are right and wrong moments to make one's move, either as a participant or as an intervenor.

Timing and ripeness are more than abstract or subjective concepts. They are real in the minds and hearts of disputants. This volume contains a number of extremely insightful contributions on these twin topics. It now remains for readers to carry on, not to abandon the study of timing and ripeness to a host of qualifying conditions and perceptions. As long as one remembers that a moment may be ripe for many things, not only the settlement of conflict, and that there are likely to be many such ripe moments, then there is every reason to pursue the study of timing and ripeness with greater vigor than before. The moment to study timing is ripe. And the time to study ripeness is now.

NOTES

1. Of course, as several authors have pointed out, the passage of time may change things differentially, as when one side becomes more motivated to move toward settlement even as the other is less inclined. Inaction is a crap shoot in which the limited opportunities of today are traded against the uncertain promise of tomorrow.

2. In this vein, the story (perhaps apocryphal) is told of a foreign exchange student who came in to visit his faculty advisor one day. He told her that, because his roommate had refused to pay his share of the rent, he felt obliged (by the constraints of his culture) to take his roommate's life. The advisor pleaded with this student to do no such thing, at which point he responded, thankfully: "Aha. You, a woman, have asked me not to take my roommate's life. That's different. I am now obliged [in accordance with the norms and values of my culture] to listen to what you, a woman, have asked me to do." This is an example of a de-committing formula, albeit one that was applied unwittingly.

11

FROM THEORY TO PRACTICE AND BACK
Research Directions

JAMES P. BENNETT, GOODWIN COOKE, and STUART J. THORSON

INTRODUCTION

W E ARE IMPRESSED by the community of interest shown by the participants in this extended seminar. Coming to the problem for several directions, both from scholarly analysis and from considerable experience in various types of negotiations, they demonstrate a shared sense of the problem and a refreshing awareness of the possible utility of interaction between scholarship and practice. Indeed, it may be that too much is made of this division: many of those involved in international negotiations are scholars in their own right, and scholars are often called upon to join or advise negotiating delegations. But the gap remains, and it is vividly illustrated by the language used by the contributors to this volume. Theoretical and practical approaches to negotiation—and, indeed, to other subjects—are frequently marked by a disparity of vocabulary and style that tends to make one less than optimally useful to the other. The juxtaposition of essays on this topic from both approaches and the discussion between *thinkers* and *doers* is an admirable undertaking.

We are asked to suggest directions for further research on the negotiating process and on timing in particular. There is obviously great interest among historians in the analysis of what went wrong, or right, and why, in a given negotiation process. We would like to propose that the most important long-range application of scholarly research in this area is the provision of assistance, guidelines, and even norms for those who are responsible for negotiation. Of course, if workable norms for

247

successful de-escalation of international conflicts were readily available, the world would presumably be a much safer place than it is. As Louis Kriesberg points out, however, "Analyses can only be about past events," and decisions about a single case can be "aided by scientific generalizations but never wholly determined by them." Further, the contextual implications for negotiation processes involving major world issues are numerous and unpredictable to the point of chaos. And if negotiations occur in a chaotic milieu that everywhere impinges on the process, how can the negotiator profit from past examples that took place in greatly differing circumstances?

Despite these difficulties, the effort to establish lessons from these examples is, as the papers presented at this seminar illustrate, most worthwhile. The scholar analyzing negotiations from the point of view of, say, game theory should not lose track of context; and the practitioner should be aware of and reflect upon what scholarship can offer. If nothing else, scholarship should reduce, or at least identify, sources of uncertainty in the negotiating process. And if the effort to understand the role of timing in de-escalation will never be completely successful, that is no reason not to continue the effort.

The authors of this chapter come from backgrounds as diverse as those of the conference participants: two are, by training, scholars, and one is a retired diplomat. Without apology, we note that these differences may produce some disunity of language and approach. In this chapter, we do not purport to give a comprehensive critique of research in progress; our focus in substantially narrower. Based upon discussion at the conference and upon our own observations, we identify a number of themes—each potentially a direction for further research—related to timing in negotiations and the de-escalation of international conflicts.

Several of these themes revolve around the relationship between negotiators and students of negotiations. This relationship cannot be said to reflect the dichotomy between theory and practice. It is more complex. First, as we noted earlier, scholars often move into and out of the role of practitioner. We are not convinced that when scholars do move into positions of public office that, as Henry Kissinger claimed, they are merely consuming their stock of intellectual capital. They are at the same time learning and changing prior beliefs about international negotiation. Consequently, scholars who have also engaged in international negotiations may have a uniquely informed and insightful perspective to share.

Similarly, senior policy-making officials as well as professional Foreign Service officers frequently acquire academic roles, either temporarily or permanently. We believe that, as a general rule, the scholarly theories of negotiation do not satisfy the needs of these practitioners-turned-scholars. In part this occurs because the specialized terminology and formal methods of analysis often used in scholarly theorizing are difficult to assimilate. But more fundamentally, the concerns of theorists—the ways they formulate problems, what they take to be interesting problems, their assumptions about human and organizational participants in negotiations, and the linkages they seek to draw with other bodies of social and political theory—do not address the understandings of practitioners about "how the world works" or how to work within the world.

Because these difficulties are pervasive (and surfaced repeatedly at our conference) and because scholars and practitioners depend upon one another for information and shared understandings, we shall organize the several themes of this chapter around needs to bridge gaps and strengthen ties between these two communities.

As a result, the organization of our suggestions is somewhat different from that of Kriesberg's questions in the Introduction and from Husbands's categories of boundaries, process, and timing. We are looking more narrowly at prospective research that would assist our comprehension of the significance of timing in negotiation and assist our implementation of policies to support the de-escalation of conflicts.

RESEARCH DIRECTIONS PRODUCTIVE FOR BOTH
SCHOLARS AND PRACTITIONERS

The conference papers are useful to historians and to those who follow scholarship in the area of negotiation theory. But an equally important purpose of the enterprise must be to influence practice. To influence practice more constructively, we urge research that shares three attributes: it should make practitioners more reflective about what they do; it should contribute to producing results that are usefully predictive; and it should ultimately be normative; that is, it should help practitioners understand how they might conduct specific negotiations in particular contexts.

Among sources of data about international negotiations, some of the most useful to scholars and practitioners alike are the memoirs and first-person accounts of negotiators. We have in mind the accounts of former diplomats (such as Ambassador William Jorden's narrative [1984] of the Panama Canal negotiations), scholars-turned-practitioners (such as William Quandt's analysis [1986] of the shifting negotiating positions at Camp David), and practitioners-scholars (such as Raymond Garthoff's commentaries [1985] on the accounts of others about strategic arms negotiations). Practitioners who are reflective about what they do in negotiations and who are conscious of the reasons why they choose some course of action and avoid others greatly enhance the richness and utility of their accounts.

Several of the contributions in this volume describe conflict situations from the perspective of state leaders, for whom claims of understanding the process are often foundations for the exercise of influence over the process. In this regard, consider the connection drawn between Zartman and Aurik's analysis of power strategies and Kriesberg's and Rubin's cautions that claims about timing and ripeness can be used to attempt to manipulate the pace and direction of negotiations. Researchers must anticipate a tight feedback loop by which their *findings*, as effectively communicated to leaders, can alter practice in unanticipated ways. The enterprise of learning about negotiation repeatedly moves back and forth between theory and practice. Thus it would be prudent to explore some contemporary conflict cases with particular emphasis upon discovering from whom and by which processes political leaders take advice, inspiration, and encouragement.

In a crucial sense, detailed descriptive studies must precede the formulation of prescriptions for de-escalation and policy advocacy. All the contributors to this volume have made intensive studies of conflicts and have grounded their analyses in case materials. Insights emerge that could not be derived from either laboratory studies of small group conflicts or from global-level quantitative analysis of patterns of interstate conflict. Nevertheless, case materials alone are insufficient without a "higher-order" organization to relate them to one another. Hurwitz's chapter typifies research that seeks to identify informal *models* in decision-makers' minds. These models are drawn from decision-makers' individual experiences and general understandings of *history* and its lessons (as Richard Neustadt and Ernest May point out [1986]). From this perspective, learning how key leaders viewed their working environments is a prerequisite to prescribing how negotiations might be done more effectively.

Research results can be usefully predictive in a number of ways. First, they can reduce uncertainties about how a particular negotiation will unfold. This is an essential preliminary step to prescribing rules for negotiators (especially for persons new to international negotiation, who are by and large "learning by doing") about what not to do—the *don'ts* that were repeatedly emphasized by practitioners at the seminar. Research results might be more positively predictive by reducing the number of plausible courses that a negotiation might take. This approach would enable practitioners to focus on exercising influence at those critical junctures that determine the course of a negotiation. It would seem that much of the policy-relevant theory about timing in negotiations is of this sort. As a practitioner, one wants to make a move (proposal, concession, coordinated external pressure, delay, etc.) at the most influential time. One can begin to calculate the appropriate time only when one has confidence that one can identify critical points for the future course of the negotiations. Of course, like all knowledge about strategic social processes in which one party sometimes has an incentive to attempt to undermine the sense of control or predictability claimed by the other, research directed at issues of critical timing can be no stronger than the realism of models of the negotiating parties that it employs. So one sees again why the collaboration between scholar and practitioner is so important.

From validated research findings of a predictive character, one can begin to fashion constructive (as opposed to merely cautionary) guidelines for practitioners. We believe that it is a major fallacy to envision such guidelines as determinative or even controlling in international negotiations. The title of Howard Raiffa's textbook (1982) on negotiation is *The Art and Science of Negotiation*. He has the order of importance right. Nevertheless, collaboration between scholars and practitioners has produced several useful "handbooks" of guidelines (notably, from Roger Fisher and his colleagues, *International Mediation, A Working Guide*). Such handbooks are useful for training and for *reminding*, a function whose importance is often overlooked. Guidelines should be developed that distinguish between negotiating structures (e.g., bilateral, multilateral, mediated), issues (e.g., economic relations, human rights, etc.), and forums or settings (e.g., institutionalized, multiround, crisis management, and multitiered). In the future, individually tailored sets of guidelines might be developed for negotiators representing different bureaucracies or constituencies and for negotiators occupying different roles (e.g., head of delegation, specialist, backstopping staff).

Although much of the research in progress on negotiation aspires to the objectives set forth, its products have fallen short of the needs of practitioners. It would be a mistake to remove scholars from the design of research about negotiation on the grounds that practitioners know what the "real problems are" and what knowledge they need to address these problems. But by the same token, research that ignores the needs and understandings of practitioners cannot expect to influence practice in any coherent way.

THE CHOICE OF CONCEPTS INFLUENCES
THE STUDY OF NEGOTIATION

Much of the discussion at the seminar involved how the timing of an intervention might affect the way a conflict is resolved. Several points that came out of these discussions are noteworthy. First, one conceptual way to approach the timing question is via a life-cycle metaphor. The basic idea here is that conflicts are organic entities that go through a sequence of developmental stages. From this perspective it is but a small step to suggest that at some points in this process a conflict may be more amenable to resolution (of particular sorts) than at other points. Haass notes an occasion during the INF negotiation when an official German decision to forego replacement of short-range missiles gracefully provided the principal negotiators with space for constructive maneuvers. Kriesberg uses the term *ripeness* to refer to points in a conflict where intervention is especially likely to produce *fruitful* results. In the INF negotiations, ripeness was frequently the product of inter-NATO discussions, and timing was no less a negotiated aspect of the process than were substantive concessions. From the studies in this volume one learns that ripeness might be a *natural* phenomenon—deriving, for instance, from unrelated events elsewhere—or it might be a condition deliberately cultivated by one or both of the disputants.

The life-cycle metaphor is just that—a metaphor. As such, it is useful to consider some of the implications of using such a metaphor. First, viewing a conflict as an organic unit would seem to commit the researcher to studying conflicts as natural objects that occur externally to human observers. A goal of research, then, is to try to develop a theory of the evolution of conflicts so that indicators of appropriate points for intervention can be identified. Here some interesting questions arise about the nature of the time scale along which conflicts develop.

One possibility is to assume that conflicts follow a natural path of development that can be measured in conventional clock time (for problems with this approach in a specifically international politics context, see the work of Allan [1987] and Tamashiro [1991]). If such an assumption is correct, then it might make sense to do comparative studies of conflicts (and associated interventions) to try to identify empirically appropriate indicators of ripeness. The design of such studies would assume that the state of the conflict could be correlated with (and thus, ultimately, identified by) the length of clock time that had expired since the conflict began. Conceptually at least, one might not expect perfect correlations because clock time is a continuous variable, and it might be thought that conflicts would go through a (perhaps small) finite set of states.

This last possibility gives rise to an alternative sense of time that might be employed. This can be termed event time (rather than clock time). In an event time–driven system, it is the occurrence of a particular event (or, more precisely, the conjunction of an event with a particular class of system states) that moves the system into a new class of states. A particular kind of event time-driven system of possible interest here is that based upon a sequence of developmental stages. As an example, the psychologist Piaget (1965) has argued that a child's cognitive system goes through a predictable sequence of developmental stages. To Piaget it is less important how long a child stays in a stage than it is that the stages must be passed in sequence. In a study using Piaget's theory, Inhelder found that children at a particular cognitive stage did not have the requisite concepts, and thus simply could not understand that, just as people from another country were *foreigners*, they themselves would be foreigners in another country. Once the children developed concepts of reciprocity and reversibility, the idea that *foreignness* depended on the context became available to them. From examples like this it is clear that, for example, parent interventions that are appropriate if a child is at one stage might be inappropriate at another.

If a similar notion underlies a life-cycle interpretation of conflicts, then it would seem that research ought to move in the direction of identifying stages and seeing whether there may be larger patterns (corresponding to stages of development) through which conflicts move in predictable ways. From this perspective, however, one would not be primarily interested in looking for correlations between clock time and conflict states. Of interest also is that there might appear to be times (now interpreted as stages) at which conflicts are especially amenable to resolution attempts. It might also be the case that resolution attempts should be different depending upon the stage of the conflict. For example, Kohlberg's (1984) work on moral development suggests that at certain stages, arguments that depend on abstract principles will not be well understood. Kohlberg extends Piaget's concepts from the cognitive domain to moral reasoning and finds that just as children go through cognitive developmental stages, so do people go through stages with regard to their moral reasoning. More precisely, Kohlberg argues that at the lower stages people act in response to an external authority that has established the *rules*, whereas at higher stages their actions are self-consciously informed by reference to general principles (such as justice, equity, etc.). From this perspective, interesting research would ask how the type of arguments that would be effective for a mediator to use might vary depending on the stages of moral reasoning that character-ized the conflicting parties.

We looked at time flow by using the life-cycle metaphor of con-flict. However, it should be noted that there are plausible reasons why the life-cycle metaphor may be misleading when applied to international conflicts. Conflicts may not be the naturally occurring sort of organic object the metaphor requires. As an alternative example, one can look at *conflict* as a particular kind of classification used to decontextualize a history of social interaction. From this perspective, conflicts would not be independent organic objects but would be partial descriptions of interactions. Indeed, on such accounts *conflicts* would not even form conceptual equivalence classes (for a parallel argument with respect to *revolutions*, see Farr). Rather, notions such as what it means to *resolve* a conflict would become problematized and, consequently, legitimate areas for research.

Aspects of life-cycle and developmental metaphors apply to the organizational nexus underlying interstate negotiations. Both Haass in this volume and Quandt (1986) show that domestic political cycles can generate their own *stages* of relative attention to and investment in solving persistent disputes. For instance, democratic governments are unlikely either to undertake risky negotiating initiatives soon before elections or to sustain a commitment to long-term negotiating strategies in periods of political uncertainty. The cases studied by Rikhye, Zartman and Aurik, and McDonald, suggest that skillful political maneuvers can at least mitigate the effects of electoral cycles. Judicious organization of a state's national security bureaucracy can help to *decouple* the pursuit of international negotiated solutions from transient pressures in domes-tic politics. In this regard, prospects for constructing attractive careers in international negotiation deserve attention from the scholars of orga-nizational design. Track Two diplomacy might be warranted as an ap-proach to permit further decoupling of long-term negotiating strategies from the vagaries of domestic politics. However, at some stage, political accountability must be exercised, as Husbands emphasizes. Her chapter is especially rich in its suggestions for focusing additional research in ways immediately applicable to providing guidance for high-level policy makers.

In short, how one perceives international conflicts influences the features that one chooses to study and the criteria that one brings to bear to evaluate strategies of de-escalation and conflict resolution. No *neutral* way to envision conflicts in this regard is available. But some metaphors and frameworks are undoubtedly superior to others. A more comprehensive survey of images of conflicts (those in different cultures and those used by scholars compared to practitioners) would be a useful first step to concepts whose uncritical application prejudices the development of practical knowledge for negotiation in subtle ways.

We would also like to see more research with the explicit objective of identifying conditions for serious negotiations aimed at de-escalating or settling conflicts. For instance, Haass notes that rough parity of capabilities has often been cited as conducive to U.S.-Soviet strategic arms negotiations. Although military stalemate does not always indicate a state of parity in military capabilities, stalemate is found by Zartman and Aurik to be a prominent feature of several contemporary conflicts prior to serious efforts by the combatants to de-escalate. Indeed, "mutual hurting" is identified by Zartman as a key inducement to de-escalate. In addition, conceptual linkages among key terms used by different researchers should be probed. How, for instance, does Zartman's *ripeness* relate to Dedring's use of "critical juncture?"

Hopmann's contribution flags another direction for inquiry. He notes that ripeness is in part a function of the general state of relations among disputants: in one sense it is a background condition that affects the viability of productive negotiations at any point. This is close to Garthoff's (1985) position, systematically espoused in *Détente and Confrontation*, that the general tenor of U.S.-Soviet relations conditions (without fully determining) what is negotiable at any particular time.

SHOULD WE BE NEGOTIATING? WHEN?

Few would claim that negotiation is always a suitable way to address an international conflict. There are, no doubt, times in particular conflicts when one should walk out of negotiations. Ikle centered his analysis of international negotiation around the practitioner's "three-fold choice": accept the terms one can get now, continue negotiating, or quit. There are, of course, a variety of ways to quit, and considerable art attaches to the selection of any one in a particular case. Research to support making the choice is addressed next.

At the outset, given the recognition of a troublesome international conflict, one must decide whether to begin to negotiate and, if so, when and how to start. Beginning to negotiate can, in many circumstances, convey to an opponent the impression of one's weakness, a situation that generally one should try to avoid. Historians of international negotiation are familiar with a number of tactics conventionally employed to try to minimize the sense that one is eager to negotiate. Third parties are often used as intermediaries, both to convey the invitation to negotiate and to make it appear that they are the source of the initiative. *Deniable* initiatives, often through semiauthoritative channels, are frequently observed. Prenegotiation negotiations can be used to clarify the agenda, to set procedures, and to control the public's perceptions of what is happening. All these are tactical moves suitable once one has decided to begin negotiating. But there are two additional dimensions on which research findings are lacking.

First, one wants to know when efforts at de-escalation, as an object of negotiation, are misplaced or dangerous. Negotiation is not always the most suitable means for dealing with international conflicts, especially those of very high and very low intensities. A hurdle in the way of resolving very low-intensity conflicts is to get them onto the necessarily very short active agenda of senior government officials so that initiatives can be taken or proposals from below in the bureaucracy can receive a fair hearing.

Manipulating the image of a conflict to motivate political leaders to address it is a very delicate, risk-laden enterprise. Husbands's chapter cites cautionary evidence that the attitude taken toward a conflict during the prenegotiation phase can severely circumscribe negotiating tactics available later. Wisely, we think, none of the contributors to this volume recommend deliberately escalating conflicts as an expedient short-term measure. Nevertheless, state representatives sometimes appear to do precisely that, especially to gain the attention and involvement of third parties.

Research that links the timing of negotiating initiatives with extension or escalation of the conflict being negotiated would be welcome. Agreements that are nearly reached but which then are abandoned or come unraveled pose particular interest for students of timing. Hopmann's study of the long-running efforts to reduce European military forces is instructive. Sometimes parties to a negotiation abandon the process for reasons having little to do with the matters on the table. The Soviet

Union's intervention in Afghanistan gave occasion for the interruption of several negotiating processes and prompted the abandonment of the U.S.-Soviet agreed draft to prohibit radiological weapons. One might think that political leaders would be tempted to return to nearly completed negotiations in search of quick foreign policy successes. However, at least in U.S.-Soviet affairs, any temptation to return to nearly completed agreements, such as the Radiological Convention, or to completed but unratified agreements, such as the Threshhold Test Ban Treaty, has been tempered by opposition from those parts of the foreign policy bureaucracies that were "burned" or disappointed earlier. In such instances, simply reopening dialogue on issues once abandoned may be the major hurdle.

Varieties of nonofficial prenegotiation discussion need further exploration for use in such contexts. Perhaps nonofficial but expert discussion can serve as a catalyst to ripen the conflict in such a way that solutions once proposed are no longer rejected out of hand. In politics there is a tendency to presume, in the absence of hard evidence to the contrary, that if a proposed settlement was rejected in the past, it was rejected with good reason. This presumption is clearly unjustified if external events and no *decision* prompted the rejection. It can also be unjustified when circumstances have changed significantly, say, owing to improvements in the technology for verifying agreements.

We would like to encourage research directed at identifying those circumstances in which historical negotiating initiatives were well chosen and those in which such initiatives were harmful. This is a difficult question to ask systematically. It presumes that the researcher can separate effects produced by the negotiating initiative itself from those produced by the skill with which negotiations were conducted as well as from effects produced by parallel, unrelated processes in the world. There is one historically rich study of the conditions under which attempts by nonstate actors (such as intergovernmental organizations) to intervene in international conflicts were accepted and when they were fruitful (Sherman and the sources cited there). But a more difficult study would extend that analysis to negotiating initiatives from individual states and from coalitions (such as the Contadora Group or ASEAN).

One would have to define operationally the "negotiating initiative," empirically identify the time it begins (which is difficult for cases such as the Soviet-Afghan or U.S.-PLO talks in which intermediaries are used for much of the negotiation), and identify the communication channels used as well as the immediate effects or impact upon the relations of the parties. Nor can one assume that, if negotiations produced a settlement, beginning to negotiate was thus the proper policy decision. Other modes of conduct might have produced a superior settlement, and the actual settlement could have been produced by other mechanisms. Was the United States correct to begin negotiating a limited test ban treaty with the Soviet Union in 1963 to reciprocate the end of Soviet pressure against Berlin, or should the United States have waited for better terms? The Soviets possibly entered negotiations to gain an image of improved relations with the West with which to pressure the Chinese in (what now appear to have been for the Soviets) more important contemporary negotiations. More recently, we have encountered the claim that, by refusing to negotiate in good faith for the reduction or elimination of nuclear weapons in 1981, the Reagan administration gained time to engage in a military buildup that helped to assure superior terms from the Soviets in the INF Treaty of 1988. Issues of timing are central to such claims, but contemporary research about international negotiations seems to bring analysts no closer to developing ways to get even rough and ready answers.

The experience of the Reagan administration's early talks with the Soviets introduces another element: When should one negotiate for "side effects" (as Ikle [1964] termed effects that are not the ostensible objectives of the negotiations)? When should one negotiate *sincerely*? When should one combine a strategy of negotiating "on the issues" and for side effects, such as influencing world public opinion, getting reelected, or buying time? To develop research designs to answer such questions, analysts will have to make hard judgments about motive, intention, and strategy of the negotiating parties. They cannot do this without assistance from practitioners who were involved in the negotiations or in policy circles when the choices were made. (Other pertinent sources of information, of course, are equally essential.) The third theme emerges as a requirement for closer collaboration between historians and experienced practitioners in the conduct of inquiry as well as in the sharing of its product.

HOW CAN THE FOREIGN POLICY APPARATUS ORGANIZE INFORMATION FLOWS TO MAKE GOOD DECISIONS ABOUT NEGOTIATION?

Two facets are intertwined: the speed of organizational response and the quality of that response. Decisions about timing initiatives and responses are usually made at the highest political levels in important negotiations. But much of the information pertinent to making good decisions originates at lower levels. We need to know more about how foreign policy bureaucracies accumulate and channel information and about how they share information with one another and with higher political levels. As issues of organizational design, we need grounded advice of three dimensions:

—To what extent can planning for and managing negotiations be decentralized?

—Which individuals and units should be given which functions?

—And at which loci, by what channels or authorization and communication, can effective decision making be accomplished?

This is a tall order. But there is a growing body of relevant material on some protracted international negotiations, such as SALT/START (in which an unprecedented view into political reporting on negotiating sessions surfaced during the recent dispute over the interpretation of the ABM Treaty).

Calculations of timing in negotiations are particularly sensitive in organizational performance at acquiring and sharing relevant information. Within the U.S. government, two occasions for political disputes have often impeded negotiating progress. One occasion is the issuance of formal instructions to negotiators and representatives. Delegations have often been without realistic instructions for prolonged periods. At other times, delegations have sought revision of their instructions but received no timely response from the White House either because there was no consensus about what instructions to issue or because the request failed to get attention at the proper level (these two reasons are often just symptoms of the same condition).

The second occasion is the development of responses to counterparts' proposals. In both foreign economic negotiations and strategic arms negotiations, the proposals of others have often lain "on the table" for extended periods because the bureaucracy was unable or unwilling to develop a response.

We recognize that leaving a proposal unanswered and (less frequently) leaving a delegation without instructions can serve as conscious instruments for delay, shifting position, and otherwise gaining flexibility. But at least as frequent as deliberate tactical moves have been delays that were unintended or unavoidable. Clearly, until the organizational interfaces are improved to enable quicker, thoroughly "staffed-out" performance, many opportunities for controlling the pace of negotiations and timing of one's own moves must remain moot. An additional consequence of poor bureaucratic performance is that "end-runs" and political "back-channels" are encouraged. We believe that, although the availability of alternative channels and processes is an asset to negotiation (and these mechanisms should be constructed or cultivated, as appropriate, as part of the preparation for a negotiation), reliance upon procedures that tend to circumvent wholesale, or to exclude unpredictably, the relevant foreign policy bureaucracies makes generally for poor negotiating results.

Yet before we can advance these beliefs as part of validated guidance for the conduct of negotiation, more detailed and focused research about the bureaucratic performance in particular historical cases is required. This is an area of inquiry where the experiences and observations of practitioners at lower organizational levels may prove to balance and enlighten the memories of senior political officials.

Evaluative histories of the performance of the separate bureaucracies are helpful (e.g., Clarke's [1979] study of the ACDA), although they may not bear centrally on any negotiating case. Beyond these one requires a more extensive set of organizationally informed negotiating histories (e.g., Gerard Smith's *Doubletalk* [1980] rather than Kissinger's *White House Years* [1979] on SALT I). Certainly, we should be more attentive to non-U.S. and non-Western accounts of organizational factors, although even apart from the language barriers, less systematic material seems to be available outside European and other Western experiences.

Consistency or coherence of state policy should be critically assessed, particularly in complex regional disputes. Dedring notes that actions of the superpowers in Lebanon cannot easily be reconciled with their actions in the United Nations. Identifying such situations—when the very notion of *rational* state action is challenged—pushes inquiry to the next question. Do such disparities reflect deliberate attempts to mislead, self-consciously hypocritical political positions, governmental fragmentation, inattention to the conflict, or a combination of all four? Answers should significantly influence our prescriptions to achieve de-escalation.

Yet there are other conflict situations in which rational state policy—or, at least, the coherence of efforts at all political levels—appears to be the norm. Earle notes that in U.S.-Soviet strategic arms negotiations, the negotiating activities of state representatives, the public stances of governments, and the decisions made at the top political levels seem to present a consistent and organized image, what we usually mean by *policy*. In such a setting there would appear to be little room for the multitrack diplomacy that McDonald advocates.

McDonald's multitrack diplomacy is not, however, simply the juxtaposition of official diplomacy and private diplomacy. Underlying his prescription is the necessity for participants in each track to share general objectives and to attend to the processes on the other tracks. The unofficial tracks are not of equal importance throughout the course of a negotiation: McDonald and other proponents find it to be most valuable in exploring other parties' positions, testing the waters for launching diplomatic initiatives or shifting negotiating positions.

The inherently less-organized images created by private diplomacy, notes Earle, restrict its use to an occasional adjunct to interstate negotiations (although skilled private individuals may be more systematically used to acquire information in preparation for negotiations). But in complex regional conflicts, such as Dedring studied, it is difficult for many governments to exclude private individuals, private voluntary organizations, and other sorts of nongovernmental actors from important and regular involvement. Research directed at clarifying the assets and liabilities of nonstate third parties, emissaries, and intermediaries by type of conflict and by stage of the negotiating process would be most welcome.

HOW DOES ONE MONITOR WHERE ONE IS AT ANY TIME IN A PROCESS OF NEGOTIATION?

Students of strategy games such as chess and GO conventionally distinguish among beginning, middle, and end-game. The distinction helps convey contextual limits to prescriptions for playing effectively. Although the objective of international negotiations cannot be to defeat the opponent, a parallel form of situational or positional reasoning is sometimes helpful. Practitioners need fixed points of reference to mark their positions in a negotiation. To some extent, formal instructions serve this function. More generally, though, one seeks a way to measure the evolving mix of conflictual and cooperative interests in any negotiation. This measurement appears to us to be an absolute prerequisite to using practically the sort of game theoretic analyses advocated in many of the contributions presented in this volume.

Substantial attention is now being given by both scholars and practitioners to the prenegotiation stage: how to prepare the setting, plan the logistics, select parties and personnel, organize communications and reporting requirements, integrate the conduct of negotiations into other governmental processes, and formulate agendas. Although scholars have not been much concerned with this stage, practitioners have placed great emphasis on the importance of final stages in a negotiation, what many have called "the last five minutes." But applying this advice, however well grounded it is empirically, requires one to know when one is involved in the opening phases or in an endgame. Such determinations at first sight may seem to be what any competent political analyst can discern. But there are enough historical instances of negotiations that appear to have skipped entirely the usual opening moves (e.g., the limited test ban negotiations mentioned and the Reykjavík summit) or to have been limited intentionally to endless repetition of opening positions. Eleventh-hour introduction of new issues that can prolong or unravel the final stages of a negotiation are also common (e.g., recent French insistence on reviewing basic positions in talks to reduce and restrict chemical weapons or the DeConcini reservation during ratification of the Panama Canal Treaty).

We do not wish to reduce the problem of determining "where one is" in a negotiation simply to problems of measurement. There is also a conceptual dimension that relates to the functions one sees any particular negotiations as serving, namely, the parties' objectives. Practitioners recognize that objectives are not fixed at the outset; neither are they complete nor unambiguous. Scholars often overlook this point. Objectives can change as the result of political changes within one party (e.g., U.S. objectives during the Law of the Sea negotiations), discovery by a party of what is possible (e.g., on the down side, Anwar Sadat's incrementally reduced expectations at Camp David; on the up side, stiffening U.S. terms in negotiating with the Franco government of Spain for military base rights), experience from previous negotiations on the same issues (e.g., British objectives set for the second "Cod War" with Iceland compared to their objectives in the first), or simply changing the basic purpose for negotiating (e.g., Argentine-Chilean negotiations about the Beagle Channel shifting from the role of a convenient instrument to focus domestic dissatisfactions against foreigners to a forum to remove a mutually troubling problem). When radical reinterpretations of ongoing negotiations are made by one or more parties, determining "where one is now" in a timely and accurate fashion can be vital to success.

This problem afflicts not only the participants in the negotiation. Senior political figures (whose watch may begin after negotiations have been in progress for a long time, developing their own dynamics of interaction and their own "mythologies" of justification) have to be informed "where things stand now." Publics—the public at large, interested constituencies, and bodies that must ratify or implement any agreement reached—must periodically have the negotiations described in a way that is at once nondisruptive and (at an appropriate level of summarization) truthful.

In the United States, the political leadership typically understands "managing negotiations" (Winham 1977) to involve at a minimum: inducing the press to report on them in a way that avoids raising unrealistic expectations (except when political leaders succumb to transient needs for support, often on issues entirely unrelated); avoiding lulling the public into a sense of complacency derived from a belief that successful negotiations will definitively solve a problem; and avoiding premature release of negotiating positions (except, again, when that may serve political needs such as exposing opposition within the government). So far as we are aware, how to integrate the larger public management of negotiations within a democracy has not been the focus of research. Building upon Husbands's work to formulate useful guidance on this matter presupposes that the leadership itself can discern "where it is" in the course of a negotiation.

Much of the analytic machinery of scholars presumes that one can determine where one is in a timely fashion during negotiations. We are not persuaded that this is generally the case. Research addressing some of the issues raised here should be given high priority if the results of scholars are to be made useful to practitioners.

WHEN AND HOW SHOULD ONE MAKE CONCESSIONS?

Making concessions can fulfill many functions within the course of negotiations so determining how and when one should make concessions must be subordinated to one's particular objectives at the time. Thus there can be no fully general answer to this question.

One can make a concession to reciprocate another concession, either to draw both parties closer to an agreement (*convergence*), or to indicate that one is still serious about reaching agreement (*holding*). The magnitude, composition, and timing of concessions can be intended to communicate such basic messages as a change in negotiating position, a revision in one party's understanding of the issues on the table, even a rejection of the other's concession or repudiation of some claim it has made. Further, the patterns and styles of concessions by different states suggest that there is no dominant set of conventions that governs either the etiquette or substance of the practice of conceding (see Jensen [1984] on postwar U.S.-Soviet patterns of concessions).

It is a rare negotiation indeed in which one party has to make no concessions on the road to an agreement. Some might distinguish negotiation from dictate on precisely this ground. Even in highly asymmetric power situations, such as the end of the second Russo-Finnish War, the Soviets made a couple of small concessions on the timing and amount of reparations. A government often wants to minimize its concessions to its own citizens while maximizing their value to the other negotiating party.

How and when to make concessions has, surprisingly, not received much attention from scholars. A major exception is the community of convergence theorists who attend to how much to concede but for whom, how, or when to concede is largely nonproblematic. Ikle (1964) offers the advice to "reciprocate concessions" but under the dominating injunction of doing as well as possible. Presumably, one needs to make a reciprocal concession soon to establish its linkage to the original concession. Practitioners work with adages, such as whenever possible, make a procedural concession in exchange for one of substance. But such rules of thumb admit exceptions and are not wise in all situations.

A number of linguistic devices indicate that one is making a concession (Weiss 1985). One is silence: a party can drop a demand by not mentioning it. Negotiators commonly introduce concessions by changing the argument or justification adduced in support of a demand in such a way that it elicits inquiry from the counterpart negotiator about the magnitude of the demand. Concessions, like other vehicles to indicate a change in negotiating position, can be made contingent or noncontingent; linked to another issue or unlinked; clear or ambiguous; retractable or irreversible; and so on. But despite the diversity of phenomena that is called *concession*, the category seems to most practitioners to be a natural one, whose patterns and possibilities should not be ignored.

Theorists conceive of concessions at three levels of abstraction. There are calculations about concessions made during planning for a negotiation: for instance, one demands payment of $X million but anticipates accepting payment of $X − Y million. Concessions are also tactical devices and may be used to avoid the breakup of a negotiation, to attempt to introduce momentum, to approach a settlement, to re-move last-minute obstacles to completing a settlement, and so on. Fi-nally, language used by negotiators can be concessionary (or not) and substantive concessions can be expressed (or not) in explicitly conces-sionary terms: for instance, "We're prepared to admit only forty inspec-tors if you can accept five more inspections."

An in-depth research program to explain (descriptively) the ways in which, and occasion on which, concessions are offered and to under-stand (prescriptively) the opportunities and limits to various ways of making concessions must grapple with some fundamental problems of political reasoning and justification. For instance, considering only the linguistic encoding of concessions, the analyst must examine the negotiator's (speaker's) utterance, infer the intended meaning, draw fur-ther inferences (perhaps assisted with information about the hearer's utterance in response) about the meaning that the hearer inferred, and perhaps also (for "strategic speech") about the speaker's intentions for the hearer's inferences about the speaker. This is sometimes referred to as reflective modeling of the negotiators' relationship (Alker, Bennett, and Mefford 1980; Alker 1988) and is commonly applied with impres-sive sophistication in formal, sociolinguistic analyses (Bach and Harnish 1979; Mefford 1988; Karapin and Alker 1985).

The subject of how and when to make concessions is indeed a complex and deep one. If the essence of reaching negotiated agreements involves the judicious calculation of how and when to reduce demands, the study of negotiation cannot avoid the study of how and when to concede.

SYMBIOSIS OF TWO COMMUNITIES:
SCHOLARS AND PRACTITIONERS

The final theme that emerged in the seminar—one that in a sense legiti-mates and motivates the others—is that we need research that makes the assumptions and claims of scholars accessible to practitioners and research that makes the experience and presuppositions of practitioners accessible to scholars. In an ideal world, a single research program could be designed to advance both contributions. Realistically, we will settle for the state of affairs in which (1) essentially artificial dichoto-mies between theory and practice are removed; (2) both communities variously share in the roles of producers and consumers of knowledge; and (3) each community becomes both more cognizant of the difficulties faced by the other and more appreciative of the potential and the need for symbiosis.

In the realm of negotiation, theory must be derived in large measure from examining practice (which is not at all to say that theory can only codify current practice). And practice, if it is to be done systematically with continual efforts at improvement, must be informed by theory. We urge the sort of role for theorists that Harold Lasswell (1974) prescribed for the "policy sciences" and the role for practitioners that McGeorge Bundy 1988, chap. 13) aspires to in drawing lessons from what happened and what might have happened in nuclear history.

Without the contributions of practitioners, theorists can access only the observations and understandings of external observers. Theorists can employ only those conceptual categories and images thrown up by other problems of the social sciences (with no assurance that they are appropriate for understanding negotiation). And they must try to extrapolate from experiments and simulations in artificial environments to patterns of thought and action in realistic settings. For these reasons, theorists and other scholars cannot make much progress alone.

The culture of the practitioner must limit self-doubts and critical reflection when they begin to limit effective political action. Practical reasoning that justifies action cannot be either logically unassailable or empirically definitive. It is the nature of foreign affairs that choice must be exercised under conditions of incomplete knowledge of the pertinent facts and often doubtful understandings of the links between intervention and outcome. The culture of the scholar should encourage a critical stance toward one's claimed understanding; to do this it encourages clashes of interpretations that a community of practitioners cannot afford. So it is not easy to construct reliable bridges between these two cultures. Just as international negotiations can only succeed when two parties acknowledge their interdependence, research joining the unique talents and perspectives of scholars and practitioners cannot be productive unless each community reaches a fair and balanced assessment of its own needs and potential contributions.

How these cultures can best relate to one another remains an important open question. The participants in this seminar gained considerably, we believe, from their exchanges. The challenge is to develop ways of accomplishing this sort of interchange on a larger and continuing basis.

EPILOGUE
War in the Persian Gulf

LOUIS KRIESBERG and STUART J. THORSON

T HE ERUPTION OF WAR in the Persian Gulf serves to illustrate points made in this book. During a few months, the world watched as an intensifying conflict led to the Iraqi invasion of Kuwait on August 2, 1990. The conflict escalated rapidly after that, resulting on January 16, 1991, in the launching of a massive air campaign against Iraq by the U.S.-led coalition forces. The war further escalated with the onset of large-scale ground operations on February 23, 1991.

Although these events are far too recent to allow any definitive account of them, they are also far too important to ignore in a book dealing with the role of timing in the de-escalation of international conflicts. It should be emphasized that these reflections represent our views and not necessarily those of the other contributors to this volume.

Several de-escalating efforts were made throughout this time as more parties entered the conflict. Obviously, the efforts did not de-escalate the conflict or even stop its expansion. Was the time not ripe for any de-escalating negotiations or was there a failure to use the right de-escalating strategy at the appropriate time? We will discuss answers to those questions for the period immediately before the Iraqi invasion, for the period between the invasion and the onset of the air war, and for the period of the actual fighting.

FAILED DE-ESCALATING EFFORTS BEFORE AUGUST 2, 1990

Even before the end of the Iran-Iraq war in August 1988, Iraqi officials had made claims against Kuwait relating to the border between them and to access to the Persian Gulf. Shortly after the end of the war, clear signs of the emerging Iraq-Kuwait conflict began to appear, with Iraqi officials articulating many specific grievances. Their major grievances related to the overproduction of OPEC quotas by Kuwait and the United Arab Emirates (UAE), the Iraqi debt to Kuwait, and excess oil allegedly taken by Kuwait from the Rumaila field.

On February 19, 1990, the Prime Ministers of the Arab Cooperation Council (ACC) met in Baghdad. Formed a year earlier, its membership consisted of Iraq, Yemen, Jordan, and Egypt. At the meeting, President Saddam Hussein demanded the withdrawal of U.S. ships from the Persian Gulf. At a subsequent summit meeting of the ACC on February 24, President Hussein privately made clear he wanted more money from the Gulf states and warned that he would take it if it were not given to him. In late May, at the Arab League meeting in Baghdad, he called for the Arab liberation of Jerusalem and said that he wanted $27 billion from Kuwait alone.

After an Iraqi official visited Kuwait and other sheikdoms, pressing them not to exceed their OPEC-determined production quotas, Gulf oil ministers met on July 10 in Jidda, Saudi Arabia, to decide a response. Kuwait and the UAE, under pressure, agreed to adhere strictly to their quotas. Some observers thought the crisis had been resolved, with Iraq serving as the enforcer of OPEC rules. However, Iraq military forces near Kuwait were increased, not decreased.

On July 24, the United States conducted joint military maneuvers with the UAE in the Persian Gulf. The next day, U.S. Ambassador April Glaspie was called to meet with President Hussein. Although what transpired at the meeting remains in dispute; certainly President Hussein did not infer that the U.S. government would wage a devastating war against Iraq to protect Kuwaiti independence. On July 31, U.S. Assistant Secretary of State John Kelly testified at a congressional hearing and affirmed that the United States did not have a defense treaty with any Gulf country.

The Iraqi government was on a course of escalation to gain objectives whose limits were not clear to its opponents. Some isolated concessions were made, but no comprehensive negotiated settlement was sought. Such a settlement might have been based on the existing power imbalance of the primary adversaries or on a more symmetric balance of power that might have been attained by Kuwait gathering support from its allies (cf. Zartman and Aurik; Haass).

The Iraqi government relied heavily on threats to gain what it wanted in negotiations. This strategy is generally not an effective inducement for de-escalation, particularly when the terms of settlement seem open ended (cf. Hopmann).

Discussions took place bilaterally or at meetings of regional organizations. No major party undertook an energetic mediating role or stressed the consequences of continuing escalation. The times may not have been propitious for de-escalation, but failure to make a major effort to accomplish it can certainly be regarded as a mistake by some potential mediators and by at least one party to the fight, the Iraqi people.

FAILED DE-ESCALATING EFFORTS BETWEEN
AUGUST 2, 1990, AND JANUARY 15, 1991

The Iraqi invasion of Kuwait marked a great heightening of the conflict and resulted in rapid, further escalation. President Hussein initially said that Iraq would withdraw in two days. Later that statement was made conditional, and still later Kuwait was proclaimed to be an eternal part of Iraq.

The Arab League immediately condemned the Iraqi invasion. The UN Security Council, with U.S. leadership, moved quickly to pass resolutions calling for Iraqi withdrawal and a strict economic blockade to win compliance. Additional resolutions imposing further demands followed. U.S. and coalition military forces were swiftly assembled in Saudi Arabia. It was said that the forces were deployed to enforce the embargo and to deter any attacks on Saudi Arabia. Then on November 9, President George Bush announced that military forces in the Gulf would be sharply increased. On November 29, in Resolution 678, the Security Council authorized member states cooperating with Kuwait to use all necessary means after January 15, 1991, to enforce the previous council resolutions.

Several mediating efforts were undertaken to de-escalate the conflict, most notably those made immediately by King Hussein of Jordan. But his and other such attempts were given little room for maneuver by the U.S. government, other governments in the coalition, or the UN Security Council, which with the end of the Cold War was allowed to act forcefully as a party to the fight (cf. Dedring; Rikhye). Mediating and negotiating efforts were also attempted immediately before the January 15 deadline. Iraq released the civilian "hostages" it was holding, and U.S. Secretary of State James Baker and Iraqi Foreign Minister Tariq Aziz did manage to have one face-to-face meeting.

Once Kuwait had been invaded, the time did not seem ripe for de-escalation. Each side moved to commit itself to its course of action, hoping and expecting that the other side would yield, which in turn reduced the possibility for each to find a de-escalating solution that would not appear to be capitulation by one side to the other. At the same time, mobilization of popular support in the United States was rapid and widespread (cf. Husbands).

The conflict may have become more intractable because of the different ways in which the parties were framing the issues and, more importantly, the ways in which each believed the other to be framing the issues. What were the objectives of Iraq? Depending upon one's answer to this question, different sorts of compromises are possible. What were the objectives of the United States and of coalition members? It may be that early mixed signals about United States objectives led President Hussein to doubt U.S. commitment. In any event, what developed during this period often appeared to be a game of chicken, in which each party tried to show its resolve by taking actions that made any subsequent de-escalations increasingly unlikely (cf. Hurwitz).

Given the vague objectives of the primary adversaries, could any unilateral de-escalating strategy have been effective? We think not. For a strategy to be effective, at least one of the adversaries would have had to change its objectives, perhaps by accepting that its goals were unattainable and that to pursue them could result in worse than a negotiated settlement. Such repositioning would have required large-scale domestic pressures in at least one of the primary adversary countries or in a major coalition ally.

The concern about domestic forces weakening the solidarity of the coalition probably stiffened the resolve of the U.S. leaders to move swiftly beyond economic sanctions toward the employment of military force. That option also seemed to promise gains (destroying President Hussein's power and the Iraqi offensive military capability) that would not readily be acceptable to the coalition as a whole.

FAILED DE-ESCALATING EFFORTS BETWEEN
JANUARY 16, 1991, AND FEBRUARY 23, 1991

An intense air war was waged against Iraqi military forces, aircraft, power plants, bridges, factories producing military weapons, and other targets. As the air campaign went on and talk of an imminent ground war grew, new efforts at settling the war were initiated before the next great step up the escalation ladder was taken. For example, just before the ground campaign was started, the Soviet government played an active mediating role; and President Hussein gave signs of much greater flexibility. The U.S. government, on its side, was able to maintain the coalition and continued to insist that the Iraqis simply withdraw from Kuwait and agree to all the UN Security Council resolutions.

Given the uncompromising position of the U.S.-led coalition, could any de-escalating strategy have produced a negotiated settlement? The President of Iraq could have made much more dramatic de-escalating moves, renouncing the incorporation of Kuwait into Iraq and beginning a large-scale withdrawal of Iraqi military forces from Kuwait. Such action might then have broken the solidarity of the coalition sufficiently to allow some bargaining on the other UN Security Council resolutions.

The momentum of military operations made stopping the war short of an imposed victory (or drawn-out stalemate) unlikely. Furthermore, leaders on both sides had already considered what they believed would be the costs of pursuing the war. U.S. government leaders had seen the war go extremely well, and each Iraqi effort to break-up the coalition was readily thwarted; total victory seemed near with little additional cost. For the Iraqi leaders, continuation of the war probably seemed the most effective way to negotiate better terms than had they capitulated before the ground war started (cf. Rubin).

GENERAL OBSERVATIONS

Once the Iraqi government started making claims and threats against Kuwait, circumstances offered little hope for a mutually acceptable agreement among the primary adversaries. They deteriorated further after the invasion of Kuwait and became even less conducive to such an outcome after the increased buildup of U.S. military forces in November made redeployments home more difficult.

Reliance on threats as a way to induce the other side to yield required taking actions to make the threats credible. Resolve had to be shown. Those very demonstrations locked the parties into escalating the conflict, not de-escalating it. The almost universal condemnation of the Iraqi invasion and annexation of Kuwait not only isolated Iraq but also reduced the opportunities for major governments to play mediating roles.

Although the chapters in this book generally did not address international conflicts at the crisis and war stages we have discussed here, the analyses presented are relevant. The context of a conflict clearly has great effects on the course of that conflict and its de-escalation. For example, the availability of various kinds of nonofficial relations between countries can facilitate unofficial diplomacy that in turn may contribute to de-escalating negotiations (cf. McDonald and Earle). The relative paucity of nonofficial exchanges between Iraq and the United States reduced such opportunities as well as contributed to the misunderstandings and miscalculations in the crisis.

The fundamental question about de-escalating the crisis in the Gulf has to do with evaluating when which parties, if any, should have worked harder and taken greater risks to de-escalate the conflict before the crisis escalated into an invasion, before the air campaign was launched, or before the ground war was begun. The answers to such a question depend on our values and on whom we feel we represent (for example, the president of the United States, the American people, the Ba'ath party of Iraq, The Soviet leadership, the peoples of the Persian Gulf region, or the people of the earth).

We offer a possible answer. This answer is based upon a long time frame, together with serious consideration of the interests of people in the region, treasuring the lives of the people in Kuwait and in Iraq as well as those from the United States and other countries in the coalition, giving high priority to the social and economic needs of the American people, and valuing the creation of precedents in the United States and in the world generally for international norms being upheld by minimally violent means as prove effective.

During the period immediately before the Iraqi invasion of Kuwait, the U.S. and Kuwaiti governments should have been clearer about the consequences of a possible invasion and should have attempted negotiations with the Iraqi government regarding the many issues in contention. During the period when the United Nations was responding to the Iraqi invasion by imposing economic sanctions, various parties should have taken greater risks to de-escalate the conflict. Anticipating, as many observers did, the likely aftermath of a war, a negotiated withdrawal of Iraqi forces from Kuwait, induced by economic sanctions, might have achieved much of what the war achieved and at much less cost. The chances of improving economic and social conditions both within and between the societies in the region would have been enhanced by more gradual changes, unencumbered by the burdens of recovering from a devastating war.

During the period of the air war, de-escalating negotiations could have been undertaken while the air campaign and trade sanctions continued. The mediation efforts of President Mikhail Gorbachev suggest that such negotiations could have resulted in the Iraqi withdrawal from Kuwait.

Although this book is about de-escalating international conflicts, we do not argue that every conflict should be de-escalated. Conflict should often be escalated to yield more just and enduring outcomes. Most people in the United States appeared to believe that such was the case for the conflict in the Persian Gulf. Based on this analysis, we agree that the almost universal condemnation of the Iraqi invasion of Kuwait and the support for economic sanctions to end it were prerequisite for an acceptable de-escalation later.

REFERENCES

Abel, Elsie. 1966. *The Missile Crisis*. Philadelphia: Lippincott.

Alexeyev, Boris. 1988. "Time to Remove Barriers and Build Bridges." *Soviet Life* (June): 6–8.

Alker, Hayward R., Jr. 1988. "Politics as Political Argumentation: Towards Regrounding a Global Discipline." Paper presented at the 14th World Conference of the International Political Science Association, August.

Alker, Hayward R., Jr., James P. Bennett, and Dwain Mefford. 1980. "Generalized Precedent Logics for Resolving Insecurity Dilemmas." *International Relations* 7:165–200.

Alker, Haywood, and Roger Hurwitz. 1980. *Resolving the Prisoner's Dilemma*. Washington, D.C.: APSA.

Allan, Pierre. 1983. *Crisis Bargaining and the Arms Race: A Theoretical Model*. Cambridge: Ballinger.

———. 1987. "Social Time." In *Communication and Interaction in Global Politics*, ed. C. Cioffi-Revilla, R. Merritt, and D. Zinnes, 95–114. Beverly Hills: Sage Publications.

Allison, Graham T. 1971. *Essence of Decision: Explaining the Cuban Missile Crisis*. Boston: Little, Brown.

Americans Talk Security. 1990. "The Peace Dividend as the Public Sees It." Survey no. 13. Winchester, Mass.: Americans Talk Security.

Attalides, Michael. 1979. *Cyprus: Neutralism and International Politics*. New York: St. Martin's Press.

Axelrod, Robert. 1977. "Argumentation in Foreign Policy Settings:" Britain in 1918, Munich in 1938 and Japan in 1970. In *Journal of Conflict Resolution*, 21, no. 4:727–56. In *The 50% Solution*, ed. Zartman. New Haven: Yale Univ. Press.

———. 1984. *The Evolution of Cooperation*. New York: Basic Books.

Azar, Edward E. 1986. "Mediation in Middle East Conflicts." Maxwell Summer Lecture series, Syracuse Univ.; Syracuse, N.Y.

Azar, Edward E., and John W. Burton. 1986. *International Conflict Resolution-Theory and Practice*. Sussex, England: Wheatsheaf Books.

Bach, Kent, and Robert M. Harnish. 1979. *Linguistic Communication and Speech Acts*. Cambridge: MIT Press.

Barnett, Richard. 1972. *The Roots of War: The Men and Institutions Behind U.S. Foreign Policy*. New York: Atheneum Publishers.

Bavly, Dan, and Eliahu Salpeter. 1984. *Fire in Beirut: Israel's War in Lebanon with the PLO*. New York: Stein and Day.

Bender, Gerald et al. 1985. *African Crisis Areas and U.S. Foreign Policy*. Berkeley: Univ. of California Press.

Bennett, James. 1986. "Subjunctive Reasoning in Security Studies." Informal handout for a talk at Bryn Mawr College, Bryn Mawr, Pa. Photocopy.

Bercovitch, Jacob. 1984. *Social Conflicts and Third Parties: Strategies for Conflict Resolution*. Boulder, Colo.: Westview Press.

Berger, Earl. 1965. *The Covenant and the Sword: Arab-Israeli Relations 1948–56*. London: Routledge and Kegan Paul.

Berman, Maureen R., and Joseph E. Johnson, eds. 1977. *Unofficial Diplomats*. New York: Columbia Univ. Press.

Berry, Jeffrey M. 1977. *Lobbying for the People*. Princeton, N.J.: Princeton Univ. Press.

Bill, James. 1988. "Why Iran Wants Peace." *Washington Post*, August 28.

Binder, Leonard. 1985. "United States Policy in the Middle East." *Current History* 84, no. 498 (January): 1–4, 35, 36.

Blainey, Geoffrey. 1973. *The Causes of War*. New York: Free Press.

Blight, James, and D. Welch. 1989. *On the Brink*. New York: Hill and Wang.

Borker, Susan, Louis Kriesberg, and Abu Abdul-Quader. 1985. "Conciliation, Confrontation, and Approval of the President," *Peace and Change 11*, no. 1 (Spring): 31–48.

Brams, Steven. 1985. *Superpower Games: Applying Game Theory to Superpower Conflict*. New Haven: Yale Univ. Press.

Brockner, Joel, and J. Z. Rubin. 1985. *Entrapment in Escalating Conflicts: A Social Psychological Analysis*. New York: Springer-Verlag.

Bundy, McGeorge. 1988. *Danger and Survival: Choices about the Bomb in the First Fifty Years*. New York: Random House.

Burton, John W. 1987. *Resolving Deep-Rooted Conflict: A Handbook*. Lanham, Md.: University Press of America.

Bush, George. *NBC-TV Evening News*. Interview on July 28, 1988.

Camp, Glen. 1980. "Greek-Turkish Conflict over Cyprus." *Political Science Quarterly 95*, no. 1:43–70.

Campbell, John C. 1983. "The Security Factor in U.S. Middle East Policy." *American-Arab Affairs* no. 5 (Summer): 1–9.

Carnesale, Albert, and Richard N. Haass, eds. 1987. *Superpower Arms Control: Setting the Record Straight*. Cambridge: Ballinger.

Carnevale, Peter. 1986. "Strategic Choice in Mediation." *Negotiation Journal 2*, no. 1:41–56.

Clarke, Duncan L. 1979. *Politics of Arms Control: The Role and Effectiveness of the U.S. Arms Control and Disarmament Agency.* New York: Free Press.

Claude, Inis L., Jr. 1963. *Swords into Plowshares: The Problems and Progress of International Organizations.* New York: Random House.

Clifford, Clark. 1981. Quoted in Lawrence Freedman, *The Evolution of Nuclear Strategy.* New York: St. Martin's Press.

Cohen, Bernard C. 1973. *The Public's Impact on Foreign Policy.* Boston: Little, Brown.

Coleman, Milton. 1983. "Jackson Set to Visit Syria, Discuss Flier." *Washington Post,* December 26.

Cordesman, Anthony H. 1986. "The Middle East and the Cost of the Politics of Force." *Middle East Journal* 40, no. 1 (Winter): 5–15.

Corson, Walter H. 1970. "Measuring Conflict and Cooperation Intensity in East-West Relations: A Manual and Codebook." Ann Arbor: Univ. of Michigan Institute of Social Research.

Cotton, Timothy. 1986. "War and American Democracy: Electoral Costs of the Last Five American Wars." *Journal of Conflict Resolution* 30, no. 4:616–35.

Couve de Murville. 1965. Speech to the French National Assembly, June 16, 1965 (New York: Ambassade de France: Service de Presse at d'Information), p. 8.

Dahl, Robert. 1976. *Modern Political Analysis.* Englewood Cliffs, N.J.: Prentice Hall.

Dawisha, Karen. 1982–83. "The U.S.S.R. in the Middle East." *Foreign Affairs* 61, no. 2 (Winter): 438–52.

Dean, Jonathan. 1983. "MBFR: From Apathy to Accord." *International Security* 7, no. 4:116–39.

———. 1987. *Watershed in Europe: Dismantling the East-West Military Confrontation.* Boston: Lexington.

Deeb, Marius. 1985. "Lebanon's Continuing Conflict." *Current History* 84, no. 498 (January): 13–15, 34.

Deering, Christopher J. 1980. "The Turkish Arms Embargo: Arms Transfers, European Security, and Domestic Politics." Paper presented at the Annual Meeting of the International Studies Association, Los Angeles.

de Soto, Albaro. 1989. "On Language: Diplomatese." *New York Times Magazine,* September 10, 36.

Destler, I. M., Leslie H. Gelb, and Anthony Lake. 1984. *Our Own Worst Enemy: The Unmaking of American Foreign Policy.* New York: Simon and Schuster.

Deutsch, Morton. 1973. *The Resolution of Conflict: Constructive and Destructive Processes.* New Haven: Yale Univ. Press.

de Young, Karen. 1988. "Iran Weakened by Years of War." *Washington Post,* July 10.

Divine, Robert. 1978. *Blowing on the Wind: The Nuclear Test Ban Debate, 1954–60.* New York: Oxford Univ. Press.

Dowty, Alan. 1984. "Israel: A Time of Retrenchment." *Current History* 83, no. 498 (January): 13–16, 37, 38.

Dragsdahl. 1989. "How Peace Research Has Reshaped the European Arms Dialogue." *The Annual Review of Peace Activism, 1989.* Boston: Winston Foundation for World Peace, 39–45.

Druckman, Daniel. 1973. *Human Factors in International Negotiations: Social-Psychological Aspects of International Conflict.* Beverly Hills: Sage Professional Paper 02-020.

———. 1977. "Boundary Role Conflict: Negotiation as Dual Responsiveness." *Journal of Conflict Resolution* 21, no. 4:639–62.

———. 1986. "Stages, Turning Points and Crises." *Journal of Conflict Resolution* 30, no. 2:327–60.

Druckman, Daniel, Benjamin Broome, and Susan Korper. 1988. "Value Differences and Conflict Resolution: Facilitation or Delinking?" *Journal of Conflict Resolution* 32, no. 3:489–510.

Druckman, Daniel, and P. Terrence Hopmann. 1989. "Behavioral Aspects of Negotiations on Mutual Security." In *Behavior, Society, and Nuclear War,* ed. Philip Tetlock, Jo Husbands, Robert Jervis, Paul Stern, and Charles Tilly, 85–173. Vol. 1. Oxford: Oxford Univ. Press.

Duffy, Gavan. 1991. "Time Space: Representing the Temporal Domain of International Conflict Events." In *Artificial Intelligence and International Politics,* ed. Valerie Hudson, 386–405. Boulder, Colo.: Westview Press.

Duncan, George T., and Brian L. Job. 1980. "Probability Forecasting in International Affairs." Final report to the U.S. Defense Advanced Research Projects Agency.

Elster, Jon. 1979. *Ulysses and the Sirens: Studies in Rationality and Irrationality.* Cambridge: Cambridge Univ. Press.

Emshoff, James, and Russell Ackoff. 1970. "Explanatory Models of Interactive Behavior." *Journal of Conflict Resolution* 14:77–89.

Etzioni, Amitai. 1967. "The Kennedy Experiment." *Western Political Quarterly* 20(June): 361–80.

———. 1986. "The Kennedy Experiment: Unilateral Initiatives." In *Psychology and the Prevention of Nuclear War,* ed. Ralph White, 204–7. New York: New York Univ. Press.

Fabian, Larry L. 1983. "The Middle East." *Foreign Affairs* 62, no. 3:632–58.

Facts on File. 1983. Vol. 43, December 31.

Fisher, Roger. 1964. "Fractionating Conflict." In *International Conflict and Behavioral Sciences: The Craigville Papers,* ed. Roger Fisher, 91–110. New York: Basic Books.

———. 1978. *International Mediation, A Working Guide: Ideas for the Practitioner.* Cambridge: Harvard Negotiating Project.

Fisher, Roger, and William Ury. 1981. *Getting to YES.* Boston: Houghton Mifflin.

Forsythe, David P. 1972. *United Nations Peacemaking.* Baltimore: Johns Hopkins Univ. Press.

Forum Institute. 1983. *Handbook of Arms Control and Peace Organizations/ Activities.* Washington, D.C.: Forum Institute.

French draft resolution (S/15255/Rev. 2); (S/16351/Rev. 2).

Freedman, Lawrence. 1981. *The Evolution of Nuclear Strategy.* New York: St. Martin's Press.

Fuller, Graham. 1988. "Why Iran Wants Peace." *Washington Post,* July 24.

Galston, William A., and Christopher J. Makins. 1988. "Campaign '88 and Foreign Policy." *Foreign Policy* 71:3–21.

Garelick, Glenn. 1987. "The Grounds for a Test Ban Treaty." *Discover* (June): 50–65.

Garfinkle, Adam M. 1984. *The Nuclear Weapons Freeze and Arms Control.* Cambridge, Mass.: Ballinger Publishing.

Garthoff, Raymond L. 1985. *Détente and Confrontation.* Washington, D.C.: Brookings Institution.

Gelb, Leslie, and Richard Betts. 1979. *The Irony of Vietnam: The System Worked.* Washington, D.C.: Brookings Institution.

George, Alexander et al. 1971. *The Limits of Coercive Diplomacy.* Boston: Little, Brown.

George, Alexander, P. J. Farley, and A. Dallin. 1988. *U.S.-Soviet Security Cooperation: Achievements, Failures, Lessons.* Oxford: Oxford Univ. Press.

Goffman, Erving. 1972. *Frame Analysis.* New York: Harper and Row.

Golan, Galia. 1982–83. "The Soviet Union and the Israeli Action in Lebanon." *International Affairs* 59, no. 1 (Winter): 7–16.

Goldman, Marshall and Raymond Vernon. 1984. "Economic Relations." In *The Making of America's Soviet Policy,* ed. Joseph Nye. 159–81. New Haven: Yale Univ. Press.

Goldstein, J., and J. Freeman. 1987. "Containment Theory and Reality: the Strategic Triangle, 1948–1978." Paper presented at the American Political Science Association annual meeting, Chicago.

———. 1988. "Reciprocity in U.S.-Soviet Chinese Relations." Paper presented to the American Political Science Association annual meeting, Washington, D.C.

Gordon, Michael. 1981. "Right-of-Center Defense Groups—The Pendulum Has Swung Their Way." *National Journal* 13, no. 4 (January 25): 128–32.

Haass, Richard N. 1988. "Ripeness and the Settlement of International Disputes." *Survival* (May/June): 232–51.

Hagan, Joe D. 1986. "Domestic Political Conflict, Issue Areas, and Some Dimensions of Foreign Policy Behavior Other Than Conflict." *International Interactions* 12, no. 4:291–313.

Hasan, Sabiha. 1982. "Super Powers in the Middle East: An Overview." *Pakistan Horizon 35*, no. 4:68–83.

Hatfield, Mark O. 1983–84. "U.S. Policy in the Middle East: A Program for Failure." *American-Arab Affairs* no. 7 (Winter): 17–23.

Hersh, Seymour. 1983. *The Price of Power.* New York: Summit.

Hilsman, Roger. 1967. *To Move a Nation.* New York: Dell Publishing.

Holsti, Ole, and James Rosenau. 1984. *American Leadership in World Affairs: Vietnam and the Breakdown of Consensus.* Boston: Allen and Unwin.

Hopmann, P. Terrence. 1981. "Détente and the European Force Reduction Negotiations." Philadelphia, Pa.: Paper presented to the 22d annual convention of the International Studies Association, March 18–21.

———. Forthcoming. *Negotiating Mutual Security in Europe.*

Hopmann, P. Terrence, and Timothy D. King. 1976. "Interactions and Perceptions in the Test Ban Negotiations." *International Studies Quarterly* 20:105–42.

———. 1980. "From Cold War to Détente: The Role of the Cuban Missile Crisis and the Partial Nuclear Test Ban Treaty." In *Change in the International System,* ed. Alexander L. George, Ole R. Holsti, and Randolph M. Siverson, 163–88. Boulder, Colo.: Westview Press.

Hopmann, P. Terrence, and Teresa C. Smith. 1978. "An Application of a Richardson Process Model: Soviet-American Interactions in the Test Ban Negotiations, 1962–63." In *The Negotiation Process,* ed. I. William Zartman, 149–74. Beverly Hills: Sage Publications.

Hopmann, P. Terrence, and Charles E. Walcott. 1977. "The Impact of External Stresses and Tensions on Negotiations." In *Negotiations: Social-Psychological Perspectives,* ed. Daniel Druckman, 301–23. Beverly Hills: Sage Publications.

Hottinger, Arnold. 1983. "Syrien im Widerstand gegen einen 'amerikanischen' Frieden." *Europa-Archiv* 3:65–72.

Howard, Michael. 1978. *War and the Liberal Conscience.* New Brunswick, N.J.: Rutgers Univ. Press.

Hudson, Michael C. 1985. "The Palestinians After Lebanon." *Current History* 84, no. 49 (January): 16–20, 38, 39.

Hurwitz, Roger, and John Mallery. 1989. "Using New Techniques of Semantic Content Analysis to Identify Normative Orientations in Textual Accounts of Game Playing." Paper presented the annual meeting of the American Political Science Association, Washington, D.C., September.

Husbands, Jo L. 1977. "Non-Aligned Nations in the Eighteen Nation Disarmament Conference: Mexico, Brazil, and Argentina, 1962–1975." Working Paper Series, Center for Arms Control and International Security Studies, Univ. of Pittsburgh.

——— 1979. "The Conventional Arms Transfers Talks: Negotiation as Proselytization." Paper presented at the Annual Meeting of the American Political Science Association, Washington, D.C., August.

Ikle, Fred Charles. 1964. *How Nations Negotiate.* New York: Frederick A. Praeger Publishers.

Institute on Soviet-American Relations. 1986. *Organizations Involved in Soviet-American Relations.* Washington, D.C.: Institute on Soviet-American Relations.

Interview with Harold Saunders. 1983. *American-Arab Affairs* no. 4 (Spring): 32–39.

Isaak, Robert A. 1975. *Individuals and World Politics.* Belmont, Calif.: Wadsworth Publishing.

Jackson, Elmore. 1983. *Middle East Mission.* New York: Norton.

James, P. 1987. "Externalization of Conflict: Testing a Crisis-based Model." *Canadian Journal of Political Science* 3, no. 30:573–98.

Jensen, Lloyd. 1968. "Approach-Avoidance Bargaining in the Test Ban Negotiations." *International Studies Quarterly* 12, no. 2:152–60.

———. 1984. "Negotiating Strategic Arms Control, 1969–1979." *Journal of Conflict Resolution* 28, no. 3:535–59.

Jerusalem Post. 1988. Int. ed., March 5.

Jorden, William J. 1984. *Panama Odyssey.* Austin: Univ. of Texas Press.

Karapin, Roger S., and Hayward R. Alker, Jr. 1985. "Argument Analysis: A Post-Modern, Dialectical, Graphical Approach." MIT Department of Science, Mimeograph.

Kearney, Kevin. 1987. "Private Citizens in Foreign Affairs." *Emory Law Journal* 36.

Kegley, Charles, and Eugene Wittkopf. 1987. *American Foreign Policy: Pattern and Process.* 3d ed. New York: St. Martin's Press.

Kelman, Herbert C. 1982–83. "Talk with Arafat." *Foreign Policy* no. 49 (Winter): 119–39.

Kennan, George. 1959. *American Diplomacy, 1900–1950.* New York: New American World Library.

Kennedy, Robert. 1968. "Three Days." *New York Sunday Times,* October 27.

———. 1969. *Thirteen Days: A Memoir of the Cuban Missile Crisis.* New York: Norton.

Kernell, Samuel. 1978. "Explaining Presidential Popularity." *American Political Science Review* 72, no. 2:506–22.

Key, V. O., Jr. 1961. *Public Opinion and American Democracy.* New York: Knopf.

Khalidi, Rashid. 1983–84. "Problems of Foreign Intervention Lebanon." *American-Arab Affairs* no. 7 (Winter): 24–30.

Khouri, Fred J. 1985. *The Arab-Israeli Dilemma,* 3d ed. Syracuse, N.Y.: Syracuse Univ. Press.

Kincade, William H. 1987. "Periods of Peril Revisited: A Public Opinion Perspective." Paper presented at the Annual Meeting of the Section on Military Studies, International Studies Association, Atlanta, Ga., September.

Kissinger, Henry. 1979. *White House Years.* Boston: Little, Brown.

———. 1982. *Years of Upheaval.* Boston: Little, Brown.

Klass, Rosanne. 1988. "Afghanistan: The Accords." *Foreign Affairs* 65, no. 5:922–45.

Kohlberg, Lawrence. 1984. *The Psychology of Moral Development: The Nature and Validity of Moral Stages.* San Francisco: Harper and Row.

Koumoulides, John, ed. 1986. *Cyprus in Transition 1960–1985.* London: Trigraph.

Krasner, Stephen, ed. 1983. *International Regimes.* Ithaca, N.Y.: Cornell Univ. Press.

Kreczko, Alan J. 1982–83. "Support Reagan's Initiative." *Foreign Policy* no. 49 (Winter): 140–53.

Krepon, Michael. 1984. *Strategic Stalemate: Nuclear Weapons and Arms Control in American Politics.* New York: St. Martin's Press.

Kriesberg, Louis. 1972. "International Non-Government Organizations and Transnational Integration." *International Associations* 24 (November): 521–24.

———. 1980. "Interlocking Conflicts in the Middle East." In *Research in Social Movements, Conflicts and Change,* ed. Louis Kriesberg. Vol. 3:99–118. Greenwich, Conn.: JAI Press.

———. 1981. "Noncoercive Inducements in U.S.-Soviet Conflicts: Ending the Occupation of Austria and Nuclear Weapons Tests." *Journal of Political and Military Sociology* 9 (Spring): 1–16.

———. 1982. *Social Conflicts.* 2d ed. Englewood Cliffs, N.J.: Prentice Hall.

———. 1987. "Timing and the Initiation of De-escalation Moves." *Negotiation Journal* 3:378–84.

———. 1989. "Transforming Intractable Conflicts: Cases from the Middle East and Central Europe." In *Intractable Conflicts and Their Transformation,* ed. Louis Kriesberg, Terrell A. Northrup, and Stuart J. Thorson, 109–31. Syracuse: Syracuse Univ. Press.

———. 1992. *De-escalation and Transformation of International Conflicts.* New Haven: Yale Univ. Press.

Kull, Steven. 1988. *Minds at War.* New York: Basic Books.

Larson, Arthur D. 1986. "Game Theory and the Psychology of Reciprocity." Paper presented at the Annual Meeting of the American Political Science Association, Washington, D.C., September.

———. 1987. "The Psychology of Reciprocity in U.S.-Soviet Relations: Beliefs, Perceptions and Motives." Political Science Dept., Columbia Univ., New York. Mimeograph.

Lasswell, Harold. 1974. *Prologemena to the Policy Sciences.* New York: Elsevier.

Lazarus, R. S., and S. Folkman. 1984. *Stress, Appraisal, and Coping.* New York: Springer-Verlag.

Lebow, Richard Ned. 1981. *Between Peace and War.* Baltimore: Johns Hopkins Univ. Press.

Levine, S., and H. Ursin. 1980. *Coping and Health.* New York: Plenum Press.

Lévi-Strauss, Claude. 1962. *The Savage Mind.* Chicago: Univ. of Chicago Press.

Levy, Jack. 1989. "The Causes of War: A Review Theories and Evidence." In *Behavior, Society, and Nuclear War,* ed. Philip Tetlock, Jo Husbands, Robert Jervis, Paul Stern, and Charles Tilly, 209–334. Oxford: Oxford Univ. Press.

Lewis, Flora. 1987. "The Wiles of Teheran." *New York Times,* August 3.

Low, Stephen. 1985. "The Zimbabwe Settlement." In *International Mediation in Theory and Practice,* ed. Saadia Touval and I. William Zartman. Boulder, Colo.: Westview Press.

Luard, Evan. 1986. "Superpowers and Regional Conflicts." *Foreign Affairs* 64, no. 5 (Summer): 1006–25.

McDonald, John, and Diane B. Bendahmane, ed. 1987. *Conflict Resolution: Track Two Diplomacy.* Foreign Service Institute, U.S. Department of State. Washington, D.C.: GPO.

———. 1986. *Perspectives on Negotiation.* Washington, D.C.: State Department Foreign Service Institute.

McDonald, John. 1988. "Guidelines for Track Two Diplomats." *Peace in Action.* George Mason University, March.

Macpherson, C. B. 1964. *The Political Theory of Possessive Individualism.* London: Oxford Univ. Press.

Mallery, John. 1988. "Beyond Correlation: Reconstructing the Relational Structures of Conflict Processes from Sherfacs Data." Paper presented at the International Studies Association annual meeting, St. Louis, Mo., March.

Mallison, Sally V., and W. Thomas Mallison. 1983. "Israel in Lebanon: Aggression or Self-Defense?" *American-Arab Affairs* no. 5 (Summer): 39–49.

Mandelbaum, Michael. 1983. *The Nuclear Future.* Ithaca, N.Y.: Cornell Univ. Press.

Marantz, Paul, and Blema S. Steinberg, eds. 1985. *Superpower Involvement in the Middle East. Dynamics of Foreign Policy.* Westview Special Studies in International Relations. Boulder: Westview Press.

Marcum, John. 1978. *The Angolan Revolution.* Vol. 2. Cambridge, Mass.: MIT Press.

Mefford, Dwaqin. 1988. "Cognitive Models and U.S. Interventions: The Function of Stories in the Formulation of Foreign Policy." Paper presented at the Harvard-MIT Seminar on Rethinking Security Relationships, May.

Melnikov, Igor, and Nikolai Potapov. 1988. "Citizen Diplomacy Brings People Together." *Soviet Life* (July): 28–29.

Miller, Aaron David. 1984. "Palestinians in the 1980's." *Current History* 83, no. 489 (January): 17–20, 34–36.

Montville, Joseph V. 1988. "Transnationalism and the Birth of Track Two Diplomacy." Paper delivered at the United States Institute of Peace Conference, June.

Montville, Joseph V., and William D. Davidson. 1981–82. "Foreign Policy According to Freud." *Foreign Policy:* 145–47.

Morgan, Dan. 1979. *Merchants of Grain.* New York: Viking Press.

Mueller, John. 1973. *War, Presidents, and Public Opinion.* New York: Wiley.

Nathan, James, and J. K. Oliver. 1983. *Foreign Policy Making and the American Political System.* Boston: Little, Brown.

National Academy of Sciences. 1988. *Reykjavík and Beyond: Deep Reductions in Strategic Nuclear Arsenals and the Future Direction of Arms Control.* Washington, D.C.: National Academy of Sciences Press.

Neidle, Alan F., ed. 1982. *Nuclear Negotiations: Reassessing Arms Control Goals in U.S.-Soviet Relations.* Austin: Lyndon B. Johnson School of Public Affairs, Monograph, Univ. of Texas.

Neumann, Robert G. 1983–84. "Assad and the Future of the Middle East." *Foreign Affairs* 62, no. 2 (Winter): 237–56.

———. 1984. "United States Policy in the Middle East." *Current History* 83, no. 489 (January): 1–4, 39, 40.

Neustadt, Richard E., and Ernest R. May. 1986. *Thinking in Time: The Uses of History for Decision-Makers.* New York: Free Press.

Newhouse, John. 1973. *Cold Dawn: The Story of SALT.* New York: Holt, Rinehart, and Winston.

New York Times. 1984. "Reagan Praises Navy Flier and Jackson." January 5.

New York Times. 1987. "The Wiles of Teheran." August 3.

Nincic, Miroslav. 1988. "America's Soviet Policy and the Politics of Opposites." *Journal of Conflict Resolution* 32, no. 2:452–75.

Norton, Augustus Richard. 1983. "Israel and South Lebanon." *American-Arab Affairs* no. 4 (Spring): 1–11.

Nye, Joseph. 1984. "The Domestic Roots of American Policy." In *The Making of America's Soviet Policy,* ed. Joseph Nye, 1–8. New Haven: Yale Univ. Press.

Olson, Robert. 1984. "Syria in the Maelstrom." *Current History* 83, no. 489 (January): 25–28, 33, 34.

Osgood, Charles E. 1960. *Graduated Reciprocation in Tension-Reduction: A Key to Initiative in Foreign Policy.* Institute of Communications Research. Urbana: Univ. of Illinois Press.

———. 1962. *An Alternative to War or Surrender.* Urbana: Univ. of Illinois Press.

———. 1986. "Graduated and Reciprocated Initiatives in Tension Reduction." In *Psychology and the Prevention of Nuclear War: A Book of Readings,* ed. Ralph White. New York: New York Univ. Press.

Ostrom, Charles, and Brian Job. 1986. "The President and the Political Use of Force." *American Political Science Review* 80, no. 2:541–66.

Ostrom, Charles, and Dennis Simon. 1985. "Promise and Performance: A Dynamic Model of Presidential Popularity." *American Political Science Review* 79, no. 2:334–58.

Page, Benjamin, I., and Robert Y. Shapiro. 1983. "Effects of Public Opinion on Policy." *American Political Science Review* 77, no. 1:175–90.

———. 1984. "Presidents as Opinion Leaders: Some New Evidence." *Policy Studies Journal* 12, no. 4:669–62.

Pentz, Michael J., and Gillian Slovo. 1981. "The Political Significance of Pugwash." In *Knowledge and Power in a Global Society,* ed. William M. Evan, 175–203. Beverly Hills: Sage Publications.

Perlmutter, Amos. 1982. "Begin's Rhetoric and Sharon's Tactics." *Foreign Affairs* 61, no. 1 (Fall): 67–83.

Piaget, Jean. 1965. *The Moral Judgment of the Child.* New York: Basic Books.

Preece, Richard. 1988. *Iran-Iraq War.* Issue Brief 88060. Washington, D.C.: Congressional Research Service.

Pruitt, Dean. 1981. *Negotiation Behavior.* New York: Academic Press.

Pruitt, Dean, and J. Z. Rubin. 1986. *Social Conflict: Escalation, Stalemate, and Settlement.* New York: Random House.

Public Agenda Foundation. 1984. *Voter Options on Nuclear Arms Policy: A Briefing Book for the 1984 Elections.* New York: Public Agenda Foundation.

Quandt, William B. 1986. *Camp David.* Washington, D.C.: Brookings Institution.

Raiffa, Howard. 1982. *The Art and Science of Negotiation.* Cambridge: Harvard Univ. Press.

Rapoport, Anatol. 1960. *Fights, Games, and Debates.* Ann Arbor: Univ. of Michigan Press.

Rapoport, Anatol, and A. Chammah. 1965. *Prisoner's Dilemma: A Study in Conflict and Cooperation.* Ann Arbor: Univ. of Michigan.

Razwi, Mujtaba. 1982. "The Search for Peace in the Arab World." *Pakistan Horizon* 35, no. 4:10–20.

Reagan, Ronald. 1988. Press conference, March 19.

Revel, Jean-François. 1983. *How Democracies Perish.* New York: Harper and Row.

Rikhye, Indar Jit. 1978. *The Sinai Blunder.* New Delhi: Oxford and IBH.

Rosenbaum, Aaron D. 1982–83. "Discard Conventional Wisdom." *Foreign Policy* no. 49 (Winter): 154–67.

Rubin, Barry, and Laura Blum. 1987. *The May 1983 Agreement over Lebanon.* Lanham, Md.: University Press of America.

Rubin, Jeffrey, and B. Brown. 1975. *The Social Psychology of Bargaining and Negotiations.* New York: Academic Press.

Russett, Bruce. 1989. "Democracy, Public Opinion, and Nuclear Weapons." In *Behavior, Society, and Nuclear War,* ed. Philip Tetlock, Jo Husbands, Robert Jervis, Paul Stern, and Charles Tilly, 174–208. Oxford: Oxford Univ. Press.

Rustow, Dankwart A. 1984. "Realignments in the Middle East." *Foreign Affairs* 63, no. 3:581–601.

Sadat, Awar el-. 1978. *In Search of Identity.* New York: Harper and Row.

Sanders, Jerry W. 1983. *Peddlers of Crisis.* Boston: South End Press.

Saunders, Harold H. 1982. "An Israeli-Palestinian Peace." *Foreign Affairs* 61, no. 1 (Fall): 100–21.

————. 1984. "The Pre-Negotiation Phase." In *International Negotiations: Art and Science,* ed. John McDonald and Diane Bendahmane, 47–56. Washington, D.C.: Foreign Service Institute, U.S. Department of State.

————. 1985. *The Other Walls: The Politics of the Arab-Israeli Peace Process.* Washington, D.C.: American Enterprise Institute.

Sauvignon, Edouard. 1984–85. "Les Etats-Unis au Liban dans la deuxieme force multinationale 1982–1984." *Ares: Defense et Securite* 7:453–66.

Schahgaldian, Nikola B. 1984. "Prospects for a Unified Lebanon." *Current History* 83, no. 489 (January): 5–8, 41, 48.

Schelling, Thomas. 1960. *The Strategy of Conflict.* Cambridge: Harvard Univ. Press.

Schiff, Zeev. 1983. "Green Light, Lebanon." *Foreign Policy* 50 (Spring): 73–85.

Schlesinger, Arthur M., Jr. 1965. *A Thousand Days: John F. Kenndy in the White House.* Boston: Houghton Mifflin.

Schneider, William. 1984. "Public Opinion." In *The Making of America's Soviet Policy,* ed. Joseph Nye, 11–35. New Haven: Yale Univ. Press.

Schon, Donald A. 1983. *The Reflective Practitioner: How Professionals Think in Action.* New York: Basic Books.

Seaborg, Glenn T. 1981. *Kennedy, Krushchev and the Test Ban.* Berkeley: Univ. of California Press.

Sergeev, V., V. Akimov, V. Lukov, and P. Parshin. 1987. "Interdependence in a Crisis Situation: Simulating the Caribbean Crisis." USA-Canada Institute, Moscow. Mimeograph.

Shakespeare, William. 1901. *Henry IV, Part II.* New York: University Society Edition.

Sheehan, Edward R. F. 1976. "Step by Step in the Middle East." *Foreign Policy* 22 (Spring): 3–70.

Sherif, Muzafer. 1966. *In Common Predicament.* Boston: Houghton Mifflin.

Sherman, Frank. 1985. "Quarrels and Disputes; An Expansion of the Phase/Actor Disaggregated Butterworth-Scranton Codebook." Center for International Studies, MIT, Cambridge. Mimeograph.

————. 1987. "Partway to Peace: The United Nations and the Road to Nowhere." Ph.D. dis., Pennsylvania State University, University Park.

Shubik, M. 1970. "Game Theory, Behavior and the Paradox of the Prisoner's Dilemma: Three Solutions." *Journal of Conflict Resolution* 14:181–93.

Simon, Herbert. 1957. *Models of Man.* New York: Wiley.

Singer, J. David. 1962. *Deterrence, Arms Control, and Disarmament.* Columbus: Ohio State Univ. Press.

Singer, J. David, and Melvin Small. 1972. *The Wages of War, 1816–1965: A Statistical Handbook.* New York: Wiley.

Sisco, Joseph J. 1982. "Middle East: Progress or Lost Opportunity." *Foreign Affairs* 61, no. 3:611–40.

Sivard, Ruth Leger. 1987–88. "World Military and Social Expenditures." *World Priorities*. Washington, D.C. Monograph.

Smith, Gerard. 1980. *Doubletalk, The Story of the First Strategic Arms Limitation Talks*. Garden City, N.J.: Doubleday.

Smith, Tom W. 1983. "The Polls: American Attitudes Toward the Soviet Union and Communism." *Public Opinion Quarterly* 47, no. 2:277–92.

Smoke, Richard. 1979. *War: Controlling Escalation*. Cambridge, Mass.: Harvard Univ. Press.

Solo, Pam. 1988. *From Protest to Policy: Beyond the Freeze to Common Security*. Cambridge, Mass.: Ballinger Publishing.

Soudan, Françoise et al. 1988. "Pourquoi l'Iran a cede." *Jeune Afrique* 1439:20–5.

Spechler, Dina Rome. 1987. "The Politics of Intervention: The Soviet Union and the Crisis in Lebanon." *Studies in Comparative Communism* 20, no. 2 (Summer): 115–43.

Stein, Janice. 1989. *Getting to the Table: The Processes of International Prenegotiation*. Baltimore: Johns Hopkins Univ. Press.

———. 1991. "Deterrence and Reassurance." In *Behavior, Society, and Nuclear War*, ed. Philip Tetlock, Jo Husbands, Robert Jarvis, Paul Stern, and Charles Tilly, 8–74. Vol. 2. Oxford: Oxford Univ. Press.

Steinberg, B. 1989. "Shame and Humiliation in the Cuban Missile Crisis: A Psychoanalytic Perspective." Paper presented at the Annual Meeting of the International Society for Political Psychology, Tel Aviv, Israel, July.

Stohl, Michael. 1980. "The Nexus of Civil and International Conflict." In *Handbook of Political Conflict,* ed. Ted Gurr, 293–330. New York: Free Press.

Stoll, Richard. 1984. "The Guns of November: Presidential Reelections and the Use of Force." *Journal of Conflict Resolution* 28, no. 2:231–46.

Strauss, Leo. 1936. *The Political Philosophy of Hobbes: Its Basis and Its Genesis*. Oxford: Oxford Univ. Press.

Suedfeld, Peter, and Philip Tetlock. 1977. "Integrative Complexity and Communication in International Crises." *Journal of Conflict Resolution* 21, no. 1:169–84.

Szulc, Tad. 1978. *The Illusion of Peace*. New York: Viking.

———. 1974. "Behind the Vietnam Ceasefire Agreement." *Foreign Policy* 15, (Summer): 21–69.

Talbott, Strobe. 1979. *Endgame: The inside Story of SALT II*. New York: Harper and Row.

———. 1984. *Deadly Gambits: The Reagan Administration and the Stalemate in Nuclear Arms Control*. New York: Knopf.

———. 1987. "The Road to Zero." *Time*, December 14, 18–30.

Tamashiro, Howard. 1991. "The Computational Modeling of Strategic Time." In *Artificial Intelligence and International Politics*, ed. Valerie Hudson, 149–65. Boulder, Colo.: Westview Press.

Tetlock, Philip, and C. McGuire. 1985. "Integrative Complexity as a Predictor of Soviet Foreign Policy Behavior." *International Journal of Group Tensions* 14, no. 2:113–28.

Thant, U. 1971. "The Role of the Secretary-General." *U.N. Monthly Chronicle* 8:1979–80.

Thomas, Hugh. 1971. *Cuba: The Pursuit of Freedom*. New York: Harper and Row.

Tillman, Seth P. 1983. "U.S. Middle East Policy: Theory and Practice." *American-Arab Affairs* no. 4 (Spring):1–11.

Timerman, J. 1981. *Prisoner Without a Name, Cell Without a Number*. New York: Knopf.

Touval, Saadia. 1982. *The Peace Brokers*. Princeton: Princeton Univ. Press.

Touval, Saadia, and I. William Zartman, eds. 1985. *International Mediation in Theory and Practice*. Boulder, Colo.: Westview Press.

Tuchman, Barbara. 1962. *The Guns of August*. New York: Macmillan.

Turner, Victor. 1974. *Dramas, Fields and Metaphors*. Ithaca: Cornell Univ. Press.

United Nations. Resolution 186 (S2), May 14, 1948; 34/102, December 14, 1979; 35/160, December 15, 1980; 36/10, December 10, 1981.

United Nations Charter 1945. I, Art. 2; IV, Arts. 13, 15; XV, Arts. 97–100.

United Nations General Assembly. 1982a. Document A/C./37/L.2, October 21.

———. 1982b. Official Records. 36th session Supplement no. 1 (A/36/1). *Report of the Secretary-General on the Work of the Organization.*

United Nations Security Council. 1946. Resolution 15. 1963. Document S/5331 June 11.

———. 1984. Proceedings at the 2,519th meeting, February 17.

United States Arms Control and Disarmament Agency. 1987. "INF Chronology." Issues brief.

UN Monthly Chronicle. 1971. 8:59 (August-September).

U.S. Code, Title 18, Section 953.

Walcott, Charles E., and P. Terrence Hopmann. 1978. "Interaction Analysis and Bargaining Behavior." In *The Small Group in Political Science: The Last Two Decades of Development*, ed. Robert T. Golembiewski, 251–61. Athens, Ga.: Univ. of Georgia Press.

Waller, Douglas C. 1987. *Congress and the Nuclear Freeze*. Amherst: Univ. of Massachusetts Press.

WAND (Women's Action for Nuclear Disarmament). 1987. *Turnabout: The National Survey on Arms Control*. Cambridge, Mass.: Women's Action for Nuclear Disarmament.

Washington Post. 1981. "Jesse Jackson in Syria." January 1.

———. 1983. "Linowitz Warns on Jackson Trip." December 27.

———. 1984. "He Shouldn't Have Done It." January 4.

———. 1984. "Jackson Talks With President Assad about Fate of Captured U.S. Airman." January 3.

———. 1989. President, Hill Rebuke Hansen for Iran Mission." November 27.

Weiss, Stephen. 1985. "The Language of Successful Negotiators: A Study of

Communicative Competence in Intergroup Negotiation Simulations." Ph.D. diss., Univ. of Pennsylvania, Philadelphia.

Will, George. 1984. "Jesse Jackson in Syria." *Washington Post,* January 1.

Wilson, George. 1986. *Super Carrier.* New York: Berkeley.

Winham, Gilbert R. 1977. "Complexity and International Negotiation." In *Negotiations: Social-Psychological Perspectives,* ed. Daniel Druckman, 247–66. Beverly Hills: Sage Publications.

Yaniv, Avner. 1987. *Dilemmas of Security.* New York: Oxford Univ. Press.

Yaniv, Avner, and Robert J. Lieber. 1983a. "Personal Whim or Strategic Imperative? The Israeli Invasion." *International Security* 8, no. 2 (Fall): 117–42.

———. 1983b. "Reagan and the Middle East." *Washington Quarterly* 6, no. 4 (Autumn): 125–37.

Young, Oran, ed. 1975. *Bargaining: Formal Theories of Negotiation.* Urbana: Univ. of Illinois Press.

Young, Ronald J. 1987. *Missed Opportunities for Peace—U.S. Middle East Policy 1981–1986.* Philadelphia: American Friends Service Committee.

Zartman, William I. 1974. "The Political Analysis of Negotiation: How Who Gets What When." *World Politics* 26, 3 (April): 385–99.

———. 1977. "Negotiations as a Joint Decision-Making Process." In *The Negotiation Process,* ed. I. William Zartman, 67–86. Beverly Hills: Sage Publications.

———, ed. 1987. *The 50% Solution.* New Haven: Yale Univ. Press.

———. 1986. "Ripening Conflict, Ripe Moments, Formula, and Mediation." In *Perspectives on Negotiation: Four Case Studies and Interpretations,* ed. Diane B. Bendahmane and John W. McDonald, 205–27. Washington, D.C.: Foreign Service Institute, U.S. Department of State.

———. 1989. *Ripe for Resolution.* New York: Oxford Univ. Press.

Zartman, William I., and Maureen Berman. 1982. *The Practical Negotiator.* New Haven: Yale Univ. Press.

Zinnes, Dina. 1980. "Why War? Evidence on the Outbreak of International Conflict." In *Handbook of Political Conflict,* ed. Ted Gurr, 331–60. New York: Free Press.

INDEX

TIMING THE DE-ESCALATION OF INTERNATIONAL CONFLICTS
was composed in 10 on 12 Sabon on a Mergenthaler Linotronic 300
by Partners Composition;
printed by sheet-fed offset on 50-pound, acid-free Glatfelter Eggshell Cream,
Smyth-sewn and bound over binder's boards in Joanna Arrestox B
and notch bound with paper covers printed in 2 colors
by Maple-Vail Book Manufacturing Group, Inc.;
and published by
SYRACUSE UNIVERSITY PRESS
SYRACUSE, NEW YORK 13244-5160

Syracuse Studies on Peace and Conflict Resolution
HARRIET HYMAN ALONSO, CHARLES CHATFIELD, and LOUIS KRIESBERG,
Series Editors

A series devoted to readable books on the history of peace movements, the lives of peace advocates, and the search for ways to mitigate conflict, both domestic and international. At a time when profound and exciting political and social developments are happening around the world, this series seeks to stimulate a wider awareness and appreciation of the search for peaceful resolution to strife in all its forms and to promote linkages among theorists, practitioners, social scientists, and humanists engaged in this work throughout the world. Other titles in the series are:

An American Ordeal: The Antiwar Movement of the Vietnam Era. CHARLES DE BENEDETTI; CHARLES CHATFIELD, Assisting Author

Building a Global Civic Culture: Education for an Interdependent World. ELISE BOULDING

The Eagle and the Dove: The American Peace Movement and U.S. Foreign Policy, 1900–1922. JOHN WHITECLAY CHAMBERS II

Intractable Conflicts and Their Transformation. LOUIS KRIESBERG, TERRELL A. NORTHRUP, and STUART J. THORSON, eds.

Israeli Pacifist: The Life of Joseph Abileah. ANTHONY BING

The Road to Greenham Common: Feminism and Anti-Militarism in Britain Since 1820. JILL LIDDINGTON

Virginia Woolf and War: Fiction, Reality, and Myth. MARK HUSSEY, ed.